"Hello, Mrs. Lockwood, Can Billy Come Out to Play?"

"Hello, Mrs. Lockwood, Can Billy Come Out to Play?"

and Other Probing Questions

A MEMOIR

by

BILL LOCKWOOD

Library of Congress Control Number:		2008911474
ISBN:	Hardcover	978-1-4363-9232-7
	Softcover	978-1-4363-9231-0

This book was printed in the United States of America.

To order additional copies of this book, contact:
Xlibris Corporation
1-888-795-4274
www.Xlibris.com
Orders@Xlibris.com
51439

CONTENTS

ACKNOWLEDGMENTS

Had my Mother not suggested that I take the typing class in my sophomore year in high school when I had a free period, I probably would not have had the typing skills to be able to tackle this project. I was the only guy in that class, and while my buddies ridiculed me for taking the "sissy class," I not only learned an invaluable skill that stayed with me for the rest of my life but I also met just about every one of the most attractive girls in school. My date book and dance card were filled for the entire year and beyond. I became the envy of all my friends and actually started a trend that became legend at Grover Cleveland High School—"take typing class and meet girls." Thanks, Mom, you'll never know how much I truly appreciated that bit of advice.

I also want to acknowledge every one I ever talked to about their childhood. They are the ones who deserve a loud round of applause because it was they who unlocked the door to my memory bank that allowed me to dredge up so many more memories than I would have been able to do on my own. Specifically, my friends Dick Roethel, John Perri, Tom Burke, my fantastic sister Patricia and my beautiful and loving wife, Connie, are the ones who come quickly to mind; but there were many more who casually mentioned their growing up in Bay Ridge, Queens Village, Glendale, Long Island City, or Flatbush and the things they did or saw, and it was those passing comments that ignited additional thoughts. In particular, all my friends at the Garden City Casino where their childhoods are regularly discussed every Saturday and Sunday morning as they wait for a tennis court to come free.

Patricia actually had an early draft of the first two chapters of this book way back in 1993 and was able to give me a great deal of feedback about things I had totally overlooked or forgotten about our early life. She went so far as to write down her thoughts about our early years and our family and they were so enlightening that I made them an addendum to this book. See "Patricia's Remembrances—Another View." I must also acknowledge the support and encouragement that Connie gave me during the last twenty years. Her memory remains a lockbox of events and people where mine was a complete blank.

My nephew and godson, John W. Lockwood, was very helpful in scanning Mom's entire photo album page by page so that I could share those wonderful pictures. Unfortunately, there is no one around to help us in identifying many of those relatives and friends from the twenties and thirties who appear in those photos. The same is true of Dad's album from his days in the army during World War I and his famous picture posing with a .45 Colt automatic strapped on his hip. I wonder if he ever used it.

Thanks also go to Wiley Miller for his most apropos cartoon that appeared in the *New York Post* on July 9, 2008, as I was finalizing this last revision. Of course, everything I've said is the truth, the whole truth, and nothing but the truth, so help me God.

NON SEQUITUR © 2008 Wiley Miller. Dist. By Universal Press Syndicate. Reprinted with permission. All rights reserved

PREFACE

It was the late eighties or early nineties, Mark was in Alaska, I had just gotten a laptop, and I had the distinct feeling that he would never really know much about his mother and I and his ancestry unless I put it down somewhere. My brother Jack and I had spoken about our family tree from time to time, but we didn't know much, if anything, beyond our grandparents on my mother's side.

It also struck me that we grew up in an entirely different world than what was happening in the '80s. There was a major world war going on in the '40s; there was no television, no computers, no organized kids sports like Little League, cars were still a developing phenomenon, airline travel was in its infancy, there was no rock 'n' roll music or rap, and we were being introduced to 78 rpm vinyl records with music on them and there wasn't any "taped" music. Looking back at that I thought, wouldn't it be great to pass on to Mark and the rest of the family a glimpse into who we were and what it was like when we were growing up.

The original project was supposed to take us up through high school only and that would be it. But then I thought: as long as we've come this far, I might as well describe the next four years of air force life. Okay, just another chapter. The rest of the book just followed along its natural path after that: What about after the Air Force? What was it like getting a job? Starting night school? Getting married? Becoming a father? Developing a career? Working on hobbies and making friends? How could I leave those things out? They are all much too important in making up my seventy-odd years. So I gave in to my urge and wrote about everything.

I'm not a talented writer so the prose and style may be a bit disjointed, for that I apologize. For the rest, there is no apology. It is the unabridged mostly chronological firsthand summary of the last seventy-four or so years of my life, for better or for worse.

There are four family trees also included as exhibits. I constructed them based on the facts I collected and stitched together over the course of writing the book. Perhaps others can add to what I've done. I've exhausted my sources of information.

I also used *Wikipedia* on Google to add tidbits of history into each chapter to give you a flavor of what was happening in the world around us during each decade. I hope you enjoy those references to history. It is by no stretch of the imagination a complete list of events, only those that I think were important. There was clearly a lot going on in the world in each decade, but in the more recent decades, things seem to have exploded with the number of people and events in the news. Obviously my thumbnail sketches of history have not done justice to those times.

And finally, I don't want to leave without commenting about certain things in this life in which I believe strongly. Throughout my seventy-plus years, I think I have maintained a pretty steady position on a number of major issues confronting mankind: national security, ability to earn a living, the right to free speech, the right to life, and the right to worship one's God. I've also tried to live a reasonably moral life, respecting others and behaving as a responsible member of our community. But over my adult life, the fundamental underpinnings on which our Christian/Judeo ethics were built have changed. There has been a corruption of our basic moral and ethical code—premarital sex; abortion; divorce; the widespread use of mind-numbing drugs; the gradual erosion of basic respect for privacy, women, and religion. I've also considered myself to be a strong political conservative. I've voted the straight party line of the Republican Party—the GOP—as far back as I can remember, except in the election of JFK when I voted for the man and not the party. That's not to say I've agreed with what the Republican hacks have done during this time. The latest Bush administration will probably go down as one of the worst governments in the history of this country. And I couldn't agree more. It has been a complete disaster. But will the Democrats do any better? I strongly doubt it.

I believe that the political machinery in the United States has been severely corrupted over the past fifty years to a point of no return. Each political party and their respective candidates in both houses of Congress have forsaken their oath of office for power and the almighty dollar. For the politicians in Washington, it's not what's right for the country but rather what's good for me and my few constituents who vote for me and what I have to do to get reelected. You can say it goes back to the Watergate scandal of Richard Nixon, but it was certainly there well before that and it went further with Bill Clinton who was the consummate politician bent on nothing more than bettering his own and his wife's position of power and money. His shenanigans in the Oval Office with Monica Lewinsky and the aftermath of lies and denials will forever be indelibly etched in our minds as an unforgivable humiliation for this country. It's just another reason for the rest of the world to hate America that is not going to go away in our lifetimes or the lifetimes of our children and grandchildren.

Then came 9/11 and the world went into a tailspin. The Islamic fanatics of the world have chosen America as the country to hate. Most of it, I believe, is fueled by our support of Israel, which above all is the most hated country in the world. In our desire to be the protectors of the world and the downtrodden, we have gotten ourselves into two gigantic unwinnable wars: Afghanistan and Iraq. How on earth are we ever going to be able to win back the hearts and minds of the fanatics who are killing not only Americans but also anyone who even associates with Americans, even their own people? We will never see the end of the Islamic fanaticism in our lifetime. How do you fight an enemy that wants to die? I haven't a clue as to how one even protects against this kind of craziness.

It gets worse. During this very month we have witnessed the complete breakdown of our banking system brought about by greed and mismanagement at the very top of our government institutions that were put in place to protect every American. We are now faced with the government bailout of Freddie Mac and Fannie Mae, two quasi-governmental mortgage bankers who have betrayed the very people they were there to protect. In the process, the banking system as we know it in the United States has been severely hurt. Again, the greed of the executives running these organizations and the ineffectiveness of the Democratic-controlled Congress allowed this debacle to ruin the lifesavings of millions of Americans while the executives walk away with millions of dollars.

Now, we're coming up on a presidential election where the Democratic front-runner is not only black but who has deep roots to radical socialism which could turn this country into a welfare state that could destroy the very basis of our capitalistic system. Our one hope may hinge on John McCain and a young lady from Alaska, Sarah Palin, who are running on the Republican ticket. God help us, please.

My fervent hope and prayer is that Mark, Sharon, Robin, and Pearl are able to grow up in a peaceful, healthy, and happy environment free from the craziness that's all around us. And I hope they are able to live long fruitful lives and be able to eventually see their grandchildren as we have seen ours. There is no greater joy. God love you all.

WAL
Garden City, New York
September 2008

Life and Memories

Life a bundle of memories
Numerical age a benchmark
The more we remember
The fuller the life

Someone with short recall
whether Fifty or Ninety
is like a teenager

Statistical age
is for actuaries
Stretching the reminiscence
stretches the life force

Memories are personal
Others living the same moment
will bring it back differently

So what!
It's your remembrance

Morrie R. Yohai
September 2007

CHAPTER I

The Beginning—1934 to 1948

A. The Family Tree: Getting to the Roots

Monday, September 10, 1934, started out as a pleasant, sunny sixty-eight-degree day in Brooklyn. That was the day Patricia[1] and I were born sometime in the early morning; "around 8:25 a.m."[2] is how Mom remembered the time. It was also made pointedly clear to everyone that Patricia was born twenty minutes before me, so clearly I was the youngest. My response has always been "It was the only courteous thing to do as the youngest Lockwood male."

Patricia and I were born into the Lockwood family, daughter and son of John Charles and Elsie Magdalene Lockwood of 1870 Linden Street in the Ridgewood section of Queens County, New York City. We[3] had two brothers, John C. "Jack" Lockwood Jr.[4] and George Francis Lockwood.[5] Jack was nine years and George five years older than us. Patricia's full name is Patricia Elsie (Theresa) Lockwood. Mine is William August (Robert) Lockwood.[6]

[1.] Growing up she was "Pat" but now she prefers to be addressed as "Patricia."

[2.] Coincidentally, that was the same time Mark was born.

[3.] In using "we," it will generally refer to Patricia and me or our immediate family.

[4.] Born March 31, 1925, died July 20, 1991.

[5.] Born February 22, 1929, died November 1969.

[6.] The names in parenthesis are our confirmation names.

1. The Lockwoods—Dad's Family

My father was the son of Margaret A. Jenkins[7] and Joseph T. Lockwood.[8] Grandpa Lockwood was a Brooklyn City[9] policeman. (Dad said that his beat was walking around the farms in Richmond Hill, Queens. But I don't think Richmond Hill was part of Brooklyn then so I'm not sure if Dad was kidding or perhaps he was referring to Grandpa in his retirement years.) He and Grandma were married in 1891 and had three boys: Joseph T. Jr. ("Joe"),[10] John C.,[11] and Theodore R. ("Ted").[12]

They were brought up in the Richmond Hill section of Queens County on 117th Street off Liberty Avenue in a wooden house with a beautiful porch around the front and one side. There was a driveway on one side with a garage at the back of the property. Grandpa Lockwood actually died on April 30, 1933, before I was born and Grandma Lockwood eleven years later on February 1, 1944. We used to go to the Richmond Hill house for Sunday dinner from time to time. As the pictures will show, Grandma Lockwood was a tall slender lady with little granny glasses. I seem to remember her being very aloof and formal, but I might be wrong about that. (Above are Grandma and Grandpa Lockwood with Dad, probably in around 1905. Dad would have been ten years old. The picture was reproduced from a tinplate photograph. I am frankly not at all certain that it is Dad. The boy seems to resemble Uncle Ted more than Dad.)

My great-grandparents on the Lockwood side—to the best of my knowledge—came from the Williamsburg section of Brooklyn. Grandpa Joe was one of ten children born to John Martin and

---

[7.] Born October 1872.

[8.] Born in Brooklyn, August 1865.

[9.] At one time Brooklyn was actually a separate city from New York.

[10.] Born August 1893.

[11.] Born August 30, 1895, died August 25, 1963.

[12.] Born July 1899, died February 15, 1971.

Adelaide (nee Wilson) Lockwood. John and Adelaide's ten children were the following: Ida F.,[13] Henry S.,[14] Joseph F.,[15] Martha,[16] Nathan B.,[17] Minnie,[18] William B.,[19] John M.,[20] Daisy,[21] and Jenny A.[22] My great-great-grandfather (John Martin Lockwood) was listed as a "Cooper" in the census report of 1870. It's interesting to note that Daisy and Jenny were both reportedly born in 1879, presumably twins. That may be the twin gene that spawned Patricia and me. To date, I can only trace Henry S., John M., and Jennie into adulthood and their marriages. Henry actually married twice to Lillian Wacker in 1886 and to Katherine in 1874. His three children—Florence, Harry, and Charles—were from his first marriage. John M. married another Lillian and had one daughter whom they also named Lillian. She was born in 1904. Jennie was married to William Carpenter and they had two sons, William E. and Frank D.

If the records are correct, my great-grandmother, Adelaide Wilson, came over from Liverpool, England, on the good ship *Robert Kelly* in 1854. She married John Martin Lockwood in 1860. (See the family tree for details.) Interestingly, the ship's manifest of passengers shows only two "cabin passengers"—Adelaide Wilson and Henrietta Dunbar. Both women are shown as "returning to the United States."[23] So Adelaide

---

13. Born 1860.
14. Born 1862.
15. Born 1865.
16. Born 1867.
17. Born 1869.
18. Born 1871.
19. Born August 1873.
20. Born June 1875.
21. Born 1879.
22. Born July 1879.
23. All other passengers aboard *Robert Kelly* were in "steerage."

may have only been visiting England. Timing seems a bit off however; she supposedly was twenty in 1854 according to the ship's manifest, but the census of 1880—that's twenty-six years later—showed her as being forty-two and John as forty-five as of that year.

Now, back to the twenty-first century. As I said, my grandparents had three boys, Joe, John, and Ted. Uncle Joe[24] had three children: Joseph III, Robert (he was called "Sonny"), and Sally (she was called either "Sissy" or "Sister"). (They would be my first cousins.) Cousin Joe had two daughters, Jane and Nancy, who lives in Glen Head, Long Island, where he did,[25] and a son, Christopher, who lives in Northport, Long Island, and Park City, Utah. Dad didn't get along with his brother Joe so we didn't see much of that family. In fact, I can remember visiting them only once and I must have been real young then because I cannot recall anything about it. Patricia thought they didn't like Mom because she was Catholic. I'm not sure what religion they practiced, if any or if that played a role in their relationship with our family.

Uncle Ted[26] and his wife Gertrude[27] had a son, Harold, who died as an infant in April 1925 and one daughter, Marjorie (Margie)[28]. We would see Uncle Ted and Aunt Gertrude from time to time. Uncle Ted worked for the insurance agency, Johnson & Higgins in Manhattan. Margie married Paul Lemieux[29] and they had a son, Theodore

---

24. Patricia's recollection of Uncle Joe was very negative. He pinched her thigh every time she saw him. And she recalls that there was a lot of yelling, shouting, and cursing in his house. His kids were all smart alecks in her memory.

25. In the nineties, Cousin Joe stopped by to drop off some pictures of Dad, but he didn't leave a phone number or an address. He told Connie that he lived in Virginia and came up for the holidays. Eventually we got in touch with him and had planned to see him the next year when he was coming to New York. He died on May 2003, and no one bothered to notify us. It would have been a chance to meet other members of that side of the family.

26. Patricia remembers Ted as being very quiet. He had a burn scar on the right side of his face. He died February 1971.

27. She died December 3, 1960.

28. Born 12/10/35.

29. He died on September 19, 2001.

("Teddy"),[30] and a daughter, Patricia,[31] and lived in Flushing, Queens. Today, Teddy has two sons, Paul and Michael.[32] We saw Margie and Paul from time to time in the midsixties when Teddy and Patricia were pretty young but didn't keep up the contact beyond then.

2. The Stumpfs—Mom's Family

Mom was the daughter of Agatha Kress[33] and August Stumpf[34] who lived on St. Nicholas Avenue in Ridgewood, which was right on the Brooklyn/Queens border, a few blocks from our house on Linden Street. The Stumpfs had a total of seven children, but only four survived to adulthood: August ("Gus"),[35] William ("Will"),[36] Henry ("Harry"),[37] and Elsie Magdalene ("Elsie").[38]

Grandma apparently emigrated from Baden-Baden in Bavaria, Germany. When Grandma's parents died, the family farm was

---

30. Born March 27, 1960.
31. Born January 28, 1965.
32. Born 1/6/89 and 10/15/90 respectively.
33. Born January 6, 1867, died January 11, 1931.
34. Born January 7, 1861, died July 16, 1917.
35. Born July 14, 1890, died December 29, 1955.
36. Born March 24, 1893, died July 3, 1958.
37. Born July 20, 1895, died 1960s.
38. Born January 21, 1900, died November 17, 1961.

inherited by the eldest male in the family and the rest of his siblings had to fend for themselves America was apparently their only option. Agatha Kress met August Stumpf in this country and they were married probably sometime in the 1880s. According to the census of 1910, Grandpa Stumpf was born in the USA. I can't be sure, but there was one Stumpf family that had a son August born around 1861 living in Queens County. What intrigued me with it was that the father, Martin, was born in Baden, Germany, the same place Agatha Kress came from. Also Martin was a baker; Grandpa Stumpf delivered yeast to bakeries in Brooklyn and Queens. Perhaps Grandma met with some landsmen when she arrived and somehow was introduced to August and eventually got married. It's not too far-fetched, but it's the only thing I have on the Stumpfs.

Grandma Stumpf had several siblings who came to this country with her. One was Jacob Kress who was Aunt Peggy Poetz's father. You'll meet Aunt Peg later in this best seller. I could find no trace of the rest of the Kress siblings.

a. Uncle Gus

Uncle Gus was a big man both in height and width. He was married to Charlotte ("Lottie"). Gus and Lottie had two children, Henry (Harry) and Beatrice. Gus had been a very successful businessman. His toy store in Grand Central Station was one of only two large toy stores in the city at the time. The other was F. A. O. Schwarz. Gus sold toys and games and magic tricks as well as sporting goods and sheet and roll music. He had an electric piano in the store that played the music rolls. Much of what he sold was imported from Germany (he spoke fluent German and also sang in a German choir at a German Platt-Deutsche Club in Ridgewood). Gus's store was the largest in Grand Central Station, and many of the great magicians bought their tricks from him. We had a wonderful German toy that came from his store, which I'll never forget. It was a papier-mâché fortress with a drawbridge. Inside the fortress were little houses and a courtyard. There were two armies of knights on horseback and foot soldiers carrying swords or spears. The men were dressed in different kinds of armor and were painted with great detail. I played with that fortress and the knights for many years. It was beautifully made, and we took great care not to damage it. The knights and other men were stored in the bottom of the fortress. When I finished playing with it each day, all the knights and horses had to be put back in their storage place. When Beatrice had a son, Danny, in the fifties, Mom gave her the toy.

Patricia remembers a whole set of Shirley Temple dolls with porcelain heads and other dolls with costumes representing different countries like Greece, Germany, France, China, Turkey, and Japan. The costumes were very ornate and detailed, and each pair came in its own box. We can't remember what happened to those dolls. Most likely Mom gave them to Beatrice when Christine was old enough to enjoy them.

Uncle Gus's business flourished, but in the late twenties, he lost his lease to a giant bookstore that wanted the plum location and offered a huge premium to the MTA[39] for the lease. Gus was effectively forced out of business. Then came the Depression and for a while Gus worked for F. A. O. Schwarz, but the Depression affected that retailer along with every other business and he eventually found himself out of work. Prompted by his son, Harry, who had trained as a plumber, Gus opened a small hardware store in the Laurelton section of Queens which he operated until his death.

Unfortunately, the Grand Central store continued to plague Gus and his family. It seems that there was a judgment against the corporation, which Gus was unaware of when he bought the business. He was hauled in to court and spent years fighting the case, but eventually paid what amounted to a "substantial" judgment. Unfortunately, the pressure brought on by the lawsuits and her appearances in court while this was going on was too much for Aunt Lottie. She wound up in a mental institution and died there at seventy-two in 1955. She had been institutionalized for twenty-three years.

[39.] Metropolitan Transit Authority which owned Grand Central Station.

As I mentioned earlier, Lottie and Gus had two children, Henry[40] (whom they also called "Harry") and Beatrice.[41] Harry wound up working in his father's hardware store after training as a plumber. Sometime in the early forties, Harry's wife, Mildred, divorced him and for spite reported him to the Selective Service wherein he was promptly drafted into the army.[42] He wound up having a sad life and eventually became an alcoholic. He continued  to run the store after his father died, but the neighborhood was changing for the worse and he couldn't hold on. He died sadly, having lived the latter part of his life in a run-down apartment in a two-family house with no friends or family except his sister. Tom Marblo, Beatrice's husband, devoted a great deal of time taking care of him in those later years.

Beatrice married Tom Marblo[43] who became a negative stripper[44] in a printing business, a union job that he got through his father who was also in that union. Bea and Tom had two children, Christine and Daniel. Christine became a nurse and married Doug Zullo, a St. John's business graduate who has worked for Olympic Optical Company since graduating from college. Chris and Doug had four children, Brian,[45] David,[46] Jeff, and Amy.[47] Brian is an air force pilot and was

---

40. Born June 30, 1912, Harry was married to Mildred Golden and was divorced. He died in the '60s.

41. Born September 7, 1919.

42. He had had a deferment because he had a couple of children.

43. Born October 31, 1917.

44. This was long before the Chippendales became popular.

45. Brian went to the Air Force Academy and wound up flying cargo planes instead of fighters. As of this writing, he is training to fly executive jets and will pilot air force brass around.

46. David graduated from Iona College in New Rochelle, New York.

47. Amy entered medical school in Manhattan in August 2001.

recently (2005) assigned to the Air Force One team of pilots flying support planes for the president of the United States. David and Jeff both graduated from college and are working either in sales or communications. Amy received her MD degree in 2005 and is currently in residency in a hospital around Washington DC. She is married to a Washington DC attorney.

Danny is a high school teacher in the Bronx and married a girl from high school, Margaret Murphy. They have one child, Matthew. Danny had a bout with drugs when he was in high school but straightened himself out and graduated from Long Island University with a degree in English. But then he got involved with the Moonies and became a follower of the Reverend Sun Yung Moon. He spent a couple of years living in Denver raising money for the church by selling straw cowboy hats at rodeos throughout the mountain states. He then moved east to the church's seminary in Upstate New York. The big event was when he married a Korean girl whom he had never met in a massive wedding ceremony in Madison Square Garden staged by the Reverend Moon where one thousand couples were wed in a single ceremony. The girl spoke no English and she returned to Korea to work for the Moonies. It was soon after that that Danny left the church to teach English in a NYC public school in the Bronx. Today, Dan and Margaret are separated and he is the dean of students at a school in the Bronx.

Bea and Tom are really fine people. Bea was particularly close to

Mom, and we saw a lot of her in the midforties before the end of World War II. I say that because it was at that time that she was dating Tom who was in the Army Air Corps, as it was known then. I remember cherishing an Army Air Corps collar pin that he gave me, a propeller with wings, the symbol of the U.S. Army Air Corps. When Tom was released from the service, he bought a Nash automobile—the first car where the front seatbacks folded down to make the entire inside of the car a bed. I remember that as being real "cool." Bea and Tom were good to Pat and me. Tom actually took me to my first (and almost

last[48]) football game between the Baltimore Colts and the New York Giants in the old Polo Grounds in the Bronx. I guess I was eleven or twelve. It snowed during the game, and besides being frozen stiff, we were seated in the end zone, so far away from the players that I had no idea what was going on. Tom loved kids and loved doing things with them. He was kind and gentle.

Another thing about Bea is that she loved to cook. She always had a pie in the oven, and her meals were always large and delicious. In addition to the pies, she was noted for her string beans with onion soup mix, which we all grew to love and expect when we were invited for dinner. Bea and Tom bought Uncle Gus's house in Bellerose and Bea continues to live there to this day. Tom died in 2005. Christine and Doug live nearby in New Hyde Park. Danny also lives nearby as do Margaret and Matthew.

b. Uncle Will

Uncle Will was a lieutenant in the New York City Fire Department stationed in the Canarsie section of Brooklyn. His wife, Emma, died in 1927[49] when their only child, Virginia, was two years old. He, Uncle Harry (whom you'll meet in a little while), and my mother owned the Linden Street house and he lived on the second floor with Virginia. Mom cooked and cleaned for them, and they were very much a part of our family. They were at the dinner table every night with us. Uncle Will never remarried although I understand he had a "lady friend" that we would see from time to time. I don't remember much about Virginia. She was two years older than Jack so she was the oldest of the children in our house. She was a beautiful girl, tall and slim. When I think of her, I see Patricia when she was a teenager. Virginia became a secretary and during the war met and eventually married Joe Donitz, a sailor from Massachusetts. They

---

48. After going to one or two more football games as an adult, I realized I did not like doing it.

49. February 7, 1927.

lived for a while in the Ford Avenue house in Glendale that Uncle Will owned. Mom and Dad didn't like Joe so we didn't see much of Virginia after the marriage. Mom was very protective of Virginia, and I think her dislike stemmed from the fact that Joe had come out of the navy and couldn't find a job and the fact that he wasn't from around Ridgewood that made everyone suspicious of his intentions toward Virginia. Virginia wound up having two children, Barbara and Joey, and tragically died at thirty from cancer sometime in the mid-'50s when I was in the service. Joe and the kids eventually moved to the Bayville house, and we lost track of them completely.

As a fire lieutenant, Uncle Will seemed always to be fighting brush fires in the flat fields near the water, not far from Floyd Bennett Field. Mom would get calls that Uncle Will was in the hospital suffering from smoke inhalation. The worst ones were the used automobile tire yards where I imagine in those days having not yet figured a way to dispose of the old tires they would store them on huge lots and eventually sell them off. If the market wasn't right, there was always a  convenient fire to solve the problem. Those fires were very smoky, and as the lieutenant, Uncle Will would be the first person on the scene to assess the problem and direct the firemen under him. That meant rushing in where the smoke was the heaviest.

Uncle Will was around the house during the day when he was not on duty. He loved to sit in his Morris chair and smoke his pipe and listen to the radio. He was always playing with his pipe, either cleaning it out or lighting it up. From chewing on the pipe, he had ground down his teeth so that they were straight across and the ends were black. We used to ask him to "show us your teeth." He always had a number of pipes lying around, too; the mouthpieces were all chewed down and probably no longer useable, but they were all there for the viewing. His Morris chair was an old recliner. On the wooden arm was a black button to release the mechanism to recline the back. The right arm of the chair was gouged out from him playing with the pointed end of his pipe cleaner.

Uncle Will was a wonderful, gentle man. He loved us as if we were his own children. He was always available to take us here or

there. And if things had to be done in the house, he would always ask me, Jack, or George to help him. He also took me to the firehouse from time to time so I could slide down the fire pole. That was exciting!

Uncle Will had a set of barbells and a rowing machine that we all were allowed to use when he was home. George and Jack would go upstairs to Uncle Will's apartment to work out with the weights after dinner and also use the rowing machine. I occasionally lifted some weights and rowed, but I didn't really enjoy it. Uncle Will was a broad-shouldered squat man about five feet eight or nine. He had powerful arms and shoulders, and his stomach was as hard as a rock. We had a standing contest to see if I could hurt him by punching him in the stomach. My punches never fazed him.

c. Uncle Harry

Uncle Henry ("Harry"), the youngest of the Stumpf boys, was a motion picture camera operator in a big movie house in Brooklyn. The big fuss with him was that he married a divorced woman, Margaret Miller, who had one son, Henry Miller.[50] As the story goes, Harry met Margaret at the movie theater where he worked; her husband was the piano player during the silent film era. Harry and Margaret ran off together, leaving her son Henry sitting in the theater. In the divorce, she lost custody of her son for having left him. According to Beatrice, Harry had promised to marry Margaret but then got cold feet. Apparently everyone in the family was against him marrying her as was Harry himself. But she threatened to sue him for breach of contract since he had promised, so eventually they wed.

Harry owned a two-family house in the Bushwick section of Brooklyn, just over the Queens border and very close to us in Ridgewood. Harry was known for making his own wine in his

---

[50]. We actually visited him when we were in New Mexico with Mark and Sharon in 1991 or 1992.

basement, which I was never allowed to taste, but Jack and George used to take sips from the wine bottles when they visited him. Harry also had two or three pet box turtles that he kept in the backyard where he also raised a variety of roses. When I visited him on my return from the air force, all he liked to do was drink beer and smoke cigars. Margaret complained constantly over the fact that he had all these cases of beer in the basement.[51]

Harry and Margaret never had children of their own. While initially Margaret was not welcomed by the Stumpf family, when Grandma took ill, she was always there ready to help out. She was a lovely person in her own right while Harry was sort of a gruff-talk-tough type of guy who always needed a shave. In fact, when we were small, we hated it when he came to visit because he would grab us up in his arms and rub our faces on his very rough stubble. I remember Pat actually crying from it and maybe I did too. Harry thought that was great fun. Margaret was also into astrology and was forever telling people their fortunes based on the stars. I don't think anyone in the Stumpf family listened, however.

In addition to being an astrologer Margaret also knew a lot about plants and flowers. When Pat was about eight, she fell against a kerosene heater in one of her girlfriends' house and burned her forehead badly. Mom called Margaret who immediately rushed over with a leaf from an aloe plant. She covered the burn with the liquid from the aloe leaf and miraculously the scar disappeared in a matter of days.

During World War I, Harry went into the army but contracted typhoid fever and almost died at an army base in New Jersey. So sick was he that they actually thought he had died and his name was actually included on a monument on Myrtle Avenue in Ridgewood, dedicated to the soldiers from the area that died in World War I. One of these days I'll find that monument. When Harry recovered, the army discharged him as unfit to serve. Because of the fever, his hair had turned pure white when he was still in his twenties.

The Stumpf family was reasonably close-knit. Gus and Harry and Will were always around at Thanksgiving. Uncle Gus sang with the

---

[51] He spent most of his time in the basement because he wasn't allowed to sit in the living room because he would dirty the furniture with his dirty pants and cigar ashes.

German group every Thursday night, which was only a few blocks from our house, so he would drop in sometimes for dinner before going off to sing.

We saw much less of the Lockwood side of the family. It was only when we were quite young that I can remember visiting Uncle Ted and Uncle Joe. There was also some relative who lived in New Jersey whom we visited who was some sort of policeman or state trooper, but I have no idea who that was.

The only other people who visited us that I can recall were the Dietricks (Mr. and Mrs. Arthur Dietrick) and the Poetzes. Arthur Dietrick was my father's best man at his wedding. He and his wife lived in Huntington and was evidently a very successful insurance man. Peggy Poetz was my mom's first cousin who lived in Jamaica, Queens. She and her husband Ted would visit from time to time. Be patient, their story later.

B. Early Childhood—The Lockwood/Stumpf Branch

Mom was delighted with having twins, although financially I imagine it was difficult since we were in the depth of the Great Depression and Dad was either working as an Eskimo Pie salesman or on welfare. He eventually landed a job with the Works Project Administration (WPA), a government-sponsored jobs program of sorts. Living at 1870 Linden Street in Ridgewood was a benefit to us as a family because Mom, Uncle Will, and Uncle Harry owned equal shares in the house and therefore we lived rent-free. Mom kept the place clean, and Dad and Uncle Will kept the house in good repair. In addition, I suspected Uncle Will gave Mom money for taking care of him and Virginia. We never seemed to want for anything.

C. 1870 Linden Street "Home Sweet Home"

1870 Linden Street was a three-story tenement with a separate railroad apartment[52] on each floor. Originally the house was the "family

---

[52]. They were called railroad apartments because the floor plan was laid out with all the rooms in a row with no hallway connecting them. You had to go through each room to get to the next room.

house." Apparently Grandma Stumpf or the four siblings bought the house as the "family house."[53] Uncle Gus was married so he took the first-floor apartment. Mom, Uncle Will, and Harry lived on the second floor with Grandma before they all were married. I'm not sure of the chronology, but Uncle Will moved out when he got married and bought a house on Ford Avenue in Glendale. Mom was married and continued to live on the second floor with Grandma. When Mom gave birth to George, things got a little tight so Uncle Gus bought a house in Bellerose and Mom  moved down to the first floor. After Emma passed away, I presume Uncle Will moved back so that Mom and Grandma could help take care of Virginia. The third floor may have been rented to defray the cost of paying the mortgage. Here is a recent picture[54] of the house. The only change is the aluminum awning over the front door, the air conditioner in the window, and the solid wood door.

The Stumpf house was the only brick house on our side of the street and also had the distinction of being the only three-story building on our side of the street. All the other houses were two-story wooden structures mostly built in the early part of the twentieth century or even the late nineteenth century. Our house had a driveway on one side and access to the backyard and a two-car garage that was shared with our neighbor on the other side of the driveway. We owned half of the garage and the other house owner the other half. It was a tin garage. Yes, it was actually made of tin sheets nailed onto wooden beams. It looked like lapped one by sixes but was actually tin. The roof was also corrugated tin sheet. When I was in high school, I had to scrape[55] and paint the whole garage. It looked awful when it

---

53. I suspect this was a move from the St. Nicholas Avenue house where Mom grew up.

54. Picture was taken on April 2003. Except for the air conditioner in the second-story window and the awning over the front door, the building had not changed from when we left there in 1961.

55. I actually burned the paint off with an old-fashioned gasoline blowtorch and gave it a coat of red lead and a topcoat.

rusted. The doors were also tin with wooden supports and they were all bent out of shape because several cars accidentally hit them from time to time, not to mention the repeated baseballs being thrown against them. Uncle Will drove into the garage one day and forgot to close the back door of his Studebaker. (It was the kind of car where the back doors opened the opposite way from the front door—from front to rear—while the front door opened like conventional car doors do today. In this case, the back door was ripped right off its hinges.) Uncle Will was furious.

Living on the first floor as we did meant we had less room because the entrance to the house itself took up that space on the first floor. Uncle Will and Virginia lived on the second floor and let George and Jack use the room over the front entrance, which was called the hall bedroom. When Virginia got married and moved out, Uncle Will let us also use the front room. Jack had the hall bedroom to himself, and George and I had bunk beds in the front room, which also served as George's studio. On the first floor, where we lived, the front room (closest to the street) was our living room. Originally, Patricia and I slept on the first floor in the second room (the small bedroom from the front, which opened up onto the living room. Actually, there were four rooms in a row: The front room, the little bedroom which came next and which was separated from the front room only by a wide archway, and next was a big room which was Mom and Dad's bedroom, and the last room at the back of the house was used as our dining room. On the side of the dining room was the kitchen, bathroom, and entrance hallway. You entered the house into the main hallway, which led either upstairs to the upper floors or

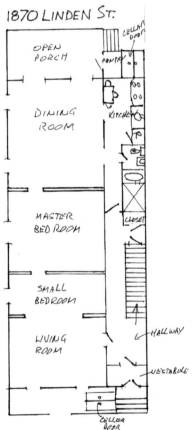

1870 LINDEN ST.

to a hallway leading toward the back of the house and the entrance to our apartment. There was also a closet under the stairs and of course the stairs to the basement. Our apartment entrance was a small hallway leading straight back to the kitchen. There was a door on the left going into the dining room and a door to the right into the bathroom. When company came, they usually were shown right into the living room from the main outer hallway, near the front of the house. The house was probably no more than fifteen feet wide so the rooms were generally pretty small.

We only had one bathroom, which was also very small. I don't remember when it was changed, but at one time, the toilet was the old-fashioned type with the water tank hanging off the wall up near the ceiling with a pull chain hanging down to flush.

The house had a set of four or five stone steps up to the front entrance and into a vestibule or foyer. The first door into the vestibule was never locked. The vestibule was probably six by eight feet. Built into the wall was a bell and mailbox system, one for each floor. Each apartment had a speaker system so that you could ask whoever was ringing the bell to identify them selves. Originally, there must have been pipes from each apartment that you spoke into and it came out in the vestibule. Our pipes didn't work. The vestibule door was opened from the inside by a buzzer. That door was always locked. We either carried our own key or we "rang the bell" to have someone release the lock electronically.

In the front of the house we also had a gated area, which ran from the side of the steps to the end of the building over to the driveway on the left. The area was fenced in with a very elaborate iron fence or gate as we called it. Inside the gated area was kept the garbage cans or bags and also the cellar door entrance to the basement.

Off the rear of the kitchen was a small pantry area that led out to a porch and a few steps down to the ground level. The pantry was not heated, so in the winter Mom could put food that needed to be kept cold when there wasn't any room in the frig or ice box. When we were in grammar school, probably around 1946

or so, the limestone pool (on the next page) that Dad and Uncle Will built when we were infants was removed and a cement patio was installed. George designed it and also laid out a design for the grass area and garden. It was really different from the conventional rectangular gardens with grass in the middle and flowerbeds around the sides. It was in a free-form design that for the time was "very

modern" and to some people "weird." In the backyard, there was also the ubiquitous clothesline that stretched from the kitchen window to the telephone pole at the back edge of the property. Mom washed the clothes in the basement then lugged it up to the kitchen to hang it out through the kitchen window. She could get to the basement either from the front hallway or down the cellar steps at the back of the house. When the new porch was built (about the same time as the cement patio went down) Mom had a clothesline from the back porch to the pole, which made her life a lot easier; she no longer had to hang out the window to hang the wash.

Since the family owned the house, we controlled the basement. It contained a coal-fired furnace for the whole building and a washing machine. Originally it was a washing machine with a wringer on top where you ran the clothes through to squeeze out as much water as possible. A large area of the basement was taken up with a coal bin for storing the coal, which was delivered by the ton to the basement through a basement window on the driveway side. The coal truck would back up into the driveway and drop the coal through the window via a metal shoot. Mom, Dad, or Uncle Will or one of us would have to shovel coal into the furnace on a regular basis in the winter. Uncle Will and probably Mom did it most of the time because they were around more than anyone else. We converted to oil probably in around 1946/'47 and the coal bin was removed and the area cleaned up and made into a storage area. That must have been some job because the coal dust was all over everything. In place of the coal bin, we then had a two-hundred-gallon oil tank in the basement.

There was a workshop in the basement too. It was well organized with a wall of shelves that held wooden cigar boxes.[56] The outside ends of the boxes were painted green, and each box had a number painted in white on its outside end. Hanging on the wall was a typed legend that told you what each box contained. It was cool; whenever you needed something, like a screw or a bolt, you just looked up on the legend what box to go to. The basement was somewhat of a retreat for me when there was nothing good on the radio or if something was going on in all the rooms and there was nowhere else for me to go. When we were real young, we had a swing bolted into the ceiling of the basement, which we used to love to swing while we were waiting to be called for dinner. You couldn't help hitting the ceiling with your feet, and it was a trick not to hit your head coming up the other way. In later years the basement became my drum studio. I fixed up the front of the basement for my drums and that's where I practiced. You could hear me all over the neighborhood.

There was also a dumbwaiter in the building that was probably used to haul coal for the coal stoves before gas was installed and maybe for heat before the radiators and central steam heat were in place. In the early forties, there was one type of gas—probably propane—being used for cooking, but sometime in the late forties, new lines brought in natural gas from the southwest and all gas appliances had to be adjusted to take the new type of fuel. The neighborhood was swarming with teams of men who went from house-to-house making those adjustments. What was different about it was that they came from far away states like Texas, Oklahoma, Arkansas, and Louisiana and their cars had strange, unfamiliar license plates. We played games to see who could see the largest number of different state plates each day.

1870 Linden Street was probably built at the turn of the century when there was no gas or electric, and actually I don't believe they even had indoor plumbing at that time so there had to be an outhouse behind each house.

But back to the dumbwaiter: it apparently took up space that was later part of the bathroom. But the trace of the dumbwaiter remained in the basement right next to the airshaft that went from the basement up to the roof with a skylight over it. We actually had

---

[56.] Uncle Will and every other male in the Stumpf family smoked cigars.

a small window in our bathroom that looked out onto the airshaft. The airshaft was about eight feet square.

The garbage for the house was kept in large cans or, at a time earlier, in large burlap bags in the front of the basement. Every other day or so, the garbage cans—or bags—had to be brought up to the front gate for pickup. That was usually my job despite my continuous squawking and crying about it. Before the house was converted to oil heat, the furnace left us with large barrels of ash that also had to be put out front for collection. That was usually Uncle Will's job. Those barrels were awfully heavy, and at that point I was still pretty young. I'm sure Jack and George did their fair share of hauling those ashes and garbage cans before I was big enough to handle them. Oh, the price of growing up! The garbage smelled too. There were no plastic bags to wrap the smelly garbage in. But our nostrils survived!

D. Ridgewood, Queens

No more than perhaps eight miles from downtown Manhattan, Ridgewood was an old community started before the turn of the century. Ridgewood was on the border with Brooklyn. This first map shows a broad view of Brooklyn and Queens and you can see where Ridgewood was situated in relation to Manhattan and to the north, the Bronx. The second map shows Ridgewood and the surrounding communities. The one thing showing up on this map is Wyckoff Heights Hospital, not a very large hospital, but it was the hospital where Mark was born and it's on the map.

On both maps you can see a piece of Forest Park where we rode our sleds in the winter or played war in the summer. Glendale was the next community to Ridgewood, and it was where Connie's parents moved when Connie graduated from college.

Ridgewood had been primarily a community of German immigrants who made it out of Manhattan or Brooklyn for more open area and possibly less crowding although I'm not sure of that. Back in the turn of century when immigration was at its peak, immigrants were drawn to communities where they felt comfortable and where they could speak their native language. That's not too different today with the barrios of the Bronx where many Puerto Rican families now live. So Ridgewood was this enclave of German families. Before Ridgewood, it was most likely the lower east side of Manhattan around Houston Street and the East River. That was one of the original German enclaves. Leaving there, the German immigrants either went to Queens or to an area in the upper part of Manhattan known as Yorkville located on the east side at 89th Street. It remained a "German neighborhood" until the fifties.

The men in the German families were hard workers: bricklayers, painters, metal workers, carpenters, truck drivers, brewery workers, and the like. There were several major breweries along the East River where some of my friends' fathers worked; Shaeffer's, Schlitz, and Rheingold were the favorites. In fact, for many years in the fifties and sixties there was a "Miss Rheingold" beauty contest that was launched in subway ads and you could vote for your favorite beauty each month. I was never too interested so I didn't know how the voting went. (It was probably done at the locate bars and grills.)[57]

[57.] One of my friends' wife, Eileen Smith, was actually a contestant but didn't win.

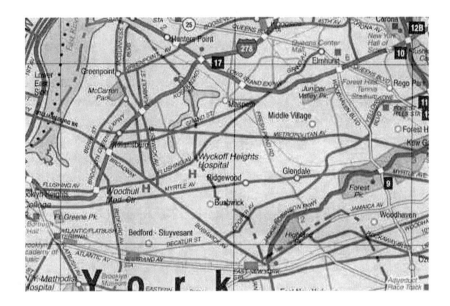

One of the most unusual occupations I heard of back then was of Henry Nigermeyer's father who lived directly across the street from us; he was a steeplejack. He traveled around the country putting up large high brick factory chimneys and was often away from home for months on end. I remember Henry telling me that his father fell on one of the jobs and broke his leg. I can still picture him limping down the street.

The late thirties and forties was the beginning of the migration of Italians out of Manhattan and Brooklyn and into Queens. So when I was in high school, while there was still a large German population in Ridgewood, some of it fueled by more recent German immigrants from World War II, there was a growing Italian element infiltrating the neighborhood. The Italian kids were for the most part not liked by other nationalities. They were arrogant, tough street fighters. The adults were noisy, argumentative, jabbering in Italian and generally did not keep their homes neat and clean like the Germans.

Ridgewood was served by an elevated subway line called the Metropolitan Line because its last stop was a station at Metropolitan Avenue. Its first stop was Bridge and Jay Streets in downtown Brooklyn. There was also an underground subway line, which ended at Myrtle and Wyckoff Avenues and went into Manhattan as far as Canal Street.

Originally the El had no windows, just canvas curtains that you could drop down if it was raining or snowing. (I actually don't remember what they were like in the winter; they must have had windows at some point.) The trains also had little platforms at each end where you got on and off. The conductor operated hand levers that opened the gates for the passengers and also took their fares, which was a nickel. We loved riding out on those end platforms; you could lean over and see what was going on below at street level.

E. The Immediate Family

Mom was born on January 21, 1900, just twenty-one days into the new century. She died on November 17, 1961, one day after having a heart attack. An ambulance rushed her to the hospital, but they didn't have the technology they have today for saving heart attack victims. Even though it was more than forty years ago, it seems like yesterday. And to this day it seems strange that there wasn't a better understanding of heart attacks at that time. My God, it was the early sixties, not the turn of the century. I strongly believe now that it was the hospital and not the lack of technology that let Mom die so young. An aspirin would have been enough.

I can't say I remember what my mom and dad's relationship was with each other in the early days. It seems to have been okay, at least until the midforties when it deteriorated and led to their separation. However, growing up it was fine, as far as I could tell. Patricia remembers there being a lot of tension in the house, a lot of fighting between the two of them. I guess I've wiped those memories away. I suspect that Dad's being on the road so much after he got the Pullman conductor job could have contributed to the tension. He would be away for sometimes weeks at a time, then come home and sleep for what seemed a few days and then off he would go again. Prior to this job, Dad had not made much of a career for himself. Suddenly, he was a world traveler, hitting every big city and small town across the country, eating a far more diversified menu of foods and meeting a lot of different kinds of people. I wouldn't be surprised that he may have found that world a much more exciting one than the one he was coming back to at 1870 Linden Street.

Dad's sleeping actually became an event when I was real young. He snored an awful lot and sometimes his head would be hanging over the side of the bed. I remember friends coming to watch him snore; the noise was overwhelming.

Mom was more of the disciplinarian than Dad. Mom gave the orders, and Dad meted out what punishment there was. There was the occasional "Wait 'til your father comes home, young man, he'll hear about your antics." But there wasn't really much punishment to speak of; we were a happy family. We all went to Mass on Sunday morning together except Dad; he wasn't Catholic, but he agreed to bring us up as Catholics. He was very encouraging when it came to religion. He saw to it that we went to church. If Mom was sick or couldn't make it, he would make sure we went to church (or drive us if we were in Bayville). But strangely he never entered the church; he waited outside reading the Sunday newspapers.

Once I remember getting a real "pants-down" spanking from Dad and then sent to bed without supper. It must have been pretty serious, whatever it was. I cried myself to sleep, but to this day, I can visually remember Dad coming in to tuck the blankets around me and pat my head. How little we know the real person sometimes. Why and how have I been able to hold that memory with me all these years? It could be that this small act of caring was so unusual that it stuck with me. Or it might be that I'm selfishly looking for reasons to think of him as someone with a real heart who loved me and everyone else far more than he showed us outwardly.

1. Mom

Mom was a great lady and a great mother. She showed a lot of love for her children. She cooked and cleaned and did the laundry, and we always had everything we wanted. We all thought she was the best cook alive. Her sauerbraten and potato dumplings were the best. And she loved to make pies. For George's birthday (February 22), she would make him a cherry pie without fail. We always seemed to have an apple pie around, and my perennial favorite was her lemon meringue pie. In the summer, there was also a strawberry/rhubarb or blueberry pie for dessert on special occasions. Mom also loved to knit and crochet. She made wonderful afghan blankets and doilies and knitted woolen sweaters and things for all of us. I was always very proud of my Mother. She could do anything. She could spell any word. And I mean *any* word. "Mom, how do you spell—?" was a daily question from just about everyone in the family. Below is her wedding picture. Aunt Peg (Poetz) was her maid of honor and Arthur Dietrick, Dad's friend, was the best man.

Mom also played the piano. We had an upright in the living room when we were kids and she would take time out regularly to play and we would stand around the piano and sing songs. She loved to play. Her favorite song was Clair de Lune. She played that so well. At one point after Dad left, when we apparently didn't have any money, she actually made the ultimate sacrifice and sold the piano; I think she got $15. If that was the case then, she indeed made a huge sacrifice for so little. I think she regretted it because it meant so much to her to be able to play, but her family came first. And even though we didn't have much money, there was always something there if we needed it.

Her faith in God was also a major factor in getting her through the rough times in her life. After I was married, she confided in me that she believed God looked out for her throughout her life and actually performed small miracles to get her through. In the '40s she had an operation, and the doctor for some reason (I believe he was going crazy) refused to give her anesthesia. She said she looked up into the operating room lights above her and prayed throughout the operation and never felt any pain. She also couldn't explain it, but she often opened her dresser drawer and found money she never knew she had, like a five- or ten-dollar bill or perhaps it was only a dollar at that time. Whatever it was, she was blessed with something.

When Mom graduated high school, the only jobs open to women were secretarial positions. She became the secretary to a Jewish businessman in Manhattan. She knew shorthand and could type sixty words a minute. In the fifties, when she went back to work as a secretary in a plumbing business on Myrtle Avenue, she was thrilled to find that she hadn't lost those skills. At the new job, she loved the challenge and meeting new people after all those years of being a housekeeper and mother.

Mom was about five feet five and a bit heavy, but not obese. She probably weighed about 150 pounds. I know she wore one of those old-styled girdles with bone ribs. She was loving and kind and you snuggled into her soft breasts and felt safe and loved. Her children were her life, and she never let them down. She was always there for us. You could talk to her about anything. She always had a solution, always listened, and above all, always understood. She didn't play any favorites although she relied a lot on Jack in later years because he was around and she respected his counsel and he was the oldest. But beyond that, her only daughter, Patricia, was her real favorite. As I try to write this, I think the most I can say is that she spread her love around so that no one felt left out. She was very concerned for George and his lifestyle but was so proud of his accomplishments and talent although she didn't understand the abstract nature of his art.

The biggest thing in Mom's life was Patricia. What mother would not have a particularly large place in her heart for an only daughter? Mom was very proud of Patricia when she went into the convent, but I don't think she was prepared for the type of relationship that came after. The cloistered life that Patricia chose cut Mom off from everyday communications, and Patricia's aloofness and religious

holier-than-thou attitude I think broke Mom's heart; she no longer had a daughter. It was too bad she didn't live long enough to regain that relationship she never had with Patricia as an adult.

Mom suffered a lot during her life from various illnesses. That operation I mentioned earlier was when we were in grammar school and she stayed in a "sanitarium" to recuperate for several months. I think it was a hysterectomy. After that, she seemed to be sick a lot. She also had her gallbladder removed, and that was also a bad operation. Mom died much too young. She was a heavy smoker, which everyone was guilty of in those days. And of course, our eating habits were different then, too. We ate a lot of meat and potatoes, gravy, bacon and eggs, bread and butter, and cheese and ice cream. Oh, how I wish she would have lived longer to see the fruits of her labor and beyond to her wonderful grandchildren. Oh, how she would have enjoyed each and every one of them and love them each to pieces. I can still remember how she loved little Jimmy, John, and then Mark when they were so little. I particularly remember her taking Mark's face in her hands and showering him with kisses. Why couldn't it be different? For all that she gave to her children, why couldn't she have enjoyed them a bit longer?

The one thing that sticks with me so vividly is the enormous influence she had on my life and conscience[58]. In the air force and even before that, in high school and grammar school, there were all kinds of opportunities to "be bad" (well, maybe not that many in grammar school), whether it was getting into trouble of one kind or another or making moves to get laid (definitely not in grammar school), the overriding, ever-present thought was always "What would Momma think?" or "How could I ever face Momma if I got caught?" It was enough to stop me dead in my tracks every time. Mom, you would have been proud of my resistance. And needless to say, there were a lot of girls who missed out on a good thing. Yeah sure.

---

[58] Coincidentally, when I mentioned this to Patricia, she felt the same way.

We were always trying to please her or making sure we didn't do anything to hurt her. Isn't it wonderful that we loved someone so much that she could have that much influence over us? Even today, I think of her regularly and feel that she would have been so very proud of all her children and their accomplishments. In many ways, I think I'm still trying to please her or at least trying not to hurt her. How do you pass that on to your children? How do you get them to be inspired the same way I was by my mother? That's an awesome power that can't be taught. Perhaps it's something that comes from religious upbringing, moral teachings, and the respect and love of others.

I feel that I left a lot undone with Mom during her lifetime. Whenever someone leaves as suddenly as she did, I guess there is always that thought that there was so much more one could have said  or should have done if she hadn't left. Would we have done more? I'm sure of it. She never lived long enough to see Mark and her other grandchildren grow up and progress. On the other hand, if she had lived just eight or nine years more, she would have seen her husband and son, George, die and that would not have been pleasant for her. What else was left undone? Did I tell her how much I loved her? Would I have told her then, or would it have been only later that I realize the enormous influence she had had on me? What this is telling me is that it's so important to say what you feel when you feel it rather than hold back. You may never get another chance otherwise.

2. Dad

Dad was sort of hard to know. He definitely was a self-centered person who loved to talk and tell jokes. (I wonder if there is any connection to yours truly.) The best thing that ever happened to Dad was his getting a job with the Pullman Company where he was meeting new people all the time. The Pullman Company was a separate company that operated the sleeping cars for

the national railway system. He loved it: traveling around the country, meeting new people and telling stories seemed to suit him just fine. Dad got that job at the beginning of World War II when troops were being transported around the country. In those early years he was a "floater," a conductor who filled in when a regular conductor was not available or when another conductor was just necessary and there was no one else to put on the job but a "recruit." Typically he would leave for an assignment and not get home for several days or weeks, and he couldn't tell us where he was going because of the troops that were being transported. Meanwhile, he would be traveling as far away as California. But when he got home, we all got souvenirs. I remember a Western-style cowboy belt from Arizona or New Mexico (or it could have been Texas, I guess) with different colored stones in it. It got banned from the house when Mom discovered that the stones scratched the back of every wooden chair that I ever sat on. Dad also sent postcards from every city he went through. Patricia saved them all and had a shoebox full. I wonder whatever happened to those cards.

John C. Lockwood loved people; he loved being around people. It was no doubt a good platform to talk about himself, but nevertheless, he listened too. He gave us our confidence in ourselves. He had a lot of good ideas and was good with his hands. He could build anything and he could repair anything. He wasn't afraid to tackle projects that looked tough. I remember when he tackled the job of putting screens in the high dining room windows. There were two awning-style windows hinged at the top that were the size of a typical cellar window about 2 ½ by 3 ½ feet but they were in our dining room and they were almost up to the ceiling. I suspect they were put there for the light; however, they opened out and I guess there was no easy way of putting a screen on the inside (which we did in the Garden City house). Dad built what amounted to a wooden frame that allowed the window to open all the way out. He covered the frame with screening to keep the flies and mosquitoes out. Everyone kidded him about putting up "birdcages" and that's what they were henceforth called.

In the thirties, Dad took motion pictures of everyone with a hand-cranked movie camera. Sometimes he cranked too fast so that Patricia and I literally flew up and down the driveway beside our house. Pictures of others showed them competing in a walking marathon race but they were actually strolling on the street. Tragically the films dried out before we knew how to save them. We also had old Mickey Mouse, Popeye, Charlie Chaplin, and Tom Mix films that we loved to watch. I can remember Charlie Chaplin in something involving cops and a big hairy guy who was menacing the neighborhood but whom Chaplin brought to his knees. And there was Tom Mix in a classic shoot-out in a saloon. By the way, these were violent films of punching and shooting but it didn't affect Patricia or me, at least I don't think so.

Dad was in the Seventy-seventh New York Infantry Division in World War I and fought in France against the Germans. At some point, he and his buddies were attacked with mustard gas and for that he was awarded the Purple Heart and sent home. Although I don't know the details, I believe that he spent some time in an army hospital recuperating before being discharged. That was an awful war and a costly one on human lives.

Dad was a sharp dresser; his shoes always had to be polished. I was responsible for keeping them polished with a high shine. What sticks in my head was the fact that he never untied his ties. They hung in his closet with a tight knot on them. I've never seen anyone else do that.

For most of his life, Dad had a problem with the skin on his hands and feet, which may have come from the mustard gas. He had to soak his hands and feet in a special purple solution that turned them purple. He then wore white socks and white gloves. He would sit in his chair in the corner of the dining room listening to the radio while soaking his hands and feet in this purple solution. Even when he was much older, when I returned from the air force, his hands were always peeling, itching, or flaking.

When he beat up on Mom in the midforties—it must have been around 1943/44—I was in grammar school. I think I both hated and feared him for a long time after that. He and Mom had been out having a few beers at the local pub down the block as they used to do from time to time. (It was before television and a lot of people frequented the local pub for some beer and conversation after dinner.) Apparently, he had had too much to drink and got angry at something Mom said and it wound up being a very nasty argument that led to him punching her around in the living room. Pat and I were in the adjoining room and saw the whole thing and could do nothing about it except scream, "Stop it!" Mom's face was all black and blue the next morning. From then on, Dad took over the front room and no one spoke to him. He eventually moved to a trailer park in Bay Shore and Mom got legally separated from him. He continued to support us, I think, but Mom wound up getting a job as a secretary at  a plumbing manufacturer, Coyne & Delaney, in Myrtle Avenue. I don't remember when I started talking to Dad again. He wasn't really around during my high school days that I can remember. I saw him before I left for Germany, and I wrote to him when I was overseas. I had a lot of trepidations about making up with him. Patricia and I had witnessed his beating Mom and I can still see it as though it was yesterday. But he was my father, and I felt an obligation to stay in touch. I respected him as my father, and in spite of what he had done, I couldn't forget that. Mom understood; it wasn't a betrayal of her.

With Jack and George, it was different. They were ready to jump on him in retaliation. Uncle Will was also very upset. I know there were a lot of recriminations but nothing physical. Jack did have a battle with Dad at a different time over something and I think fists were thrown. That had to be after Jack returned from the navy. Something also happened between George and Dad. And here, too, it resulted in a complete severing of relations. I'm certain it came primarily from Mom's beating. Neither one of them ever spoke to him again. They were also not mentioned in his will. In later years, he asked about both of them and how they were doing and about their children. But he never made any effort to contact them. I doubt very much if either one of them would have responded to his call.

Then there was Jack, George, and Patricia, my brothers and twin sister.

3. Jack

Jack was the oldest. He was nine years older than Patricia and I. He must have graduated from high school in around 1943/44 because he went straight into the navy upon graduating. I don't remember Jack very much as a kid. I guess because I never really saw him as a "kid." He didn't do anything in school that was particularly noteworthy, at least in my memory. In fact, he said he had to work after school.

Maybe because he was the oldest, but I always remembered him as being very serious, not joking around very much. When he went into the navy, I remember him coming home after boot camp from the Great Lakes Naval Training Base outside of Chicago. He was really skinny, and with the tight-fitting navy whites, he looked even thinner. In those early years when he was eighteen or nineteen, Jack was not only skinny but he also seemed to have exceptionally big ears and a lot of teeth in his mouth. The pictures of him at that time will attest to that. He and his best friend Chick Litkey were inseparable. His crowd also included Joe Dobbin and several girls on the block and some guys around the corner whose names I no longer remember. Mom always wanted us to write to him when he was in the navy. That didn't last too long with me because in my first letter I apparently spelled some word or words wrong and he wrote back and chewed me out for not knowing how to spell. Well, I showed him—I didn't write anymore!

Mom wrote to Jack regularly (as she did with all of us). After boot camp, which was another way of saying "basic training," Jack went to Norfolk, Virginia, and became a signalman; you know, the guy who hoists the various flags on the ship and sends messages using semaphore flags or Morse code with the signal lights. From Norwalk he was put on an LST (for landing ship something). This was a ship designed specifically for landing men and supplies on the beach during a land invasion.

As part of the patriotism of the times, families with members in the armed services displayed in the front window of their homes a small (twelve by eighteen inches) white flag with a red border and gold tassels hanging off the bottom and a blue star in the middle. The star represented one family member in the service.[59]

Jack's destination was obviously the Pacific campaign. But as luck would have it, the day he arrived in San Diego, having gone through the Panama Canal and up the coast to California, the Japanese surrendered and World War II was officially over. That was VJ Day (*Victory over Japan* and it's still celebrated on August 15 by a few states, i.e., Rhode Island is one). From San Diego, Jack's ship continued on to Guam where he stayed for about a year. I don't know what there was to do on Guam, but whatever it was, Jack did it and in his spare time he walked the beach and brought home a large bag of exotic seashells that he collected. He also sent home pictures of the island and some of the Japanese prisoners of war that were being held there.

Jack was released from the navy in 1945 after two years of service. The big question then was what to do with his life. Everyone was coming home from the war. Few had any schooling beyond high school, and jobs were hard to come by. When the war ended, the economy went south. Industry was trying to readjust to a peacetime mode, converting equipment and machinery to manufacture consumer items such as cars, washing machines, and refrigerators. Because of the slow economy, these items were not selling  that well in spite of the fact that new households were springing up as servicemen came out and started families. It wasn't that long after he came home that he landed a job as a bookkeeper for Royal McBee Typewriter Company and traveled into Manhattan every day on the subway to their offices at Two Park Avenue. He also enrolled in New York University's night school to earn a bachelor's degree in accounting. The job didn't pay much, but it was a job. He also talked for a while about trying out for the NYC Police Department, but that

---

59. One star for every member. Gold stars meant "killed in action" and were bordered in black. There were a lot of those on the windows around our neighborhood.

didn't materialize. He worked out with a few guys on the block who all had the same idea. But I guess the Royal McBee job turned out to be okay or there wasn't any hope of getting on the NYPD. When the war ended, Congress enacted the GI Bill to help defray the cost of education or other kinds of vocational training for GIs (GI stands for "government issue") and Jack took advantage of the program.

Jack's friend Chick Litkey became a sheet metal worker and actually stayed in that line of work for his entire career. Joe Dobbin, who lived on Menahan Street, was an only child whose widowed mother worked for the telephone company her entire life. He went off to the University of Wyoming. When he came home for the holidays, he sported cowboy boots and Levi's Jeans[60]. He claimed that cowboy boots were great for driving because of the high heels. Joe became an executive of an insurance company and eventually moved to Vermont.

I don't remember if Jack ever finished NYU. He and his friends partied every weekend and dated different girls. They all were frantically looking for Miss Right so they could settle down and raise a family. That was the thing to do at that time. When George was home, I would overhear the two of them discussing their various dates and future prospects.

Jack found Miss Right in Eileen Kennedy whom he married sometime in the midfifties while I was in Germany. They had an apartment in White Plains, and it was not long before Eileen gave birth to John William Lockwood, my godson. Patti came next and then Susan. Jack got different jobs within Royal McBee and moved into a brand-new house in Rockland County.

Looking back today, I think the saddest thing that happened to me was losing Jack as a brother in the early sixties. It happened after Mom died. Mom had little in the way of possessions, but obviously someone could make use of the beds, chairs, etc. Jack, George, and I agreed that we should take back any gifts that we had given Mom (if we wanted them), and anything else any of us might want we should write down on a piece of paper and we'd go over the list together to decide who would take these things. As it developed, George put down a few things as did I (mainly the crystal that I brought back

---

[60]. That was before Levi's jeans were popular except for cowboys.

from Germany for her). Jack and Eileen, on the other hand, listed just about everything in the apartment (including the items they knew we had given Mom, i.e., the crystal). Actually, no one really cared because we didn't want any of it. But the appearance of it looked bad. Anyway, Jack eventually came and took the beds and chairs and the other things he had put on the list and which we had agreed he could have (not the crystal) and we thought that was the end of it. There was some furniture and odd pieces no one wanted, and since Connie and I lived upstairs, we agreed to get rid of all the odds and ends and clean up the apartment.

Whatever it was, something bothered Jack and Eileen about what was left behind and what was to happen to it. We actually threw most of it out as I recall. But Jack kept harping about how since I was living there I was getting more than him. We argued about it and eventually I stopped talking to him and he to me. Unfortunately, this went on for more than twenty years (from 1961 to 1982).

We literally did not see or talk to each other until sometime in the spring or summer of 1982. We probably saw each other at George's funeral but nothing else. We learned through Beatrice that they had moved to Wayne, New Jersey, and eventually up to Vernon, Connecticut, where he had been transferred to the typewriter ribbon division of Royal McBee.

The ice was broken when I heard from Bea that Jack had lost his job when the division was sold, and not long after that, we learned that Susan had broken her neck in an auto accident on the night of her prom. I could hold back no longer; I called Jack and offered my help. The silence ended, and we got back to a normal relationship.

Unfortunately, we could never retrace those twenty-odd years that we lost. We could never go back and watch John, Patti, and Susan grow up nor could they see Mark grow up alongside them. It was a tragic part of my life. Obviously, I didn't realize what I had lost until I regained it. Jack became my best friend. He was overwhelmed when he saw the wood carvings I had done and the ducks and geese I had created. He himself found

an interest in those carvings that he never knew he had and wound up teaching duck carving in adult ed classes. When he eventually lost his next job, he went into the business of selling duck carving tools, paints, and materials and traveled around to craft shows.

My fondest times were driving to Ocean City, Maryland, with him to attend the World Decoy Show each year. We loved it. Eileen and Connie joined us one year and they too enjoyed the trip, the show, and the friendship.

I spoke to Jack by telephone and both of us made it a point of visiting each other on a regular basis. He and Eileen loved Southold, too.

Unfortunately in the early nineties, Jack learned that he had colon cancer and that it had spread to his liver. He lasted perhaps five years on chemo and didn't complain once despite suffering continually. He was so brave in front of everyone. To see him gradually fade was heart wrenching. But when he finally died, everyone was relieved; his suffering was over.

I had not really known Jack when we were younger, and maybe had we stayed close after Mom's death for those twenty years, we may not have become as close as we eventually did. It might have been entirely different, who knows. But I loved Jack and was able to tell him that before he died. He was truly a great brother and a dear, dear friend.

4. George

From the beginning, George was also a very special brother. He had a strong character and enormous talent. He was the second child, the "black sheep" of the family. He was born on February 22, George Washington's birthday, and I guess Mom and Dad had no special names that they were thinking of for their second child and/or they were just patriotic enough to hang the "George" handle on him. George was five years older than us. I don't remember much about his friends, but he was always building something or making something. His creative juices were always running.

Vivid in my memory were the "projects" he worked on in the basement after school. There was the hunting knife that he made from scratch. We had the coal furnace then and he used the coals to heat the metal, shape it, and eventually temper the steel, etc. He made the handle by using plastic strips of different colors. I used to sit in the basement and watch him work for hours.

Then there was the cross bow, a magnificent project. I don't remember if he ever completed it or shot it. It was so beautifully made, shaped from a solid piece of clear hardwood. The bow was separate and made from different types of wood. The trigger mechanism was particularly impressive, as I recall, because it was fashioned out of a new material called plastic and inserted into the frame of the wood with a spring mechanism for releasing the bowstring. Some of the projects he worked on came out of *Popular Mechanics* magazine, which he read from cover to cover.

Another project was the puppet. He carved the body out of wood and the head was formed out of some hardened material. It was a real work of art. I guess he did this throughout high school. He was truly a talented artist.

George had a great sense of humor as well. He scared Mom out of her wits one day while he was working in the basement on some project. We heard this loud scream and he came running up the stairs from the basement and into the kitchen with a little white box in his left hand. The box contained one of his fingers, which he had inserted through a hole in the bottom of the box. His finger was sitting on white cotton covered with a red substance to look like blood. The end of this finger—the end that was supposedly severed—was discolored with green and black paint to look awful. At first Mom was shocked and upset and then really laced into him for scaring her, but she was good-natured and eventually laughed about it.

While he was still in high school, George's art teacher got him a job working for a wallpaper designer who lived in Middle Village, not far from the school. George would go to the man's studio after school and finish painting the rest of the design that the designer had created. The man would do the main part of the design and leave the rest for George to fill in. It gave him spending money as well as experience. Eventually he went on his own and sold his own designs to the same people the designer was selling to. I remember him telling me that the wallpaper people liked his designs better than the guy for whom he had worked.

George was also a large influence on my life. He taught me style and probably a lot of what I did later with wood carving. He introduced our entire family to a more modern way of thinking. Nothing he did was conventional in the sense we knew it. It had to be different. It had to be innovative. He once told me that he consciously changed the way he did things so as not to have things become habits. He changed the way he tied his shoelaces starting with his left shoe first and even changing the type of knot he tied. He also put his shirt or coat on starting with his left hand instead of the right. He even experimented with different lifestyles, sleeping four hours and working four hours and other things we take for granted in our everyday life.

He went on to win a full scholarship to Cooper Union, a prestigious school for art, architecture, and engineering in Greenwich Village. He actually moved into a flat in the village and came home only occasionally to get his laundry done and get a good meal. At the time, everyone considered him a "bohemian," sort of like the forties version of a seventies hippie but not as severe. When he needed money, he would create a couple of wallpaper designs and get $50 each without much effort. The wallpaper people bought everything he produced.

I loved it when he came home from Cooper Union. He always brought a big 2 ½' x 3 ½' drawing pad with all the nudes he had drawn for his drawing class. He'd tape them up around the dining room so when we got up in the morning they'd be there for us to view. Mom thought it was terrible to have all the nudes around, but he thought we should expand our thinking. But here's another example of how great Mom was. George would never get home before twelve or one o'clock in the morning, and he immediately would wake Mom up to tell her he was there and then they would talk for several hours. He did that once when we still had Buddy the family dog, and when George went to wake Mom, the dog bit him on the hand. We ended up having to put Buddy down because he got too protective of Mom to the point where no one could touch her.

George also transformed our house into a modern apartment. He built furniture for the dining room by cutting down the big ornate mahogany expandable dining room table and making it into a modern straight-legged table. He built an indirect lighting structure on the dining room ceiling and started painting his own drapery design, but that was never completed. Actually, I think Mom and Pat were going to finish the painting but never did. Whatever it was it was hung up as is.

The design of the living room was the most controversial item in the family. He painted the ceiling yellow and the wall got covered with dark brown plain wallpaper with some Van Gogh reproductions for which he built great picture frames. He also came up with the idea of painting Pat's room pink with a dark blue ceiling. These ideas were real weird in the late forties and early fifties.

He covered our entrance door with a sheet of Masonite on each side to make it a flat door and painted it bright red. That shocked everyone.

We also redid the kitchen by taking the paint off the kitchen cabinet doors and staining the raw wood. He made a Formica-topped table for the kitchen out of an old table that was there. I actually participated in some of his projects by holding the tools or something.

There was also a love seat in the dining room with fabric that he designed and painted himself, which Patricia sewed into the covers for the foam cushions, and a funny, very modern chair made with plastic-covered telephone wire. It drew a lot of laughs, but it was very comfortable.

George didn't forget the backyard either. He landscaped the backyard with an unusual shape for the lawn and the flowerbeds and even put in a triangular-shaped patio in front of the porch, which I mentioned earlier. He went so far as to select the flowers and made up a complete plan showing where they should be planted.

I visited his "flat" in Greenwich Village once and found it amusing. His bed was a platform covered with a foam rubber mattress, longer than a conventional bed, and a bit wider than a conventional cot. The unique aspect of it was that it had a triangular hole cut near the head and side cuts for arms. The bed allowed him to read a book while lying on his stomach with his arms hanging off allowing him to turn the pages. There was also a reading light on the under side of the bed and a shelf for the reading material. The flat also had a bathtub in the kitchen, which doubled as a tabletop against the wall. George had a funny man painted on the tub's side as though he was trapped under the tabletop. In the bathroom there were two very scary eyes painted on the door, which faced you when you sat on the toilet. I loved every thing about it and actually had to report home to everyone else.

Sometime when he was home from Cooper Union he would spend part of the evening at the corner bar and actually developed a double-edged razor sharpener after discussing the need for such a thing with the regular bartender. The gadget was quite simple with fine sandpaper on two strips situated at angles so that the edges of the razor would be just right for honing the razor edges. Nothing ever happened with it, but that's the kind of challengers he liked to take on.

George was a thinker. He had ideas for everything. He was quite intelligent and tried to influence everyone's thinking at home. Jack, I think, was jealous of him and clearly didn't like his ideas or it might have been that Jack was just too conservative to accept these new bohemian ideas and designs. He thought George was real radical and laughed and ridiculed everything he did.

George graduated from Cooper Union and was soon drafted into the army. The Korean conflict was raging and George was eligible for the draft. I can only remember that he was shipped to Seoul, Korea, as an artist to draw propaganda pamphlets that were dropped onto the North Korean and Chinese troops to break their morale and get them to surrender. He did that for about a year.

When he returned, he jumped back into the art world but I don't remember exactly how. Before I went into the air force, I remember that he married a Jewish girl that he met in New York City. That didn't last too long. While I was in Germany, George went on to earn his master of fine arts degree at Yale University. He also taught at Amherst and Smith Colleges in Massachusetts.

After Connie and I were married, George came to me for a $5,000 loan to buy a studio in Boston from the girlfriend of the artist who had owned it and who had just died. We loaned him the money and he bought what became the "Impressions Workshop" which specialized in lithograph printmaking.

While in Boston, he met and married Margo Nyhan, a young poet. They had four children, Jimmy, Jennifer, Juliette, and Jonathan. Impressions Workshop flourished and George and Margo were able to buy a rundown old farmhouse in Pembroke, Massachusetts, not far from Plymouth on the Cape. George had great plans for the house and its eleven-acre site. But it was not to be. In the midst of rebuilding the barn to become his studio, George dropped dead of a heart attack at age forty, leaving Margo alone with their four children. Jimmy was probably seven or eight and Jonathan was about one or two.

Margo has survived on her wits and whatever money she got from the sale of the workshop and the farm property. At first, Margo and family moved to Ireland and the children received their education there. When they returned, Margo opened a bookstore selling rare books in Brookline, which she operated for many years. Jimmy went off to the Rhode Island School of Design on a full scholarship, and while he is a talented artist like his Dad, he instead became a successful entrepreneur with his own construction company in the Boston area. Juliet married a statistics professor at Louisiana State University in Baton Rouge, Louisiana. But they've since divorced. Jennifer married a male nurse, and at last look, they were living in one of the apartments in Margo's house. Jonathan was floating around not knowing what to do. He played rugby for a while on the U.S. team and then went back to school for art and wound up studying in Florence, Italy, for a year. In between, he also worked in his brother's construction business.

We were never particularly close to Margo and the children but not for want of trying. We tried desperately to reach out to them, sending gifts and letters, but eventually tired of the effort when we got no responses, no thank-you, no recognition that we even existed in their lives. When we did see them (at Jennifer's and at Juliette's weddings) they all expressed a great deal of interest in seeing more of us, but then nothing ever materialized. We felt it would have to come from them and we waited. There was nothing but silence.

Jonathan expressed a strong desire to stay in touch. He wanted to learn more about our side of the family. Jimmy, on the other hand, always seemed to have a chip on his shoulder, sort of like someone owed him something. I'm sure it came from the loss of his father at an age when he could remember how great it was to have him around. And then the loss.

George had by far the greatest influence on me than anyone other than my mother. He taught me to think for myself, to be self-reliant. When I was eleven or twelve and just starting to learn to play the drums for the Boy Scout drum and bugle corps, he encouraged me to be better and even paid for my drum lessons with a famous drum instructor in Manhattan. At that time, Mom couldn't afford the three dollars a week.

In the sixties, when I worked at U.S. Trust, George was very interested in knowing what I was going to do with my life. He always thought I should be doing something else other than working in the bank, but he died too early to witness what came after. I think he would be proud of me. I sure hope so.

5. Patricia

Patricia was a cute little girl with dark eyes and dark hair. I don't think we fought very much. She was a great sister. She was very supportive; she helped me with my homework from time to time although she refused to give me her work because she thought I was too lazy to do it myself. She would run to Mom and complain and Mom would make me do my own work. Clearly, what she did was the best thing for me (I guess).

Pat was an all-around nice person. She had a lot of good friends around her as we went through grammar school and high school. Her girlfriends were special to her. In grammar school there was Dorothy Jacklitch, Dorothy Remy, Dorothy Tuck ("Dorothy" was a very popular name in those days), Joan DeStefano, to name the ones I remember. Once she had a tea party for just seven of her girlfriends and I wasn't invited and I wanted desperately to attend  (because I needed the attention, I guess). I wound up getting disguised as Pat's "uncle Pierre from Paris." I had a beret, mustache, fancy tie, and sport jacket. The picture at the right tells it all.

One time in Bayville, I kiddingly pushed Patricia into a whole field of poison ivy and she wound up in bed for quite a long while with the dreaded rash over most of her body. Having had it every year when we lived in Southold in later life, I think back on that horrible deed and feel so bad having done it to her. But I was only about six or seven and didn't know the consequences of my act.

Pat took piano lessens for a while but didn't like it and dropped it; I guess she must have been nine or ten.

We generally went our separate ways on a day-to-day basis. She had her friends and I had mine. We walked to school together every morning, but I don't remember walking home together. Some of her friends lived on Grove Street, the next block over from Linden Street, so she would sometimes walk up Grove or even the next block, Menahan  Street, and then walk along Onderdonk Avenue to Linden Street.

 When we were about ten or eleven, Patricia had a date with Robert Maroney from our class. He invited her to Central Park Zoo one Sunday afternoon. Mom didn't want her to go alone so she made me go. I took Connie Runkle

whom I really liked. I'll talk about her later. But that I guess was my and Pat's first dates (as well as Connie's).

Patricia learned how to sew, and that took up a lot of her time. She made just about everything, including the slipcovers for the furniture in the living room to go with the dark brown walls and yellow ceiling. One of them was a gold-colored chair.

Patricia and I slept in the same room in bunk beds, with me on the top when we were in grammar school. I always fooled around a little. I'd try to keep her awake by shaking the bed or dangling a string or a pillow in her face while she tried to fall asleep. It would usually come down to "Maaaa, . . . Billy's bothering me, tell him to stop." Then Mom would say, "Don't make me come in there." That's when I'd stop. I moved upstairs with George when I attended high school.

Patricia attended Bishop McDonald High School in Brooklyn and thoroughly enjoyed it. It was there that she was introduced to the Daughters of Wisdom nuns who taught French. Evidently, she saw something in them that turned her on. She left for the novitiate in Connecticut almost immediately after graduating from high school. I saw her only once or twice after that before going into the air force.

Her life in the convent brought her all over. She spent some time in Canada at one of the convents and then went off to France to take her final vows. When she returned to the States, she went to Catholic University in Washington DC where she earned a degree in art and religion. I'm not sure of the dates, probably the early sixties, when Patricia wound up teaching art and religion at the Daughters of Wisdom High School in Ozone Park, not far from where we lived. The order was mellowing then and she was able to see us on a more regular basis. It was later in the sixties that her thoughts changed and leaving the order became a goal.

She finally left around 1969. She lived with Connie and I for a period of time but eventually moved to Houston, Texas, with another ex-nun whose mother had moved there to be close to her son. Patricia

came into her own once she left the convent. She became a traveling salesperson in Texas, selling art reproductions and eventually moved back to New England with the thought of selling the same pictures in that area as she did in Texas. Unfortunately, New Englanders' taste in art was quite different from that of Texans.

Patricia eventually settled into a wonderful coop apartment in an old section of Boston where she earned a nice living cleaning rich people's houses. That led her into doing basic bookkeeping for some of those same clients and

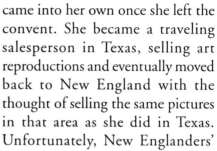

eventually became the accountant or bookkeeper for a large charitable organization in downtown Boston. Since she had little real accounting experience, she spent a lot of time learning what to do from Jack.

I don't remember the year, but she met and married a guy who seemed to be real nice but who

wound up being an alcoholic and Patricia summarily dumped him.

We were thrilled when she met Mike Davis, a retired electrical engineer who had a small house in one of Boston's suburbs. She didn't particularly like the house and he wanted a basement where he could do his puttering, which her apartment lacked. The compromise was a new house that they both loved on a quiet street across the beautiful Boston arboretum. Mike and Patricia are wonderful together. The new house needed a great deal of work, and while he was in his late sixties and through his seventies, Mike worked every day on one project to another. It took him a few years, but they ended up with practically a new house. Mike had replaced all the electric wiring, plumbing, made a new kitchen and the attic into a master suite with a new bathroom. But as they grew older, the severe Boston winters got to them and they wound up relocating to Chapel Hill, North Carolina, which they love.

Patricia is a fantastic person. She had made a wonderful life for herself and Michael and is totally absorbed in living it to the fullest. There was a time in early 2000 when they found a tumor in Patricia's midsection. It was a dark time for her, but she came through it, fought the fight, and is now cancer free. It truly hurt me seeing her suffer with that awful chemotherapy, but she doggedly stuck to it and it worked.

Patricia is a very special person, "my womb mate." How many people can actually say that about another person? I love her dearly.

6. Buddy

Last but not least there was Buddy, the family dog. Buddy was a Boston bulldog. We were in grammar school when he arrived, and I took him for a walk maybe once, that I can remember. We played with him, but he's vague in my memory. Mom was the one who fed him and cared for him. In fact, Buddy slept on top of the covers in Mom's bed. The incident with George came in the early fifties.

This apparently had been coming on for some time before that when Buddy got very jealous of anyone who paid attention to Mom, like hugging her or fooling around with her. Buddy would get quite upset. So it was decided that we had to get rid of him for fear that he might actually do some further damage to other family members. Buddy's loss really didn't have a major impact on Patricia and I. I think because he was not so much our friend but Mom's—a one-person dog—which really wasn't appropriate in a house with several kids.

So there they are: the people (and one animal[61]) that made up my early childhood. They were people I loved and who cared about me as well. They could be relied upon to be there when needed. They were family in the true sense of the word. It's too bad that families

---

61. There was also an assortment of fish, snakes, hamsters, chicks, rabbits, and I also seem to recall a canary.

break up and get blown to the four winds. Indeed, it wasn't a large family by many standards. And the people in it didn't turn out a huge number of offspring, which you would say is the way families continue to grow. But our family did grow somewhat, but it didn't stay close.

In the next chapter you'll learn what it was like growing up in Ridgewood, Queens, in a time that no one will ever forget. The Great War (World War II) affected so many lives. There was a patriotism that had not been seen before in this country. And beyond that, our world changed with the politics of aggression, communism, hatred, and mistrust for everyone. The economy also changed and brought with it an era that would forever change the very underpinnings of our society, from music to religion to communications and technology of every kind.

Stay tuned . . .

History of the Times—1930s

The **1930s** was one of the most difficult periods in modern history. The world was struggling through a global depression, which began in 1929 and lasted right up until World War II. The country actually didn't recover until the end of the war.

Because of economic conditions, parts of Europe was falling under the thumb of such dictators as Adolf Hitler in Germany who came to power in 1933, Joseph Stalin in Russia, and Benito Mussolini in Italy. Spain was engulfed in a civil war, which started in July 1936. Then as the decade was coming to a close, World War II was started with Germany's invasion of Poland on September 1, 1939. In Asia, starting in 1931, Japan began its own war with the invasion of Manchuria and expanded that to include China itself in 1937.

In the United States, Franklin D. Roosevelt's New Deal attempted to use government spending to combat unemployment.

But we also had positive things. During the **1930s,** Walt Disney developed three-color Technicolor and launched some of his most cherished characters: *Pluto* in 1930, *Goofy* in 1932, and *Donald Duck* in 1934. The movie *Snow White and the Seven Dwarfs* appeared on the screen in 1937. I didn't see it probably until I was at least five or six or perhaps a little older. *Li'l Abner* and *Flash Gordon* debuted in the comic strips. Another major film to appear first in the **1930s** was *The Wizard of Oz* with Judy Garland, Ray Bolger, Jack Haley, and Bert Lahr. Will we ever forget these treasures?

The **1930s** also is known as the Golden Age of Radio. Then in June 1938, we met *Superman* in the first action comics book. Starting in 1935 we had the "Big Band" era, which lasted until the late 1940s. Django Reinhardt, Stephane Grappelli, Benny Goodman, Fats Waller, Glenn Miller, Duke Ellington, and Louis Armstrong all became popular in the **1930s.**

Pope Pius XI began his reign in 1929, which lasted until his death on February 10, 1939

In sports, Joe Louis ("the Brown Bomber") turned pro in 1934 and reigned as heavyweight champion of the world from 1937 until 1949.

Here are some statistics from the **1930s:**

- In 1934, the population of the United States was 126.5 million. Today it's close to 300 million.
- A three-bedroom house was $2,925; today it's $200,000.
- Average annual income was $1,237 versus $46,000 now.
- Gasoline was $.19 per gallon. It's now over $4.00 per gallon.
- A pound of bread was $.08; now it's $1.12.[62]
- A gallon of milk was $.44; now it's $2.93.
- A postal stamp was $.03; now it's $.42.

By Contrast, what was it like in 1905?

Here's a sample:

- The average life expectancy in the United States was 47 years.
- Only 14 percent of the homes in the United States had a bathtub.
- Only 8 percent of the homes in the United States had a telephone.
- A three-minute call from Denver to NYC cost $11.

[62.] The federal government's ill-conceived push for alternative fuels such as ethanol made from wheat has caused a huge boost in demand and thus a spike in prices as food companies find themselves competing with ethanol makers. Food prices have been severely affected for anything using flour and animal feed.

- There were only 8,000 cars in the United States and only 144 miles of paved roads.
- The maximum speed limit in most cities was 10 miles per hour.
- With 1.4 million residents, California was the twenty-first most populous state.
- The average wage in the United States was 22¢ an hour.
- The average worker in the United States made between $200 and $400 per year.
- More than 95 percent of births in the United States took place at home.
- Ninety percent of all physicians in the United States had no college education.
- A competent accountant could expect to earn $2,000 per year.
- A dentist—$2,500 per year.
- A veterinarian between $1,500 and $4,000 per year.
- A mechanical engineer about $5,000 per year.
- Sugar cost 4¢ a pound.
- Eggs were 14¢ a dozen.
- Coffee was 15¢ a pound.

The twentieth century brought the subway to New York City. Construction began with the IRT (Interborough Rapid Transit) line in 1900. The following year it was extended into Brooklyn and three years later the Bronx. It took another eight years to connect Queens. When all the lines were completed in 1940, it would be the largest subway system in the world.

CHAPTER II

The Early Years

A. Family Life

Life as a kid growing up in Ridgewood was filled with daily options.

When Patricia and I got home from school at a little after three, I would either have to run errands for Mom or go out to play or stay in and play or study. (Given those options, which do you think I took?) Going to the store for Mom was the routine of the day (I also ran errands for some old ladies on the block). There were about four or five stores that were the regulars: the deli around the corner for a "few things," the Ridgewood Pork Store for meat (there would always be a nice thick slice of bologna waiting for me at the pork store; in fact, every butcher seem to have a long tube of bologna at his chopping block just to give to kids—think of it as a bribe for going to the store for Mom), then there was Dilbert's for groceries, the bakery for cake or Lindenmeyer's Pharmacy for medicine. There was also Morris, the dry goods store on the corner of Linden and Woodward where I'd have to get sewing thread or a hank of wool or window shades and Scheuer's hardware store for just about everything else. Except for the pharmacy, which was on the corner of Seneca and Gates avenues, the other stores were on Woodward Avenue. There was another deli on Onderdonk just down the street from Connie's house that I could opt to shop at (catchy phrase, hey?). When I was really hot for Connie, I used to actually volunteer to go to that deli so I'd have an opportunity to maybe see her sitting on her stoop or running errands herself. That particular deli had the best cod fish cakes, which we always had for Friday's dinner.

Once the errands were out of the way, it was either playtime or working around the house for Mom or doing schoolwork. The playtime I'll talk about later. If the weather was bad or if Mom was making some dinner that was especially tasty, I'd help her with it.

My favorite was helping her make meatloaf or fricadellas. I liked (and still like) mixing the ground meat with eggs and other ingredients because I'd get a chance to taste the mixture as it was progressing. I liked nothing better than raw chopped meat. Fricadellas were similar to meatballs or small hamburgers, but they were made with chopped meat mixed with leftover lamb or pork from another meal. Mom would grind it up like hamburger meat and mix it in with regular chuck chopped meat, onions, bread crumbs, and seasoning.

I'm not proud of it, but I also had the nickname "Wursty." Why? Because I loved liverwurst, and after school when I changed my clothes to go out to play, I'd always have a liverwurst sandwich in my hand. It became my trademark. I still like (love) liverwurst, but for obvious reason I try not to eat it too often. Jack called me "Hans Wurst."

Mom also had some meals that very few people seem to have ever had then or now. For example, there was baked ham and potatoes. The potatoes were sliced very thin and laid into a casserole bowl. Next came a slice of ham with the little round bone in it; then came more potato slices and more ham until the bowl was filled. Mom put some milk in the bowl and baked it. There was a slice of ham for everyone and plenty of potatoes to go around.

Then there was the infamous "tailor ham and milk" dish about which absolutely no one has ever heard outside of our family. Taylor ham was a mix between bologna, ham, and salami with a little bit of spice to it. Mom would fry up slices of tailor ham in a frying pan. When the ham was done, she would take it out of the pan and pour in a few inches of milk and heated it. The pan, with the milk in it, would be set on the dinner table while still piping hot. Everyone would dip a slice of white bread into the milk and take it out quickly (before the bread fell apart). Then put the fried tailor ham slices on the bread and cut off pieces of the bread and tailor ham together. It was delicious. Mom also liked making kidney stew, another one of my all-time favorites. I guess things were altogether different then in terms of the foods that were good for you. In fact, there was nothing better than a slice of freshly baked Levy's rye bread heaped high with salted butter. The bread came unsliced, and Uncle Will was particularly adept at giving everyone a generously thick slice.

Thanksgiving dinner was real special because Uncle Gus, Bea, Tom and Harry, Uncle Harry and Margaret, and Uncle Will and Virginia were all there. Mom would have a giant turkey with all the trimmings.

The trimmings would include mashed and sweet potatoes, creamed baby onions, string beans, cranberry sauce, creamed corn (which was called succotash. She'd also bake all the pies or maybe Bea would bring some. We had a large choice of pies: apple, pumpkin, lemon meringue, and mincemeat. After dinner, we'd all sit around, too full to do anything. All the uncles would fall asleep while the table was cleared and the dishes were washed and dried. When they awoke, it was time for a nice turkey and stuffing sandwich on Levy's rye bread and another piece of pie.

Thanksgiving reminds me that we had another tradition on that day that no longer exists. In fact, I can find few people who ever heard of it. We used to go around on Thanksgiving morning begging for money as a "trick or treat" prank, what they now do on Halloween. It seems to have been lost in this modern world, but I went around in tattered old clothing and a dirty smudged face and sang songs. We'd go into bars and the men would throw us their change. When we finished the bars, we'd jump the fences and go into the backyards in the neighborhood and sing and the residents would throw us coins wrapped in newspaper. Whatever happened to that tradition? I like it better than today's trick-or-treating at Halloween.

Mom also made another of my all-time favorite foods: hasenpfeffer (rabbit) or sauerbraten (beef) at least once or twice a year. That was also a meal to which everyone came. It was a special occasion. Mom would have to specially order the rabbits at the butcher store. They were large-range rabbits from Australia. They would be dropped into a pot of marinade at the beginning of the week. Mom would work all day Saturday cooking, peeling, and ricing the potatoes. On Sunday morning after church, we would cut up and fry little cubes of bread and make the potato dumplings with one piece of that fried bread inside each. We made over one hundred dumplings for that meal (and ate a lot of them, too). They would be dropped into boiling water, and when they rose to the top, they were done. The potatoes would be covered with a layer of bread crumbs that had been fried in butter and served on a large platter. The marinated rabbits or pot roast was served with thick sour gravy along with red cabbage. It was the best meal.

For regular nightly meals we had to be home at five o'clock for dinner every night (or it may have been six). Dad, if he was home, wanted to eat at a certain time. Everyone had to be at the dinner table. Strange, but I never remember saying grace before meals. Patricia and I had to help with setting the table and with bringing the food from the kitchen to the dining room and setting it on the table, and clearing the table and washing and drying the dishes after dinner. Dinner was the main meal, and everyone was there for it. There wasn't any ritual about it. We didn't have to recite what we did that day, but I guess that's what we probably talked about.

The main meals were the usual—pork chops, ham, chicken parts, various kinds of stews, tailor ham and milk, and I shouldn't forget soups, etc. Some of the other foods we ate that you don't see around much anymore were things like beef hearts, tongue, kidney stew, fried chicken fat, chicken livers, and liver and bacon. The latter was my all-time *least* favorite. The liver was always hard to swallow. We would bury it with catsup and fried onions when we could. We also ate an awful lot of ice cream, pies, and cakes, in addition to the Levi's rye bread.

On Friday we didn't eat meat. I don't know what the fish costs in those days, but we didn't have fish very often. What became a real staple meal on Friday was cod fish cakes. They were served with spaghetti and tomato sauce. The deli around the corner, as I said, in fact all delis, sold cod fish cakes, which they made themselves. On the deli counter, they were laid out on a tray with a little flour on the bottom so they wouldn't stick to the pan.

Saturday nights were reserved for another of my all-time favorite, "cheese surprises." They were made with english muffins, or just toast, with a slice of cheese, a slice or two of tomato topped with a few slices of bacon. It was then baked in the oven until the bacon was crisp and the cheese melted. Yummy!

When dinner was over, the table was cleared, the plates, utensils, pots, and pans were washed and dried and everything put back in their proper places; the final chore was to put out the garbage. After that, homework had to be done. Most of the time Patricia and I sat around the dinner table doing ours. Sometimes I could look over at her work and get some hints. Mom and Dad would help if we needed it. When homework was done, we had a chance to listen to our favorite radio shows or go out to play. In the spring and summer we could stay out until eight or nine o'clock.

1. Play

As a kid in grammar school, I played very little sport. I didn't play in high school either. That's one of the things in my life that I regret not having done. Sports never really interested me so I played just enough  to try to make some friends. But when they found out how bad I was at sports, I lost them. I guess I was just too lazy to make the effort to learn how to play and then exert myself doing it. None of my brothers ever played any sports either so that didn't help to encourage me into a sport. We used to play some stickball in the street. Stoopball was also a regular after-school sport. "Stoopball" was played by throwing a Spalding[63] rubber ball against the edge of the stoop. Those playing with you were aligned on the sidewalk behind the guy with the ball or in the street or even across the street. If the ball was caught on the fly, it was an "out." If it hit the very edge of the stoop, it would generally take off over the head of the guy at the curb and fall in for a run or a two-base hit or something like that if no one caught it. If you played with more than one person, it was very hard to get a run because someone in the back was bound to catch those really long balls that went across the street. Some people called this "curb ball" when you threw the ball against the edge of the curb instead of a stoop.

Another Spalding ball game was "punchball." Here you threw the ball up in the air and punched it with your fist in the same way you would hit the ball with a bat or a stick. You then ran the bases if it wasn't caught or you weren't tagged out as you ran the bases.

Being recognized by your peers was actually important even in those young years. A happy afternoon was when the front door bell rang and one of the kids on the block said, "Hello, Mrs. Lockwood, can Billy come out to play?" There were those afternoons that no one came around for one reason or another and we didn't go out to find

---

63. A Spalding ball was a pink rubber ball made by the Spalding Company used for stickball and other games and sold in any candy store for probably 5¢-10¢.

our friend, but there were other days when we were being punished and were not allowed to go out.

We played a lot of different games after school and then again after supper in the spring and fall when we were allowed out to play. In fact, if we were being punished for something, the punishment would be "not being allowed out to play after supper." The night games were ringolevio, tag, war, and hide-and-seek. There was another game we played against the wall down by Kalkorfen's Bar and Grill. It was bouncing a Spalding ball against the wall. I don't remember the details, but we played it for hours. Another was "box ball" which was played by two kids. A popsicle stick was placed on a crack in the sidewalk and each player stood one sidewalk block on either side of the stick (about three or four feet from the stick). The object of the game was to hit the stick with the Spalding ball so it would move closer to your opponents' side. The one who was successful in pushing the stick all the way to his opponent's side won.

Ringolevio was like tag. "War" was a tag game also played with a Spalding ball. We'd make a large circle in the middle of the street with a piece of chalk; the circle was divided into pie-shaped pieces based on the number of kids playing. Each kid declared himself a country (no two could be the same). One kid would be "it" and have to declare war on a country of his choosing. When he declared war he would have to hit the kid whose country he declared war on with the Spalding. Once he hit the kid, then that kid would be "it." If he didn't hit him in so many tries he was "out." The winner was the last kid left after everyone was out. The problem was that as soon as the "it" kid declared "war," the "target" kid took off. The kid with the ball had to chase him down the street and then try to hit him with the Spalding. If he missed, he would have to run after the ball and then continue chasing the "target." Punishment for losing a game in some neighborhoods could be "asses up." The loser would have to bend over with his head against a wall and everyone would have a turn throwing the Spalding and try to hit him in the ass. Another version of that was just having the kid face the wall and have everyone have a turn at hitting him in the back with the ball.

The Spalding ball was a staple in our lives. Everyone had one or more in his possession at all times. And if you ran out, there were always more on the rooftops to replenish the supply. Balls were constantly being thrown or hit over the rooftops so we'd have to go to the house and ask the "landlord or lady" (typically the one who owned the house or who was responsible for the house in the absence of the owner) if we could get our ball off the roof. Since most of the roofs were flat with a door leading out onto them, they would let us go up to the top floor of the building and out onto the roof where we would usually find a half dozen or more balls. We would also find Spaldings in our driveway from kids throwing them against our driveway door and missing.

Sometimes I'd lose one of the Spalding balls down the sewer. No one had the guts to try to retrieve it. In the sewer, they were goners.

If there were a lot of kids around, we would play "Johnnie on the Pony." The "Pony" team would have one team member stand against the wall facing out. He was the "cushion." The first "pony guy" would bend over, put his arms around the waist of the "cushion," and place his shoulder against the "cushion's" waist. The rest of the team lined up behind the first pony guy, bending over and wrapping their arms around the waist of the guy in front of them. This would make a long row of backs jutting out from the wall. The other team (the "Johnnies") had to run and jump onto the backs of the "pony" team members. The goal of the game was to get all team members onto the pony. The trick was to have the lightest, fastest guys run and jump as far forward as possible so that there would be enough room for everyone else behind him. It was great fun. If the guys on the bottom couldn't hold up the guys on top of them, the whole "pony" would collapse.

Another game played with a lot of kids was Red Rover. I don't remember the details exactly, but there'd be two rows of kids, all holding hands and they would call someone from the other side with "red rover, red rover, come on over." One of the kids from the other side would run over and try to break through the line.

In the warmer weather (when we were quite young), we also played marbles in the street. In those days the curbside was generally free of parked cars so we could play marbles up and down the block without a problem. Home would be a hole in the tarmac that we would gouge out.

I was reminded recently that just about everyone made "skateboards" when I was in grammar school. Not like today's boards, however; the old skateboards were made with a piece of two-by-four inches with a wooden orange crate nailed to one end. To the underside of the two-by-four, we fastened half of a metal skate wheel mechanism to the front end of the two-by-four and the other half of the mechanism went on the back end of the two-by-four. Then we would paint the crate some color that we had lying around the basement. Using another color, we would put big numbers on the front and sides—like our personal racing numbers. On the top of the orange crate were nailed two sticks as handles. We would race around on these contraptions as though they were massive high-speed motorcycles.

Those same skates were also used for conventional roller skating. The top of the skate was a flat piece of metal where you placed your shoe. The metal was actually in two pieces to accommodate different-sized feet. So you could slide apart or close the skate and fasten it to your shoe with a special key (called a "skate key"). The skate was held on with a strap across your instep plus two clamps that tightened down onto the edges of the soles near the toe of your shoes. That was always a pain because they would never stay on, especially if you hit something in the street to dislodge the skate. I don't remember doing a lot of skating. But I do recall how much trouble we always had trying to keep the skates on. They seemed to forever be coming off because of the clamps on the front that held your shoe to the toe part of the skate. It also depended on what kind of shoes you were wearing. Sneakers didn't work at all because there was no sole to clamp down on.

We also played "guns." Hunting down the bad guys or teaming up against the Japs or "Krauts" hiding in hallways or behind cars or in alleys and then shooting it out with the bad guys. There was a lot of "I got you. You're dead" or "No, you missed me" and "Your gun wasn't even aimed at me!" Everyone had some sort of toy gun. There weren't very many big machine guns or mortars or things like that. It was typically the six-shooter or a Colt .45 variety. As it is today, guns were not allowed in school.

While some of the girls often played these games with us, they generally played by themselves. Jump rope was a big activity. Two girls could jump rope by tying one end of the rope to a fence and one of the girls turned the other end. If there were three or more girls, they would play double jumping with two lengths of rope. If a girl was alone, she jumped rope by herself. Because it was generally a girl's activity—and also one that got the heartbeat up—I never learned to jump rope, even today.

Hopscotch was another game that showed up on every sidewalk where the boxes were marked with chalk.

Have I mentioned the ubiquitous "Good Humor" ice cream truck yet? Every night without fail, the bells would peal out the arrival of the best thing in the world. The truck would cruise up the street and stop in the middle of the crowd of kids playing in the street. Everyone would rush home to get money for ice cream. It was the thing to do.

As I mentioned earlier, trick-or-treating was not done on Halloween as the kids do it today. Instead, we'd get one of our mother's stockings and fill the foot part with flour and tie a nut at the ankle. That became a long lethal weapon with a hard ball of flour at one end. This lethal weapon would be used to hit your buddies on the back or on the legs. Sometimes we'd even go after the girls. I don't remember it hurting that much, but it left a nice white mark on your clothing. There was some egg throwing as well, but we couldn't afford that luxury.

Inevitably, someone always had a Halloween party when we were around nine or ten years old. Most of the time it was at one of the kids on the block's house or we would have it. We would have games like Pin the Tail on the Donkey and definitely do some "dunking for apples." The apples always had a penny, nickel, dime, or quarter in them—or maybe it was only certain ones that had the coins in them, I don't remember. But I remember that I always got my shirt all wet from diving into the tub of water. How come they don't do that anymore? Let me guess: AIDS or other communicable diseases. Nothing ever happened to us!

In the next step up the party ladder at about age eleven, twelve, or thirteen, prior to high school we started to experiment with the opposite sex. The parties would include some dancing and the infamous Spin the Bottle kissing game where you got the chance to kiss the girls without acting like a pervert. There seemed to be a lot of parties during those years. Unfortunately, I seem to remember that the bottle never stopped at the girl I most wanted to kiss (or maybe it was the opposite: no one wanted to kiss me!). There were too many girls on our block, but the one I liked was Dorothy Schmidt. Her girlfriend was Marie Groin who lived on Seneca Avenue.[64]

---

[64] Ironically, Marie Groin turned up living on our block in Garden City when we moved there in 1973. In fact, her daughter Diane was the same age as Mark.

In the winter, when there was snow, and there always seemed to be more than we get today, we had great fun on our American Flyer sleds. On the next block, on the other side of Woodward Avenue, Linden Street rose up, making the street a great course for sledding. The problem was that if you got up a good head of speed, you had to be very careful when you reached Woodward Avenue because of the traffic. There weren't as many cars then as there are today, but they were moving along Woodward Avenue. What saved us was the fact that it was usually very snowy and not too many cars were out in the snow, and if they were, they usually went pretty slow. Plus, the roads were generally unplowed. So we had great fun on Linden Street.

Then here was also Snake Hill by Grover Cleveland High School which was five times longer than Linden Street's run, but there were also hundreds of kids using Snake Hill and it would take us a half hour to get there.

The all-time favorite sledding was in Forest Park, but we had to take the trolley. Within the golf course, there were great hills as well as "the Bowl" with sledding on all sides and kids coming from every direction. It was surprising that no one ever got hurt.

George somehow acquired a pair of wooden skis and would travel to Forest Park to ski whenever there was snow. I can still picture him skiing along the street. This was long before skiing was even popular.

We also made great snow houses or igloos on those heavy snow days. We built ours right in front of our house from the snow from shoveling the sidewalk. Once the shoveling was completed, there were big snowball fights with every kid in the neighborhood participating. The snow houses or igloos would evolve down to a three-sided fort from which to launch the snowball battles. We'd go home with our clothes totally filled with snow and soaking wet.

One of the favorite sports on snow days was throwing snowballs at passing trucks. Coming home from school, I once threw a snowball at a fuel oil truck and hit the driver square in the cheek as he rolled down his window. He stopped the truck and chased me for what seemed to be forever. I never ran so fast in my life.

I got chased another time by the iceman. Many homes had only ice boxes instead of today's refrigerators. The iceman delivered the ice on a regular schedule. His open-backed truck was loaded with large blocks of ice maybe four feet long and two feet thick. Depending on which house he was delivering to, he would chop a piece off one of the large blocks by making a series of stabs into the ice with his ice pick. The smaller block would come off easily with his touch. He didn't like us climbing up on the truck chipping off pieces for ourselves. One day he came back from a delivery and found us all on the truck chipping off pieces. We jumped off the truck and started running with him right behind us. I ran as fast as I could, and as he ran after us, all of the change in his leather apron flew out and he had to stop to pick them up. Naturally, we avoided him for several weeks after that. Money was important to us so we did risk going back to the scene later that day to see if he missed any coins.

But back to the snow: it wasn't just fun and games on snow days. It became serious business to go out and get some snow shoveling jobs to make a few cents. I had Linden Street between Underdonk and Woodward pretty much sewed up for myself, at least on my side of the street. Everyone knew Billy Lockwood would shovel their sidewalks and clean off the stoops. I earned a dollar or two per house.

I also made money at other times by selling old newspapers at the junkyard. All the old newspapers from our house were put in a big "paper bin" in the front of the basement next to the garbage bags. Every other Saturday or so I would pile the papers into neat bundles, tie them up, and wheel them down the block in my wagon to Grenari's junkyard. Depending on the market, Grenari paid about 50¢ per hundred pounds. I would sometimes save up the papers and have to make several trips and wind up with a couple of dollars. We even had a scale in the basement so I could weigh my papers ahead of time to keep Mr. Grenari honest. I would also scavenger through the basement collecting old pieces of lead pipe or other metal objects that could be sold for scrap metal to help the war effort. Metal went for more money, but there wasn't that much around. Uncle Will would sometimes bring home some old scrap metal for me to sell to Grenari.

I also inherited the job of picking up the horse manure left in the street by the horse-drawn vegetable vendor. (I think my mother did it herself since we were often in school when the wagon came around.) Every other day or so, this horse-drawn wagon would come by piled high with all kinds of fruits and vegetables pulled by a mangy old horse. In fact, the wagon always stopped right in front of our house probably because we were right in the middle of the block. There was a wooden streetlight pole in front of our house too and the vegetable man would tie the horse up to that pole. Apparently the horse liked the wooden pole and over the years left a large indent in the wood from where he munched on it. But anyway, Mom loved flowers and had many different species of roses and other flowers in the garden. Horse manure was a great fertilizer so we were very conscientious whenever the horse left something behind. Matter of fact, when I got the job of doing the picking, it was because George didn't do it. He caught hell from Uncle Will but never did it again. I inherited the job permanently—or at least until we no longer had the horse come by with the vegetables. By the way, Mom's roses were beautiful. She prided herself on her roses and poppies and also grew some tomatoes and other vegetables. I remember so vividly having to go into the garden to cut some chives to mix with the cottage cheese (it was the chunky kind of cottage cheese).

As I got older, I also got more responsibility for working around the house. Painting was one job I did when I was in high school. That was in addition to the big job on the garage. I painted the window frames on the outside. They were always painted green. I actually had to climb up to the third story on a big extension ladder, which never bothered me. The house had a flat roof covered with tar paper, and it had to be painted with thick gooey tar that we brushed on every couple of years. I seem to remember being involved with the job on at least two separate occasions. The tar was like a liquid tar that had to be painted on with a long-handled push brush made specifically for that purpose. It was a real dirty job where everything we wore got tar on it. I had to wear only my oldest and crummiest clothes and shoes. In May there was one more job: putting up the window awnings on the front windows and the awning on the back porch.

Patricia and I were pretty healthy kids growing up. Mom's baby record for me showed chicken pox at seven months, a mastoid operation at seven weeks, whopping cough at two years, measles at just under four years (July 1938), and scarlatina[65] (commonly called scarlet fever) at seven years.

[65.] Strep throat.

I also had my tonsils out in October 1942; I had just turned eight. That was my first stay in the hospital. I got to eat a ton of ice cream for weeks afterward. The worst part of it was being in the hospital and not knowing how long I'd have to stay. I waited and waited for Mom to come the morning after the operation. I assumed she would be coming early in the morning to pick me up. It seemed like an eternity, but it was probably no more than an hour or two. Isn't it strange how I remember that small incident from such an early age. I can still picture myself in the hospital bed peering down the corridor to get an early glimpse of Mom coming for me. When she didn't come, I was filled with disappointment that still wells up when I think of it.

When I was in grammar school—probably 1943 or 1944—I had a growth on my foot. From walking around barefoot all summer long in Bayville, a piece of sand must have lodged itself into an open cut on the bottom of my left foot, right under my big toe. The cut healed, but my body wanted to reject that piece of sand and couldn't so a large lump formed. The podiatrist actually had me come back several times as he shaved away thin layers of the lump and then burned out the sand at the heart of the lump. My mother had to take an old pair of shoes and cut out the toe so I could have something to walk on.

I got into the awful habit of biting my fingernails, which I still do from time to time. The family doctor, Dr. Bongiorno, had to make a house call to examine me because I was having bad stomachaches. He blamed the stomachaches on my swallowing the nails I bit off. It was during that examination that he noticed that I needed to be circumcised. Ouch! That was in October 1945; I was eleven. It was an awful experience, which I will not bore you with the details. But it was something I will never forget. My mother should have known it was not going to work out well. The doctor who performed the circumcision was named "Dr. Butcher." Can you believe that? How's that for luck! I've always contended that he cut off much too much! Well, let's not be too shortsighted.

Fun things in those early years of my life included simple pleasures like going to the candy store. There were candy stores all over the neighborhood, one on practically every block, sometimes two. For five or ten cents, we could get a mellow roll which was ice cream on a piece of cake wrapped in thin cardboard. The ice cream might even have been some different kind of cream. Candy itself was also very cheap so we could always get a piece of chocolate or something like a piece of candy that looked like a cigarette. Some were just a white candy with a red tip while there were some that were chocolate covered with a white paper wrapping. There were also other kinds of goodies as little wax jugs filled with a sweet liquid. They all had special names, too.

Friends came and went in those early years. One friend that went pretty fast was Foster Culver. He lived right behind us on Gates Avenue. He was a tall lanky kid whose parents had died when he was young, and he was brought up by his aunt and uncle. In grammar school, Foster had a bad habit of sucking his thumb. But the real gross part was when he sucked his thumb he also stuck his pinky finger in his nose. Everyone laughed at him, but he didn't seem to know exactly what we were laughing at. I sort of hung out with Foster for a short span. We generally played guns at that age, and he would come around to our street because Gates Avenue was too busy with the buses going by all the time.

The problem with Foster was that he stole things. I wound up missing a couple of my favorite guns, and the real problem came when my father's two watches were missing from the cabinet in the dining room where he usually left them when he slept or was washing up. They wound up missing right after Foster had been in the house during the time when Dad was sleeping. My father went around to Foster's house and accused him of taking the watches but he denied it and we couldn't prove otherwise. My father was understandably furious with him and me (for letting him in the house) and I was banned from playing with him. Since I had a couple of guns missing too, I wasn't too happy with him either. So the ban didn't really hurt too much. Foster turned out to be rather weird throughout high school but I don't know what happened to him after that. We didn't talk much.

2. Radio Shows

Television didn't come to our house until about 1947-'48. Prior to that, the radio was our main source of entertainment. The radio shows we listened to were magnificent. They were a real treat. They developed our imagination beyond what anything today could do. Today, kids are not allowed to imagine anything. It's all there in front of them all wrapped up in a neat package. If someone said there was a monster with burning red eyes and smoke coming out of its nose, you could actually picture that in your mind. There were mystery shows such as *The Inner Sanctum, Lights Out Everyone*, and of course, *Gang Busters, The FBI in Peace and War, Captain Midnight, Public Enemy #1, Superman, Dick Tracy, The Green Hornet, The Shadow, Jack Armstrong—the All-American Boy*, and Westerns like *The Lone Ranger, Tom Mix*, and *Gene Autry*. There were also laugh-out-loud-funny shows like *Jack Benny, Fibber McGee and Molly*, and *Amos and Andy*. There were other shows like *Can You Top This?* a panel of comedians telling jokes on various subject matter that were picked out of a box and judged by the applause of the audience.

While we listened to the radio at night, my dad would take his beer pail down to Koenig's and return with about a quart of draft beer. The beer pail was exactly that. It was a tin pail with a wire handle and a tight-fitting lid. Sometimes I was allowed to go for the beer. There wasn't all the regulations about children drinking and smoking that there are today. I seem to recall the pail of beer costing 25¢ or 50¢.

The *Dick Tracy, Captain Midnight, Jack Armstrong*, and other shows all offered secret decoder rings and other cheap 10¢ toys that you could get by sending away to the radio station or to a cereal company along with the required number of box tops from the cereal packages. The *Captain Midnight* decoder ring was my favorite. There were also secret whistles, spyglasses, fake two-way wrist radios (used by *Dick Tracy*), and dozens more.

There were also the afternoon soaps such as *Stella Dallas, As the World Turns*, and *Helen Trent*. Mom listened to them regularly while she washed, cleaned, ironed, or just knitted. She was an ardent follower of most of those afternoon soaps.

Jack and George, at that time of my life—say, when I was between eight and twelve—were nowhere to be found in my memory.[66] I looked back and tried to picture the dinner table. They were there, but they were not talking or fooling around. Even after dinner, they are not around in my picture memory. Perhaps that's true. They may have gone off to study alone or to their room upstairs or something like that. But they weren't around.

---

[66] Except for the time spent watching George make things in the basement.

Saturday was a workday at home. There was always something that had to be done on Saturday. That philosophy actually carried over to my adult life where Saturday was always set aside for working around the house. Whatever had to be done, it was done on Saturday. It took me a long time to break that habit and realize that you could have fun on Saturday too. The rugs in the hallway on both the first and second floors had to be rolled up and swept, and the floors had to be cleaned. The rugs were sought of grass rugs that "shed" their fibers. All of that had to be swept up. The hall cleaning was primarily my job. I also had to sweep the front sidewalk, and Mom generally washed down the front stoop. And there was the ever-present shopping. On Saturday, I also had to go for the food for Sunday's meal.

Sunday's dinner was at one or two o'clock without fail. It was a big meal with all the trimmings. Everyone was always there, and everyone was dressed up since they had been to church that morning. The food was always good: roast beef, chicken, pork loin, or leg of lamb. All meals were served with vegetables and mostly mashed potatoes. We sometimes had Idaho baked potatoes, and depending on the time of the year, there were sweet potatoes. I particularly loved sweet potatoes. Mom would always make a lot of extras so the next day she would slice them up and fry them in butter. They were and still are the best. Sunday was a special day. There wasn't any playing in the street with the kids. It was quiet and calm. We didn't change back into street clothes after eating the big meal.

But back to Saturday: The big thing was the afternoon movie at the Parthenon Theater on Wyckoff and Myrtle Avenues under the elevated trains referred to as the El. The Saturday movies were a treat. There were two full-length features plus a load of cartoons to start and a newsreel of what was happening around the world, mostly connected to the war. Some of the movies were "serials" that went on from week to week, so you couldn't miss one week. There was *Buck Rogers* and *The Lone Ranger*. There was another show with a hero who rode a horse, but I don't think he was a cowboy. His headquarters were at the side of a mountain which opened up as he approached. The villains wore tin hats and caps. Patricia and I must have gone with Jack or George because I can remember tagging along with them and their friends.

One memorable movie was *Sahara* with Humphrey Bogart where he was in the army tank corps in North Africa and they were stranded at a small house in the middle of the desert and running out of water. As though it was yesterday, I remember the intellectual discussion that went on as we walked home from the movie: "What would happen if they did run out of water? Would they drink their own urine?" One answer was "Hey, stupid, if they didn't have any water to drink, they wouldn't have to piss!" It's funny the things you remember all these years.

Next door to the Parthenon Theater under the El was the Ridgewood Grove, a boxing arena. Every Friday night was "Boxing at Ridgewood Grove." Pop and Uncle Will would go practically every Friday night. Occasionally, Pop would take. It was a smoke-filled dark room with a lighted boxing ring at the center. (Why did they call it a boxing ring if it was square?) Everyone was smoking cigars, cigarettes, or pipes and we sat on wooden benches. What a treat to go to the Ridgewood Grove. When television came in, there continued to be a program called "Friday Night Fights from Ridgewood Grove" for several years until boxing lost its audience.

There were also the Sunday comics that appeared in the *New York News* or the *Post*. The big ones were *Dick Tracy*, *Li'l Abner*, and *Popeye*. And my favorite was *Prince Valiant*. There were probably a dozen or more comic strips that we read religiously every Sunday morning. There was also a period of years when the mayor of New York City, Mayor La Guardia, read the comics on the radio every Sunday morning.

3. Boy Scouts

During my grammar school days I joined the parish's Boy Scout troop.[67] We didn't do much other than practice as a marching band. Since I was a fat little kid, I got the bass drum to play. Gradually, I worked my way up to the tenor drum (that was a snare drum without snares and played with felt-tipped sticks and it had the sound of a tom-tom). Once I learned all the drum rudiments and the beats we played, I was promoted to the snare drum.

Playing the drums for the Boy Scouts was a turning point in my life. My brother George was painting and selling wallpaper designs,

---

[67.] I don't think they had a Cub Scout troop at that time.

and he was also a big fan of bebop jazz and encouraged me to learn to play the drums professionally. Since Mom didn't really have any money, he gave me three dollars a week for drum lessons. One of his friends gave him the name of this famous drum teacher in Manhattan named William Kessler on Forty-seventh Street between Sixth and Seventh avenues (ironically, the same street that my office at Chase Manhattan Bank was on more than fifty years later). And while the building itself isn't there any longer, the same music stores that make the area the heart of the musical instrument trade in Manhattan are still there. I started taking lessons from Mr. Kessler when I was about eleven or twelve. Every Thursday afternoon after school, I would take two subways to Forty-seventh Street. By the way, I never passed the Nedick's stand on the corner of Forty-seventh Street without having a hot dog or two and an orange drink. I guess I had enough money for that, probably only 25¢. Mr. Kessler was a tough taskmaster. As I improved and learned playing songs rather than just doing rudiments, he would play the xylophone and I drummed along with him to learn certain beats. Mr. Kessler was a short, funny-looking man with a very broad nose covering his face as though he once was a boxer who got hit in the nose a lot. He bragged of being the drummer at the Copacabana Nightclub, which was the place to be seen socially at the time.

When I was in twelfth grade at St. Brigid's, a few kids from the class and I formed a dance band for the first time. I don't remember much about it, but it had to be real crude. One of the members played the accordion. (There was always someone around who played the accordion in those days.) I somehow got an old set of drums from somebody. I remember taking the two drums apart and painting them blue with black trim. (There I go again with the black paint.) It was a big bass drum and a snare drum plus a terrible cymbal and a high hat (two cymbals with a foot pedal to bang them together). I remember playing at one school function at St. Brigid's and everything else is blank, thankfully.

When I was in high school, I upgraded to a used white mother-of-pearl set of drums, which I got through Mr. Kessler for $150 with a high hat and a great Zildjian ride cymbal. Jo Jones, a well-known jazz drummer at that time, had owned the set. I'll talk about that later.

Back to the Boy Scouts: The biggest thing in my life in grammar school was playing in the marching band in a parade to Ebbets Field. I can't remember what the occasion was (it could have been some sort of Catholic Day event), but I can remember being the lead drummer in the marching band and our troop marched with the school. We marched all through Brooklyn and wound up in Ebbets Field. That was the one and only time I was ever there.

I don't remember earning one merit badge in the Boy Scouts. We just didn't do things like that, apparently. We may have gone to some park once acting as though we were camping out, but we never stayed overnight or anything like that.

A lot of other things happened in grammar school too. Most of what I remember actually came in the latter years, when I was eleven and twelve. That's when you start making real friends as you mature. It was in grammar school that I met Connie. She walked down Linden Street every day just as did Patricia and I and several other kids. We were attracted to each other pretty early on, too. In fact, when I was eleven and she ten, we actually went to the movies together (that was after the Central Park Zoo date). I saved up my allowance and scrap-paper money, and we went to the Grandview movie a few blocks away. It was a little movie house and I had to stand in the back because there was only one seat left and Connie took it. The movie was 18¢. We later went for a soda at the local ice cream parlor on Woodward Avenue. (The sodas were 15¢.) I wound up using my entire 50¢ allowance for that week and even had to borrow some from Mom. That movie house, as an aside, also showed outdoor movies in the summer. The movie house was on the corner, and next to it was a vacant lot that had been paved over and which was screened off from the sidewalk with an eight-foot-high green wooden fence. The outdoor movies were projected onto the outside brick wall of the tenement house on the other side of the vacant lot, and there were rows of wooden benches for the moviegoers to sit on.

Our clothing was fairly simple. For school we wore slacks and a shirt and tie, no uniform. At one time, Mom bought me a suit with knickers. I was so big in the upper part of my body for a boy of my age that the elastic part of the knickers was almost down to my ankles. Don't laugh! I had to tuck the elastic up above my knees and blouse the pants from there. It was very uncomfortable because the elastic was tight around my upper leg, cutting off circulation to the lower part of my leg. Because

I was so fat, nothing ever fit me right. But you know, it never seemed to matter. Somehow or the other, I sloughed it off.

B. St. Brigid's Roman Catholic Church and School

Elementary school for me was St. Brigid's Roman Catholic School on St. Nicholas Avenue about four blocks down Linden Street from our house. The Sisters of Mercy nuns ran the school. We had to wear a shirt and tie every day. There wasn't anything like

jeans then. But if there were, we would not have been allowed to wear them anyway. I don't remember all the names of the nuns. Sister Vincentia was one. She would bat us around if we misbehaved. I remember once she left the room for a short break and returned to a room full of kids having a ball. Everyone was up and around doing something they shouldn't have. She promptly got the boys lined up on one side of the room and the girls on the other. As they approached her single file from each side, the boys got a smack with her right hand and the girls with her left hand—she must have been ambidextrous. That was the first time and probably the last time Patricia ever got hit and she really was upset. I remember her coming home and telling Mom that I cried and she didn't. I really don't remember if I did or not. (I think I did cry, but only because Sister Vincentia hit the boys harder than she hit the girls.)

We worked hard in school; there was always homework, and you always got called on throughout the day. If you didn't do something right, the punishment was to write it correctly twenty-five or fifty times. I failed a penmanship test and thus had to write the Lord's Prayer twenty-five times after school. I must have written it over twenty-five times before I got it right. And you know, it didn't help my penmanship one bit.

When we first started in school, the building was a real dump. The bathrooms were in the basement, and they were dark and wet all the time. Once I went to the bathroom and my pants fell on the floor, and when I put them back on, I realized that the floor was wet and so were my pants. I got ribbed for wetting my pants. Later, the building was redone with glass block walls and a complete makeover. It was quite nice after that.

It seemed as though our entire life centered on the school and church. I was an altar boy and had to serve Mass just about every day. This was a big thing, and only a few boys were selected. We had to learn the Latin responses to all the prayers and how to "serve" Mass. Each week we got a different schedule. Sometimes it was the 5:45 a.m. Mass every day for a week; the next week it was perhaps the 8:00 a.m. or 9:00 a.m. Mass or a funeral later in the morning. And we also had to serve a Sunday (and Saturday) Mass and often we had to serve at Saturday and Sunday weddings, which we liked because the best man or the groom always  gave us a dollar or two. Mom had to buy me a black cassock just like the priests wore and a white surplice that was worn over the cassock. She also had to keep the surplice clean and ironed with starch.

Before becoming an altar boy, I wanted to be in the choir, but the choir was headed by an old German organist and choirmaster who was very strict. I auditioned for the job and was practicing with the choir on the first day when I whispered something to my friend. The choirmaster heard me talking and kicked me right out. That was a real shock, but worse was having to tell Mom.

Saturday afternoon after the movies was confession time at St. Brigid's. That's when we met our friends and did some socializing. One Saturday I wound up in a big fight with Henry Braido. We were about the same size and were both altar boys. He threw me to the ground, and I hit my head on the hard concrete. I hated him after that, and it lasted right into high school. But I finally got even with him in gym class. We were all standing around trying to avoid having to do any exercises when Henry picked a fight with me again. We were at the end of the gym where all the gymnastic equipment was—floor mats, horses, parallel bars, etc. We wrestled around for a while, and to his surprise, I pinned him to the mat and won. He was mortified. A year later, he picked another fight with me and got me in a headlock where I felt like my brains were being squeezed out and my ears hurt real bad. He won that one and we didn't fight after that. Henry is one of the few guys from my class that I've actually seen in later years; he rode the Long Island Railroad to Jamaica with me several times over the years and was the only guy from my high school class that I saw at our forty-fifth class reunion. And he didn't pick a fight! I guess I showed him!

The Lockwood kids were well-known at St. Brigid's. Not only did my two older brothers go there, but Virginia went there and Mom before her. Being twins was one thing that set us apart from everyone else. Patricia was much more conscientious with school than I. I never liked to study and was probably not as smart as she. I guess in retrospect, had I studied harder, I would have been able to get into one of the Catholic high schools. I took the tests for all the schools but didn't make it. Mom really wanted me to go to one of them. But both Jack and George went to the public high school, Grover Cleveland, and so that's were I wound up. It was probably just as well since it would have cost her more money than she could afford at the time.

The big religious events in the church included first Holy Communion at age seven and confirmation at age twelve. They were both big deals, requiring Mom to spend a great deal of money she didn't have on a dress for Patricia and a dark blue serge suit for me; it probably also included shoes for both of us. For confirmation, we needed to take yet another name. I chose Robert.

Don't ask me why; it happened to be a popular name in those days. Patricia chose Theresa. Funny, but I've not liked the name Robert or Theresa since then.

The one thing about growing up when we did was that there wasn't this emphasis on "entertaining the kids" like it is today. We fended for ourselves. We had our own games to play, some with other kids, some by ourselves. I can remember playing with little lead toy soldiers on the living room floor for hours by myself—and having lots of fun. Patricia and I also played a lot of make-believe situations. The overstuffed arms of the big sofa in the living room, which folded out at night and doubled as our bed, were great galloping horses for both of us as we rode off into the sunset or chased the Indians (or ran from them) as our imaginations took us into the wild and wooly West; the big chair in the corner was a boulder to hide behind when the Indians attacked. We also had that really nice castle set from Uncle Gus, which allowed us to travel to the highlands of Scotland to defend our castle against the marauding knights from England. *Prince Valiant* was one of our favorite comic strips every Sunday morning, and we lived those times with great enthusiasm.

A big box of Lincoln Logs also took us into other wilderness areas where we built forts and bridges and farmhouses that exercised our imagination to the fullest. This was particularly the case since there wasn't anything around that remotely resembled a television set. That came much later.

The war was on too, but we didn't get the blow-by-blow reports like we do on television today. We saw pictures of the war in *Life* magazine or the newspaper or we saw newsreels at the start of the movies. We were affected most directly by the food and other rationing that was imposed on everyone. Meat, cheese, and oil, for example, were all severely rationed (that might be why we ate tailor ham and milk for dinner) as were gasoline and butter. Oleomargarine became a staple in our house. I had to mix the margarine with a dye that came in the package that would make it look more like the color of butter. Mom and Dad would have a ration book that would allow them a certain amount of meat, cheese, butter, sugar, coffee, tires, shoes, and oil per month. Cigarettes were definitely in short supply, and that was a problem in our house since both Mom and Dad were heavy smokers. Dad had a cigarette-making machine that Patricia and I learned to operate. It was a small metal gadget about the width of a cigarette with a sheet of rubber that somehow rolled the tobacco into a long round cylinder. We fed cigarette paper into one end, shook a predetermined amount of tobacco onto the rubber, and pulled the lever and voila! A cigarette would roll out the other end. Patricia and I made thousands (well, maybe hundreds) of cigarettes that way.

The war also meant that women couldn't get nylon or silk stockings to wear. There were only ten flavors of ice cream available, and beer was watered down (at least that's what I read; I was too young to drink in those days). Unless you were in a vital job such as a doctor, minister, or defense worker, you got ration cards for two gallons of gasoline per week (the vital jobholders got rations for three gallons per week). The war effort was very strong. An article I just read told of how carpooling was encouraged. A poster on carpooling read, "If you drive alone, you drive with Hitler." That same article talked of the items that were not available as Christmas presents in December 1943. They included the following: doll carriages, rubber boots, bicycles or tricycles, typewriters, toasters, hair curlers, and alarm clocks. There wasn't any tinsel for the tree either, nor gold and silver ribbon for wrapping packages.

The government (the War Production Board) actually issued directives on clothing production. Full and pleated skirts were forbidden; hemlines were raised (it was called patriotic chic) and men's pants could not have cuffs, and vests were outlawed.

We were also influenced by the war propaganda particularly as it related to the Japanese. They were described as cruel, sadistic barbarians that we should hate. And indeed that tended to work on our young minds. I can remember discussing with my friends what we would do if we had a Japanese prisoner of our own. We'd chain him to a wall in the basement and dream up ways to torture him endlessly. The old war movies of the time portrayed the Japanese soldiers just that way. In the street game "war," we were extra hard on Japan, Germany, and Italy too. (Kids tended to take countries like France or England for that reason.)

We did not know of the atrocities that were being done to the Jews in Europe so we were less hateful of the Germans and Italians. In fact, most of the residents of Ridgewood were German. We did hear that there were German spies who landed on the beaches along the south shore of Long Island from U-boats. But for whatever reason, that never bothered us as much as what we heard about the Japanese. Of course, we heard about the Bataan Death March and how some of our men were treated when captured, and the biggest thing that turned us against them was the unprovoked attack on Pearl Harbor. I was too young to have understood or read about the fact that the U.S. government actually rounded up and interned all Japanese residing in the United States into a camp in Nevada for the duration of the war. They didn't do anything like that with the Germans or Italians living in the States. I wonder why.

I was reminded recently that Dad took us to view the *Normandie*, a huge French luxury ocean liner that capsized in New York Harbor in 1942. The *Normandie* was at the time the largest and most luxurious ocean liner ever built. It was built in France in 1932 and was faster than any other ship at sea. At 83,400 tons, there was nothing bigger. In 1941, it was docked in New York when Germany invaded France. The U.S. government confiscated it and started to convert it to a troop transport ship when a spark from an acetylene torch ignited some life preservers. The New York City Fire Department apparently screwed up the efforts to bring the fire under control, which led to water filling up part of the ship and causing it to capsize. At the time it was a big event in New York Harbor. My father drove us by the site very slowly but couldn't stop. I can still remember seeing this gigantic ship lying on its side next to the dock.

When the war was over, technology advanced at a rapid pace. It was probably just after the war that we got a phonograph player. What a wonderful thing. Dad actually bought a pile of records, too. It was the centerpiece of our living room, and we played it whenever we got the chance. For me anyway, that lasted until it malfunctioned. It seemed that the turntable started slipping so that the songs slowed down. The repairman came one day when I was homesick. I remember it as though it was yesterday. He put on "Ballerina," a song by Vaughn Monroe. I grew to hate that song as the repairman played it over and over and over again, each time at a different but yet incorrect and slow speed. No one in our house ever played that record again. The songs we did get were generally the popular ones of the day. For example, "Nickelodeon" ("Put another nickel in, in the nickelodeon . . .") by Patty Brewer; a lot of Frank Sinatra and Bing Crosby—I know we had "White Christmas." Many of the songs were singles on the smaller 45 rpm-sized records. There were not a lot of record albums as we know them today. I'll talk about television later.

It was not too much before the phonograph and the television that we also got our own telephone. We were so excited to get a telephone. Of course, it was a rotary phone but we didn't know any different. The first thing we did when the telephone book arrived was turn to the *Ls* and look for our name. And to our shock we were the only "Lockwood" in the book. What a surprise. You mean there are no other Lockwoods in all of Queens County? Wow! Were we special!! At least that's what we thought. Little did we know that there are more Lockwoods than you could shake a stick at; they just didn't have telephones then, I guess.

C. Bayville—It Doesn't Get Any Better Than This

The earliest I can actually remember of my life is in Bayville, so perhaps I was two or three. We were still at the "Spanish House,"[68] and it was the Fourth of July and Uncle Will and Dad and Jack and George were shooting off fireworks. I had the measles or something and had to stay in bed. I could only look out the window next to my bed. I remember thinking about all the fun I was missing.

[68.] I think it was called the "Spanish House" because it had a red tiled roof.

Bayville was a special place. It was sparse, clean, relaxed, and just there to have fun. Oh, how I can remember the creek. At the end of  Fifth Street where we lived, there was a sandy beach and what amounted to a rather large impression in the ground that was surrounded by marsh reeds. These reeds separated the beach from the main body of water, Oyster Bay itself, which was perhaps one thousand feet or so farther out. The creek was never entirely dry. There was a stream running through it out to the bay. (Fed, I think, by an underground spring.) At low tide, we would play in the stream, which always had an abundance of killies or baby eels, and of course, there were always the ubiquitous fiddler crabs. They were everywhere, thousands of them. When the tide came in, the fiddler crabs would disappear into their holes and the creek would literally fill up with the bay water at high tide. It was our own private lagoon where only the few families who lived on Fifth Street and a few other adjourning streets ever used. The stream that ran through the creek had carved a path through the reeds, so at low tide there was a convenient way out to the bay to go clamming or for catching worms for fishing. That path through the reeds was always there when the tide came in. Boats coming in and out of the creek followed the winding path, which was probably ten or twenty feet wide, through the reeds. At the base of the reeds were real thick black mud and an abundance of mussels, which at the time, we didn't really think were edible. Only the Italians ate them, and we thought they were crazy. Had we only known then what we know now!

The creek was our hangout. After breakfast, I would run to the creek to see what was going on and to determine how the tide was going to be that day. The most fun was when the tide was up or coming up so we could swim. If the tide was coming in, that was great because I could get down there as it was coming in and stay in the water until it went back down on ebb tide. One year, someone had anchored a huge gray cork navy lifeboat-type float out in the middle of the creek. We had great fun with that. It had a floor with netting on the sides, which lasted for just one season. After that, it was just an oblong float but still great fun.

If you look at the picture of me in the boat above, right behind my head is a tree. That tree had a platform in it, which was our hiding place of refuge. There was a ladder made of pieces of wood nailed to the tree trunk for access to our tree house. Not everyone was allowed to climb those stairs and enter the inner sanctum.

Our family would go to Bayville the day school ended and literally not return until Labor Day night, just in time for school the next day. How I remember those days. The Studebaker would be packed; it was as though we were moving far away. I can even remember having to stop halfway there to let Dad take a little nap because of the long drive. We had to sit very still while he napped. (On those occasions he must have come straight from work because it was only thirty or so miles to Bayville from Ridgewood.) When we got there, off came the shoes, and for a day or so it was tough walking barefoot but then my soles got like leather and I could walk over hot coals if I had to. For the rest of the summer we only put our shoes on to go to church. Of course, I got all kinds of things stuck to the bottom of my feet. (Remember my time at the podiatrist?)

There weren't a lot of kids around to play with in Bayville. Richie Schwartz lived right next to the creek, that is, the first house closest to the creek. His father was a banker from the city, and every Friday afternoon, he would come barreling down Fifth Street in his big black Buick. The Schwartzes had three children; Richie was the youngest. He had an older sister and a brother. During  the war, his brother was a Navy Wildcat pilot on an aircraft carrier in the Pacific and was shot down during a dogfight with a Japanese fighter. He survived in a lifeboat for several days before being picked up. He came home for several weeks after that, and we would sneak into the garage to look at his shoulder holster and the .45 Colt in it, which he apparently was able to take home with him (no one seemed to care about whether us kids would shoot ourselves). Richie was a nice kid and very studious. He was always reading in contrast to yours truly who hated to read. I pestered him to come out and play, but he wanted to read. His mother constantly pushed him to read all the time so I ended up playing with Patricia a lot or just playing by myself or with whoever was around.

While Bayville was a great retreat from the hot and steamy streets of Ridgewood, the downside was that I never learned to play sports like my friends back in Ridgewood who spent their summers in the playground or in the street playing stickball or baseball. When I returned to Ridgewood, I was never asked to play ball. Teams were already sided up. And worse, as I said earlier, I really didn't know how to play. But somehow or the other, while it bothered me momentarily that I didn't know how to play or I just didn't play well when I did play, I can't remember ever getting really upset over it. It bothered me from the standpoint of not having any close friends because of not being around all summer. But once school started, everything was back to normal and we were out in the street having a good time again. As I got older, it may have bothered me more because I got fatter and lazier and then I didn't want to exert myself with sports.

But Bayville was great. We had a heavy fourteen-foot wooden rowboat (named **Pat & Bill**) with a little two-horsepower outboard. I was too young to use the motor, but that didn't stop me from rowing all over the bay. On real windy days, Richie and I would row to the southern end of the bay—particularly when the wind was coming from the South, which is where it usually  came from. We'd row the two or three miles into the wind then turn the boat around, stick an oar out the back as a rudder, and open up our big beach umbrella. One of us would hold on to the umbrella while the other would steer the boat with an oar back.

I remember very vividly playing a game of pirates with a whole group of kids right after a bad storm. In fact, I think we conceived it while we where sitting out the storm. We ended up making wooden swords, eye patches, and hats and then went out with several different rowboats and fought battles from one boat to the other. I particularly remember it because the tide was so high the water was up over the reeds and we could go places that typically were too thick with reeds to navigate.

What I don't remember much of is what Jack and George were doing while Patricia and I were playing, particularly when they were real young. I know once Jack got a severe cut on the bottom of his foot when he stepped out of a canoe onto a broken bottle. He came into the house with blood all over his shirt that he had wrapped around his foot. Uncle Will was there at that time and put him into the bathtub where he washed off the cut and then poured a whole bottle of iodine into it. Jack really screamed. It ruined the rest of the summer for him and he had to go into Oyster Bay for a tetanus shot.

Another pastime was shooting my BB gun. We shot at frogs and other small animals and birds. I don't remember hitting very many birds, but we did get quite a few frogs, fiddler crabs, etc. We also shot at tin cans for target practice. George got hit with a BB in the back of his upper leg once while riding his bike. One of his friends thought he'd be cute, never thinking he would hit him. God forbid you do something like that today. You'd be sued in a heartbeat and serve maybe even jail time.

Once, I entered a swim meet on the Sound. Why? I don't know. I guess Mom thought I was a pretty good swimmer. It turned out that I wasn't up to the competition. Apparently this was a regular event and the kids were all prepared for the race. I didn't know any of the rules or anything. I finished but not until all the other racers were long gone. But you know, at that time it didn't bother me one iota. So I didn't do well. I didn't sulk or get angry that I didn't do well. I just looked at it as another experience and went on doing what I enjoyed doing. What was that? You ask. Who knows! It certainly wasn't reading books or learning about anything. I was really lazy.

On rainy days we sometimes went to the movies in Oyster Bay. Someone would generally offer to take us along with their own kids.

We'd then stop for ice cream. Ice cream was the summer staple. The Good Humor man came around every night right after dinner, just like they did in Ridgewood. And unless we were being punished for something really egregious, we'd be allowed to have an ice cream. My favorite was vanilla ice cream with orange ice. I can taste it to this day. The traditional chocolate-covered pistachio ice cream popsicle was way up there on my favorite list too. Trying to get the chocolate coating off in one piece became my summer project for one year.

Everyone enjoyed Bayville. One year when Jack was, I guess, seventeen or so, he bought an old Model T Ford and tried to fix it up.

It ran but I don't think he went too far because he didn't have a driver's license nor was the car registered. Jack and George rode it around the back streets of Bayville and once in a while ventured out onto the main road for a block or two. They had great fun with that car. Someone else had a coupe with a rumble seat and we had the thrill of riding in that rumble seat with the wind blowing over us.

When they were in high school, Jack and George both worked as gardeners on big estates in Center Island, which was at the end of Bayville, a tip that jutted out into Oyster Bay. It was a private community of wealthy estate owners with large mansions decorating the shoreline with huge beautiful lawns running down to the water's edge. One resident that we could see from the creek even had his own seaplane that he rolled into the water every morning at about 8:25 a.m. and took off from Oyster Bay probably for his office, presumably in Manhattan. He returned every evening at about 5:25 p.m.

Dad and Uncle Will loved to fish, and they spent a lot of time out in the middle of the bay. Sometimes I would go along. I had the job of getting the worms for fishing. I'd have to wait until low tide so I could get out to the area in the bay usually covered by water. Along the shoreline of  the bay, digging with a pitchfork, I could get as many sandworms as I wanted as well as steamer clams. When the tide was out, it was also good for hard-shell clamming. Dad and Uncle Will would take several burlap bags with them and wade out into the bay to clam. Jack and George and Patricia and I would also clam. We all had the requisite clam rakes and would wade out into the shallow waters of the bay at low tide. Often, as the tide got higher we had to stop, but Dad and Uncle Will would be up to their shoulders trying to get that last dozen clams before they couldn't stand any longer. We always came back with loads of clams. Mom would make the most delicious clam chowder, clam fritters, and fried clams and we'd have them raw as well. On Saturday night we always had steamer clams, raw clams on the half shell, some kind of fish and perhaps some fried eels, which were really delicious. We also had a garden full of vegetables that Mom cared for, and we always had plenty of flowers all around the house. We may have been poor financially, but I never knew it and always felt like we had a lot more than most people.

Jack and George and I would also go spearing for eels. We had eel spears on long poles and we'd go out into the shallow waters of the Oyster Bay as the tide was coming in (or going out). One of us would very slowly paddle the boat while the other sat up on the bow of the boat (or stood) looking for eels. From the surface they looked sticks at the bottom of the water. Catching eels was a slimy business; the eels wrapped themselves around your  arm and you had to hit them in the head to knock them out. The hard part was skinning them. We nailed their head to a wooden board and peeled the skin off. They were (and still are) very good eating. Jack was old enough to operate the outboard motor above.

The Bayville house (that's Jack cleaning the windows or putting in the screens) was a large house by then standards. It had a full closed-in porch across the entire front of the house. This is where we sat at night to read or tell stories or watch the people go by.  There wasn't any TV then. We had a large set of wicker furniture, several big chairs and two couches and a rocker. One year we had the project of repainting them a light green with an insert of orange and black. Past the porch there was the living room on the right side of the house as you walk through the porch. Behind the living room was the dining room and beyond that the kitchen. The left side of the house contained three bedrooms and a bath. I can remember sleeping on the porch when we had company or even out on the side of the house in a tent.

Normally, Patricia and I slept in the middle room (that's the one with the two windows shown in the picture). We had bunk beds that Dad built with angle iron, and I slept on the top. I still carry a neat scar on my left knee from when I slid down the homemade ladder. One of the corners of the angle iron frame had not been filed off enough, and the fleshy part of my leg caught it as I slid down. I got a another scar on my other knee a few years later in Bayville. When we were playing "war," someone tossed a "grenade" that was actually a sharp piece of steel. It got me on the knee and ruined a good pair of pants with a hole in the knee. By the time I got home, there was blood dripping down my leg that also stained my pants.

Weekends were when we normally had company. Uncle Will was there regularly with Mom and Dad. Virginia and Cousin Bea and Tom  would also be there sometimes. (here are Virginia, Mom & Bea) There were also friends of Mom and Dad who would come out for the day. When the house was full of people, Jack and George would sleep out in a big army tent that was up in the lot next door (which Uncle Will also owned). Patricia and I slept out once but in a smaller tent, but we didn't like it and ran into the house in the middle of the night.

Mom also had friends who lived in Bayville. One in particular was a couple that lived a few block away. They and their daughter shared a double bungalow. The daughter was married to a New York City police detective and they had no children, so Patricia and I were their surrogate children and I remember spending a great deal of time at their house (although for the life of me I can't remember their names). They took us to the movies and the beach and they also had a canoe that they would take us out in. I remember that I could not pronounce *canoe*. I would say *hanoe*, and everyone would kid me about it. That had to be before I started grammar school. I must have been three, four, or five years old.

The people in Bayville were all very friendly and sort of took care of us if we were around. Most of the people on the block were Italian, which bothered my father and uncle a lot. The Italians always had a lot of relatives out on the weekends, and they were always very loud. The DeFillipos lived right next door to us. Our house and theirs were separated by the two adjourning driveways. Casper DeFillipo was the husband. He had a beauty parlor in Brooklyn. He had had a problem with his breathing once and wound up with a hole in his upper chest, just below his neck and he spoke with a very gravelly voice. He had an awful scar; his skin was all pulled up to the hole and was a different color around it. He didn't seem to mind it since he never covered it up. That's why I remember it so vividly. The DeFillipos had a couple of older daughters whom I really don't remember other than the fact that they always seemed to be screaming at each other. There were always a couple of old people around too: Casper's mother or his wife's mother or an aunt or two.

The other families on the street other than the Schwartzes were all Italian, and they all had a couple of daughters for Patricia to play with. I can't remember their names, but we played a lot together. One of the families that lived on the next block over had two girls, one was Patricia's age and they were very friendly. The strange thing was that their parents required them to address them as "Mother dear" and "Father dear" when they responded to them for any reason. I had a crush on the one sister who played with Patricia, but I was only ten or eleven.

Not like Ridgewood, we seemed to be forever going into town for groceries or something or other. It was only a few blocks away, but I always had to run the errands. We did it practically every day. But it wasn't a big deal. I guess we complained about it at the time, but it obviously couldn't have been much as I look back fondly.

When the tide was down during the day, it meant there was no swimming in the creek so we would often walk over to the Long Island Sound side that was just across the main street. The streets going down to the Sound were all private property so we had to walk a few blocks to Rhinehart's in order to access the Sound. Rhinehart's was a pavilion that had a dance hall and bar and was a place to buy beer, soda, and hot dogs. It also had the only public beach around. The place was packed on weekends as people came from the city to get away from the heat and swim in the Sound.

Sad to say there were periods when the Sound was really dirty. I think the garbage scows from Connecticut dumped their loads right into the Sound, and depending on the tides, it would all float over to the beaches on the north shore of Long Island. In fact, when I was quite young, I remember once proudly bringing Mom a "balloon" that I found floating among many balloons and other garbage in the water. She quickly had me throw it back and told me never to touch those balloons because they were dirty. I must have been four. I didn't learn what they actually were until I was a teenager.

Coming home on Labor Day was the hardest. Everyone had such a good time in Bayville. I can't imagine what summer would have been like without Bayville. Ridgewood was hot and muggy. Daily life would have been playing in the street or going to the park or just hanging around. I don't remember ever seeing a public pool in Ridgewood. There was a sprinkler shooting water up in the air for the kids to run through in one of the nearby parks. But it would not have been nearly as pleasant as Bayville. Nothing was better than Bayville!

Having Bayville as our annual summer retreat came to an end just at the time when we were finishing grammar school—1948. Virginia had gotten married, and she and her husband moved there either permanently or were using it for the summer. Since we were no longer speaking to Virginia and her husband, we were persona non grata.

We recently[69] visited Bayville and drove down Fifth Street where the house was. It's all built up now, no more open lots, just a lot of ugly small houses. There's no longer access to the creek and no place to swim except at Rhinehart's on the Sound or a beach on the bay down by the entrance to Center Island to which we used to go with Mark when he was little. It was a convenient place to launch the Sunfish and the water was calm. The roads had traffic lights at practically every intersection, and I can imagine what it must be like on a summer weekend with everyone trying to get to the beaches wherever they are. It'll never be the same.

Summer was the greatest time of my life. I think that was always the case. Remember though there was no air-conditioning; the three *H*'s (hazy, hot, and humid) seemed to be ever present. Back in Ridgewood where the houses were attached to one another, the air didn't move at all. Windows were kept wide open so that street noises—dogs barking, cats fighting in the backyards, people shouting "shut that damn dog up," men and women arguing, radios blaring,

---

[69.] In June 2003.

police sirens wailing at all hours, people talking as they walked by on the sidewalk in front of the house, drunks singing as they staggered down the street to get to the next bar or home, cars backfiring—it was all there. It was the fabric of the neighborhood, the sites and sounds that made it a neighborhood. On the really hot nights when the perspiration just didn't stop rolling off the body, I used to take my pillow and sleep on the floor where the air was a degree or two cooler. This was just the accepted thing to do. We didn't even know that air-conditioning existed, particularly in the early part of the forties. We did eventually have fans, but I don't remember having them when I was very young. We never had an air conditioner until the seventies when we moved to Garden City.

D. Transportation

When I was about nine or ten, my father bought me a used Schwinn bicycle; I think he paid about $15 or maybe less. The paint was all chipped; I don't remember what color it had been, but I took it down to the raw metal and with the ubiquitous can of black paint I repainted my new "wheels." It was an old balloon-tired bike, the only ones around at that time. I had some trouble with the brake mechanism and stupidly took it all apart and then couldn't get it back together. I think Jack reassembled it for me. That's another one of my shortcoming; mechanically I'm all thumbs. I could never figure out how car engines work, nor do I really care. Anything mechanical—lawn mower, power washers, chain saw—if they stopped while I was using them, I could never figure out how to start them. But I digress. My bike, and I guess some of my friends' too, didn't have a change guard. I don't see them around too much today, but I had "bike clips" that I used to hold my pants so they wouldn't get caught in the bike chain. I can only remember once getting my pants caught. It was a mess and left a big grease stain that never came out. If the clip wasn't available for whatever reason, I would roll up my right pants leg.

We weren't allowed to take our bike to school; not even in high school did I even think of it. Everyone walked. I didn't even take it to the store when I had to go. I think there was a fear that it would be stolen. We didn't have any chains with locks like they have today. But I did ride it around a lot as long as I was able to stash it somewhere where it wouldn't get taken. Once I was heading down

Linden Street standing up on the pedals and pumping real fast to get up some steam, and just after crossing over Onderdunk Avenue, WHAM! I went head over heels with the bike landing literally on top of me. What happened? I was a little banged up; we didn't wear helmets in those days. I had a couple of big scratches on my face and arms and a bruise on my knee. I limped home—it was only up the block—and examined the bike more closely. The front wheel had come loose and began to wobble and jammed up against the front fork, stopping the bike in its tracks and throwing me off as though I were a bronco rider.

What I never did learn to do was mount the bike by pushing it forward and then putting my left foot on the left pedal while the bike was rolling and then swinging my right leg over the seat and sitting down while the bike was moving. That was always the coolest thing to do, but I never learned it and that always bothered me that here was something so simple and I didn't know how. It goes back to being lazy. I wasn't willing to exert myself in order to accomplish something more. It wasn't important enough to me then.

For myself, growing up in Ridgewood and Bayville were the best. Obviously, I didn't know any better. But do I have any regrets about Ridgewood? In retrospect, I think I would have liked to have had an interest in sports. At that time it would have been primarily baseball. The fact that no one in my family ever had any real interest in sports is probably the only thing that I could say I regret. I was never in an environment that encouraged sports so I was never forced to learn about the players, their stats, etc. There was not even any encouragement to learn how to play different sports. Neither Jack nor George ever played sports that I am aware of. Nor did they ever talk about the teams and the players, etc. Whether I would have remembered them today is another issue, probably not. But given the interest today and the memories that many of my friends took with them from that period of time in the forties and fifties, I feel as though I missed something.

Starting in 1948, I spent another four years in Ridgewood; that's the subject of the next chapter, one that influenced me in so many different and wonderful ways. I often think back about how different it would have been had I gone down another path. What would have been different? And how would that have affected my life? Does it make any sense even musing over those possibilities or should I stick to what actually happened? Anyway, read on . . .

History of the Times—the 1940s

As a result of World War II, 50 million people—that's 50 million people—lost their lives somewhere in the world. This included the millions murdered by Stalin starting from his reign in the 1920s, the massacres of the Chinese by the Japanese, the soldiers from all armies, and the Jews slaughtered in the Holocaust. The first half of this decade was all war.

Our president through most of World War II was Franklin D. Roosevelt. He tragically did not live long enough to see it end. He died in office on April 12, 1945, less than a month before Germany surrendered. His successor was Harry S. Truman who will go down in history as the president that ordered the dropping of the atom bombs on Hiroshima and Nagasaki in August 1945, which is credited with ending the war with Japan.

But starting with the surrender of Germany on May 8, 1945, and followed by the Japanese surrender three months later on August 15, 1945, the world was at peace. And the free world tried to mend the wounds it had suffered and look for ways to guarantee that there could not be another world war like the one we had just experienced. The United Nations was established in September 1945 to help with that cause. That was followed in April 1949 with the North Atlantic Treaty Organization (NATO). The Marshall Plan was implemented in July 1947, and the United States pumped more than $13 billion into rebuilding war-torn Europe. That's equivalent to $100 billion in today's dollar. What thanks did we get for that?

On a lighter side, "race music" was now being called "rhythm and blues" and the great actors of Hollywood were introduced to us in more ways than we could imagine. Such greats are Abbott and Costello, Bette Davis, Bing Crosby, Frank Sinatra, Ingrid Bergman, Jimmy Stewart, and many more.

In sports, the National Basketball Association was formed in 1947; Jackie Robinson became the first black man to play major league

baseball as a Brooklyn Dodger in April 1947; Joe DiMaggio ended his fifty-six-game hitting streak on July 16, 1941, and was the first professional baseball player to sign a contract worth $100,000 ($70,000 salary plus bonus); and Ted Williams became a baseball legend with the Boston Red Sox.

CHAPTER III

The Developing Years 1948 to 1952

Nineteen forty-eight to 1952 were my high school years. I started at Grover Cleveland High School in September 1948. World War II was over, the servicemen were all home, everything was in flux. New cars were now coming off the assembly line, and young men and women were getting married and raising families. However, the economy, as I later learned in my economics classes at St. John's, was not doing well. The war debt was pulling the country down. The country was reeling from the worse deficit in its history. While production was coming back and jobs were loosening up, inflation had reared its ugly head, causing prices to go through the roof. So as these young couples saw themselves beginning to start a new life, they were suddenly hit with the realization that it was costing them a lot more than they had bargained for.

George had graduated from Grover Cleveland two or three years earlier and was attending Cooper Union. Patricia was starting at St. Barbara's, a regional Catholic school for girls in the Bushwick section of Brooklyn, not far from where we lived. St. Barbara's was a one- or two-year schools where the girls went before being transferred to Bishop McDonald's Diocesan High School in downtown Brooklyn. I was continuing to take drum lessons from William Kessler in Manhattan. However, the Boy Scouts became passé since all they had was a marching band which I was no longer interested in and I guess I grew out of it once I was playing in a real band. Anyway, there wasn't the opportunity to become an Eagle Scout nor do I remember even aspiring to that lofty goal. I had a long way to go with no merit badges.

When Jack was a Boy Scout, he actually worked on merit badges. One night, there was a contest between the various patrols, and one of the events was starting a fire with a flint and rock. Jack thought he'd get a leg up on the event by soaking the straw in gasoline. His mistake came when he tried to dry the straw by putting it in the oven.

He lost all the hair on the front part of his head and his eyebrows. I thought he was smarter than that, but we all have days like that.

George never joined the Boy Scouts that I know of.

I was now a full-fledged teenager. At the time, I was actually pretty slim, having come through grammar school as a roly-poly fat little kid. Mom was disappointed that I didn't get into one of the Catholic high schools, but it was for the best (I probably would have flunked out because scholastically I wasn't paying much attention to learning).

As the start of my high school career loomed before me in September 1948, I was suddenly invited to spend a "few weeks" with Aunt Peg and Uncle Ted at their summer home in Shinnecock, Long Island. With George no longer available to work with Uncle Ted on his various projects, I was selected to be the next Lockwood "worker bee."

A. Shinnecock

It sort of sounds dirty "Shinnecock." Actually it is the name of the local Indian tribe that inhabits a stretch of land on the shores of Shinnecock Bay located between the towns of Hampton Bays and Southampton on the south shore of Long Island. The bay is protected from the ocean by a long spit of land that wraps around from Southampton containing great sand dunes. There was a road almost all the way to the tip,  which brought you to the Shinnecock Inlet. It used to be totally closed, allowing travelers to go west along the dunes all the way to Hampton Bays and into Westhampton and beyond, but the great hurricane in the late thirties broke through the dunes and Shinnecock Bay. There was a canal with locks at Hampton Bays that connected Shinnecock Bay with Peconic Bay to the north.

Theodore ("Ted") and Margaret ("Peg" or "Peggy") Poetz were about the same age as Mom; Ted and Peggy both had good jobs, even during the Depression. Ted was a civil engineer for some department within the New York City bureaucracy. Aunt Peg was a music teacher at Andrew Jackson High School somewhere in eastern Queens County. She had been at Richmond Hill High School not far from where Dad grew up (and where Dad went to school, I think).

Uncle Ted was a good-looking Scotsman with flaming red hair and a good build. He was a champion long-distance swimmer on the Manhattan College swim team and boasted about racing from Coney Island to Manhattan; no easy swim. Aunt Peg was a large overweight woman with a big face and body—a good-looking woman. She wore fancy clothes, big pieces of jewelry, a lot of lipstick, perfume, large earrings, and big hats. She played the piano beautifully as well as the clarinet and the violin and probably other instruments. And she loved to cook. (The above picture is of Mom with Ted and Peg one Sunday morning after Mass in front of their house in Shinnecock.) Ted and Peg had one daughter, Little Peggy, as she was called. She was four years older than Patricia and I. The Poetz family lived in Jamaica Estates, Queens, in a very nice two-family house on 148th Street between Hillside Avenue and Grand Central Parkway. The first floor was rented to an FBI agent and his wife. Since they worked all winter, Peg had a live-in housekeeper, Nellie, who prepared the meals and cleaned the house. And she traveled with them to Shinnecock on the weekends and stayed with them during the summer as well.

Sometime in the early thirties, probably in the height of the Depression when people were literally giving away their assets at incredible low prices just to get money to live if they didn't have a job, Ted and Peg bought about five acres of raw land on a small pond off Shinnecock Bay and built a house there, one they figured they would eventually retire to. The house was designed and built by Ted. However, while working on the roof during its construction, Ted fell off the roof and broke his back and severely injured his ankles. He wound up supervising other workers as he lay strapped to a sheet of plywood propped up on the front lawn. Ted was very energetic and liked building and making things. He was also considered a cheap Scotsman who did everything himself because he didn't like to spend money. I'm not sure I believe the "cheap" handle however because he and Aunt Peg were very generous to Patricia, Mom, and me and other members of the family.

Uncle Ted and Aunt Peg were not really our aunt and uncle; we just called them that. Aunt Peg was Mom's first cousin, the daughter of Mom's mother's sister, Margaret Kress. Mom's mother was Agatha

Kress as you will recall. Aunt Peg and Mom were very close. In fact, Aunt Peg was Mom's maid of honor at her wedding.

Prior to my being "selected" to go to Shinnecock, George spent a few summers and/or long weekends there working with Ted on one or more projects. The big one was a two-car garage made of cinder block with a flat roof, which was set into the ground at the basement level. Ted and George built the whole thing. Eventually, Ted built a large living room over the garage. But that was after our time.

Since we no longer could use the Bayville house, Aunt Peg invited Mom, Patricia, and me to spend a few weeks in that summer of 1948. Patricia and I wound up spending the entire summer. Mom went home after two weeks because Jack was still at home. As an aside, Jack always bragged about how he got away without working for Uncle Ted in Shinnecock because he was in the service and then went to work full-time when he got out. Actually, I think he missed out on a good thing, but you couldn't convince him of that.

I had no idea what I would encounter when I first got to Shinnecock. As it turned out, I did just about anything and everything that needed to be done. I painted, I cleaned up the grounds, I weeded the garden, I mowed the lawn, and I cleared brush and bramble bushes and did some plumbing and carpentry with Ted's guidance. Before he left on Sunday night to go back to work on Monday, Ted actually left me a list of chores he wanted completed during the week. And I didn't disappoint him; most of the projects were completed by the time he drove up the driveway on Friday night.

That first summer the big project was paneling the small living room and two hallways off the living room with beautiful random-width knotty tongue and groove cypress wood that Ted acquired at a "bargain" from some lumberyard. It was gorgeous wood. I learned more about carpentry that year than in any other time of my life. We covered the ceilings and walls in the living room and the two halls. Some of the wood was warped so we had to bend it into place, cut around doors and electrical boxes, and do some intricate woodworking, but it was beautiful when completed. We also made kitchen cabinets and broke through the original concrete block foundation to install a door between the old basement and the new garage. I also broke through the concrete foundation in other places to install a couple of windows in the basement itself. That's when I learned to wield a chisel and sledgehammer. We didn't have any electrical power tools for those jobs either.

I also learned to make "sasparella" soda from Uncle Ted. He had the formula and several bottles and a bottle capper. I seem to remember that he made about a case or two. Sasparella is like root beer soda.[70]

Even when school started, I often would take the E train out to Jamaica and drive out with the Poetzes on Friday night to work with Ted for the weekend. Uncle Ted had a Willys Jeep that was cool. Before that, I remember he had a Chrysler woody station wagon. We would drive out on Jericho Turnpike[71] and always had to stop off to visit with Aunt Peg's brother, Harry Kress, who lived in Smithtown, just off Jericho Turnpike in a beautiful Tudor house with a sunken living room. Harry owned a concrete and cinder block manufacturing business on the east end of Smithtown and made a ton of money as Long Island began to grow after the war. He and his wife, Marie, had no children and he loved to fish. If I had to compare him to someone, I'd say he looked like Ernest Hemingway without the beard. He was a gentle guy, but somewhat distant. I guess for me that wouldn't have been unusual since he barely knew me and he had not had a close relationship with Mom although they were first cousins. Not long after I started going to Shinnecock, Harry sold his business and he and Marie moved to a beautiful home on the shore in Three Mile Harbor in East Hampton. He also had a nice fishing boat, which was moored in front of the house. He apparently sold his business for big bucks back then. His wife also had money, having inherited a share of the proceeds from the multimillion-dollar sale of her family's potato farm that was sold to a real estate developer for single-family housing somewhere near Smithtown. That was the beginning of the era when the Long Island farms were being bought up by developers for tract housing after the success of Levittown in East Meadows at the end of the war. If you recall, Levitt built small homes on concrete

---

70. In the dictionary there is a reference to sarsaparilla, "a sweetened carbonated beverage flavored with sassafras and oil distilled from a European birch." I'm not sure if that's it, but it's the only reference I found that's close.

71. The Long Island Expressway hadn't been built yet.

slabs for under $10,000, which was just what the young families could afford as the GIs came back to start their own businesses or get settled in a career. As the young married couples' population grew, the demand for this type of housing mushroomed and spread further out on Long Island.

That first year we were in Shinnecock.[72] I believe Ted's mother was still alive and living with them; she was quite old but chipper. Every morning she had a bottle of Guinness Stout to keep her energy up and give her some nourishment. There was also another old lady who I think was Uncle Ted's aunt Nell. They were both real nice and friendly and always seemed to be darning socks, hemming skirts, or sewing something. I remember we had fun kidding them about the pins and needles they kept stuck in their housedresses at the level of their chest. They were forever rubbing their hands over their breasts looking for those elusive needles and pins. They both told wonderful stories about their lives. I wish I could remember them. They both died that next winter.

Nellie, the housekeeper, was also there. She was a woman of German descent in her mid to late sixties with very long rusty-colored hair (and she boasted of the fact that it was the original color). She wore her hair generally in a bun or sometimes a pigtail down her back. Nellie played the mandolin beautifully; and at night, before dinner every evening, we would congregate in the living room and sing songs while Aunt Peg, Little Peggy, and Nellie played music as we waited for the food to cook. (I banged on something for the drum effect too.) We also played music and sang after dinner. Aunt Peg and her guests were always warmly treated, and Peg insisted on having cocktails before dinner. So along with the music came cocktails.

What else was good about being there was the fact that Aunt Peg treated everyone well. She included everyone in the conversation. When she had friends over for lunch or cocktails and everyone sat around in the back or on the lawn, Aunt Peg would always ask me to relate to her guests a funny story I told her previously or make the funny face I did the night before. In other words, she help us awkward teenagers to assimilate with strangers where we would otherwise be quite uncomfortable. That one experience has stayed with me, enabling me to meet strangers head-on with no inhibitions.

---

[72] I actually spent two summers in Shinnecock.

Aunt Peg loved to cook, and she would spend her summers cooking elaborate meals every day (since she worked all winter). Mom loved Shinnecock, but she claimed she never got any rest because she was always helping Aunt Peg with the cooking. Actually, everyone helped Aunt Peg with the cooking. Talk about delegation of authority, Aunt Peg won that award hands down. She would give everyone a job preparing dinner while she talked up a storm and supervised the kitchen help. If it wasn't peeling the onions, it was taking the tips off the string beans or cutting up the carrots. It was "Sunday dinner every day at the Poetzes'" as Mom was fond of saying.

I blamed Aunt Peg for getting me to smoke cigarettes. Everyone smoked in the Poetz household except Pat and me. Uncle Ted smoked a pipe all the time; Peg smoked cigarettes as did Little Peggy and even Nellie and my mother. Uncle Ted would also smoke a cigar after dinner. Aunt Peg would not leave me alone about smoking. I had vowed I would not smoke because I didn't like it, but every night after dinner, as we sat around the table with the last cup of coffee or after-dinner drink (for the adults), she'd chide me to take a puff. Eventually I did and wound up hooked.

Mom and Dad didn't know I smoked until Dad caught me one day. I was walking down Gates Avenue with a friend and Dad apparently was walking up Gates on the other side of the street and I didn't see him. That evening after dinner he casually turned to me and said, "Whose cigarettes are you smoking?" I don't remember my reply, but his was "Okay, so long as you don't take mine." That was the end of it. Mom tried to dissuade me from smoking, but everyone smoked including Jack and George and Uncle Will. But oddly enough, I don't remember Aunt Peg ever doing the same thing to Pat when she was there.

But anyway, Shinnecock was a great place to experience. Aunt Peg and Uncle Ted had a wooden canoe, which I used regularly. I had to go crabbing every Friday morning so Aunt Peg could make crabmeat salad for lunch. The pond was so full of crabs that once around, the shallow shore on foot with a crab net would yield easily a couple of dozen good-size crabs, enough for Aunt Peg's crabmeat salad. Aunt Peg also loved it when I brought back a couple of soft-shell crabs that would be hiding up in the reeds. They couldn't move because they were molting and we all know what soft-shell crabs are like. At the time I didn't like them. (Come to think of it, I never got too many of them so maybe I didn't even get offered one to eat.)

I learned a lot at Shinnecock, met a lot of people, and had some fun despite the fact that I was really there to work. I remember one fun thing the first year we were there. One day it was drizzling and there was a friend of the family, a boy my age whose name I can't remember. Patricia, Peggy, and I were sitting around wondering what to do for the rest of the day. One of us suggested we go up to see if we could get into the big old mansion straight up the hill from us. It was about a twenty- to twenty-five-bedroom mansion that had been closed and shuttered for several years. With a spirit of adventure, we got into the place through a window that was partially open. The first floor was dark because of the shuttered windows. Upstairs was light so we roamed around for about a half hour. Suddenly we heard voices coming into the house; it was a realtor with some prospective buyers. At that point we thought it would be fun to make noises as if ghosts were in the house, so we banged on the walls and made ghostlike sounds. They quickly realized that the noise was coming from a bunch of kids and so they threatened us for a while. Eventually we sheepishly came down the grand stairway with all the people staring at us, and we left peaceably. We thought they might call the police, but they didn't. We talked about that episode for the rest of the summer. Ironically, almost ten years later to the day, Peggy had her wedding reception there as it had been turned into an elegant hotel and restaurant/catering facility called the Scotch Mist Inn. We laughed about "our ten-year-ago venture" at her wedding party.

Little Peggy was not always around during the summer. She was four years older than us and was starting college at New Paltz in that first September as we were starting high school. I seem to remember that she had a job for a while that first summer. She also invited some of her friends out for a few weeks, so we got to meet them and spend time having fun with them. One thing I always did was try to peek at the girls as they used the outdoor shower, which was situated just below one of the kitchen windows. When I found out they were there, I would sneak into the kitchen and quietly open the window enough to stick my head out to see them in the shower. Once I was found out, I was barred from the kitchen during the girls' shower time.

We did other things in Shinnecock, things I probably would not have experienced had it not been for Shinnecock. Little Peggy got me a couple of dates with a beautiful local girl the second year I was there, and she stayed in my thoughts for a long time. (I actually met her fiancée when I was in basic training at Sampson Air Force Base in 1953.) I don't remember her name, but I vividly remember sitting in the backseat of Little Peggy's date's car while they were walking the beach. I had never really kissed a girl before, and I wasn't sure what to do in that situation. She was two years older than me, and I guess I was a bit intimidated by that. I wound up not kissing her and was frustrated for the rest of the summer just thinking about the opportunity lost. I naturally could never mention this to any of my friends; I'd be ridiculed.

We also went horseback riding and swam in the ocean and sailed the canoe (which had a sailing rig) and went fishing. We also went to church every Sunday at St. Dominick's, the Catholic church in Southampton. It was filled with Southampton celebrities who all sat down in the front pews of the church. Aunt Peg also sat as close to the front as she could. So we saw the Fords and the McDonalds[73] and the Murrays[74] and many celebrities from motion pictures, including Cary Grant (the only one I can remember).

The Poetzes were warm and caring, and my going to Shinnecock for those two years was a meaningful and happy part of my teenage years. Uncle Ted gave me the courage to work with my hands more than I had gotten before that. I learned to have confidence in my abilities, and he also taught me through my work with him to stick to my guns, tough things out when they're not going just right. We had much of that at every turn such as when the wood was just not working right or the angle was a difficult one or the electrical circuit was wrong. I owe a large debt of gratitude to both Peg and Ted; they were classy people. For example, they read the *New York Times*. We didn't have that at home. They also read *New Yorker* magazine. I learned to love the cartoons in that magazine and cut out all the little pen and ink pictures of musical instruments that appeared in every issue. And I also learned some social graces through their entertaining of guests. As I think about it, I think I also got hooked on conservative clothing styles from the wealthy people attending church or from the ads in the *New Yorker.*

[73.] Henry Ford of Ford Motor Company married a McDonald girl whose family had a large mansion on the beach next to the Fords' mansion.

[74.] The Murray family made their moneymaking electrical switch boxes in a factory in Brooklyn when electricity was first introduced into homes.

Our relationship with Little Peggy in later years wasn't all that close, I guess partially because everyone had their own family to bring up. She raised five kids and was always very busy. The few times we did visit her and her husband, Jim Daley, at their home in Mantoloking, New Jersey, we wound up sitting around as they went off running errands or doing things that totally left us out. For example, Jim was an avid sailor who participated in club races every weekend. Only once did I get to sail with him and that was because there were heavy winds and he needed the ballast. Connie and I are godparents to their daughter Jenny.

Peggy and Jim's five children are Jim Jr., Margaret Ellen, Jenny, and Grace. They are now scattered about the country. Jim, I believe, is the only one who lives locally in New Jersey and is an architect.

Little Peggy became a teacher after her kids grew up. Jim started out to be a priest but left and eventually married Peggy. He is a very bright engineer-type guy, much like his father-in-law, Ted, always making things. Before he got married, he actually built a nice home on the Metedeconk River, which flowed down to Barnegat Bay on which Mantoloking was located. He and Peg moved there after their marriage. After they had a couple of kids, Jim needed to get some additional space so he built another house next door and sold the first one. He also built his own boats. He primarily raced "Lightnings," which is a sixteen- to seventeen-feet day sailer. It's a class boat, which means every boat built as a Lightning has to meet stringent specifications as to every part of the boat, the sails, the rigging, etc. If a boat is certified as a Lightning, then it qualifies to race in Lightning races with all other identical boats. Jim actually raced all around the East Coast with his Lightning, and he was actually the authority on its specifications and was paid by other makers of the boat to qualify new boats for the class. Later on, he switched to Blue Jays, a smaller twelve-feet version of the Lightning. In fact, Jim wound up building Blue Jays in his garage and selling them. Originally, he built wooden models, but when he learned the technology, he switched to making the hulls out of fiberglass.

Jim had several jobs. When he was first married, he was an engineer for the navy, working on the safety cable springing system for catching planes landing on aircraft carriers. The original technology was designed for prop planes. As jets were introduced to the carriers, there was a great deal of problems trying to stop these heavier, faster jets as they hit the carrier decks to land. The cables were not holding them. Jim was involved in designing much bigger, stronger systems to accommodate these planes. After that, I think he became the commissioner for power and light for the community.

I'll never forget Shinnecock.

B. Grover Cleveland High School

High school was so different from grammar school. First, there were no more nuns to smack us around. Second, there was a whole new batch of girls that I had not seen or known before. But everyone was scared and uneasy those first few weeks of school. We were assigned a homeroom, and that's where we got the rules laid down for the year. Your homeroom teacher was your sergeant. He gave you advice and discipline, and school, in general, was different than it is now. Everyone had to get dressed: slacks, shirts, and ties. There were no jeans, no polo shirts, or skivvies. You looked good: polished shoes, nice tie, pressed shirt.

Unfortunately, the peer group pressure started almost immediately. Kids from different neighborhoods were now, for the first time, meeting other kids from surrounding neighborhoods. So there was a macho element of who's the toughest and who's the coolest, etc. (But it wasn't called cool then.) The Italian kids from Bushwick Avenue section were definitely the toughest and meanest. Not that there was a lot of fighting or anything. But they all wore pegged pants and long black hair that was combed into a "DA[75]" in the back. They talked tough and stayed together in cliques, and they were notorious for violence and having really badass gangs.

Today the ethnic deviations have changed. There used to be the Italians and the Irish. Our school had a mix of the Italian kids, other ethnicities, and the German kids. A lot of German kids came over from war-torn Europe. They did not form cliques or get into fights. In fact, there was only one black kid in our entire school of four thousand students and he was a really smart guy who got along with everyone. It wasn't until I went into the service that I actually got to meet black

---

[75]. *DA* stood for "duck's ass" because the hair was combed back where it met at the back of the head.

people. There also weren't any Puerto Rican or other Hispanic kids in school with the exception of one Cuban girl, Gladys Carbo, who played some of the percussion instruments in the band with me. I can't even remember knowing any Jewish kids except David, the son of Abe, the manager of the Dilbert's store I worked in.

The Italian and Irish (or mixed nationalities generally) kids had gangs, and there were gang fights around the neighborhood from time to time. But school was pretty calm. The fights seemed to stem from the girls and who they were dating or what someone said to one of them, etc. When I was in grammar school, I can remember worrying about being jumped by a roving gang if we were out at night. Once, coming home from Boy Scouts, we did get jumped by a bunch of guys but everyone managed to run away, except Forster Culver. He got beat up a little bit. He also happened to be the biggest kid in our group. I remember the incident well because we lived on the next block so I ran home and got my BB gun out in case they stormed the house. Patricia was home alone sewing at the time and the two of us weren't sure what to do. Fortunately, Mom came home and we felt protected.

Back to high school: I immediately signed up for the orchestra and met Ms. Smith, the music teacher. She was a ditzy lady who flitted around the school always with a big smile saying hello and giggling to everyone; most people thought she was nuts. But she knew music and conducted the orchestra and the chorus beautifully. She devoted all of her time to those challenges.

I got in the band, but it turned out to be less than exciting. I was the low man in the percussion section so I got to play the bass drum. The two other drummers were tough Italian guys who were unyielding to me. One was Pete DeLoria who was a great drummer. He also played the vibraphone. I had to carry the drums up and down the stairs to and from the storage room below the stage. I literally had to do everything. I was somewhat like their slave. That went on for the whole school year. I was miserable. One of the two, Tony, was a big brawny guy with whom I didn't get along. He was my nemesis. I hated going to band practice because of him. I should also say that both of them were much better drummers than I. It was a rude awakening to find out you're not as good as you think you are.

I dropped out of the band in my sophomore year because of them but came back in my third year after Tony graduated. Pete turned out to be okay after that. He went on to lead the school dance band and I became the drummer. Ms. Smith liked me, and I guess I got to be a better drummer then too. But I was nowhere near as good as Pete and Tony. You might ask why wasn't I as good. Well, like many things in my life, I only did as much as I had to do to make it work. In other words, I could get by with my level and I was basically too lazy to go the next level. Why? Because it would take too much of me to accomplish that; I was indeed too lazy to give it my all. I didn't have the staying power to take something all the way to the top.

Music became a big thing in my life in high school even though I wasn't in the band that second term. My friends and I formed a quintet, which we called the "Encores," and we played at all kinds of dances, weddings, parties, and the like. The money was pretty good for fifteen-year-old kids in the late forties and early fifties. I was never without money in my pocket. For a Friday night dance, we would maybe get $4 or $5 each. It doesn't  sound like much, but it was great. The band was made up of Dick Roethel on accordion, Lukie Adamzak played the clarinet and alto saxophone, Frank LaRosa played the trumpet, and the fifth guy was Eugene on guitar. Eugene was a friend of Lukie's who lived in Maspeth and went to a different school. Lukie was a character. He was a small guy with a funny personality. He kidded around a lot and was popular with everyone, but the girls thought he was too much of a character; he couldn't get a date if his life depended on it. He was a genuine guy, though, and we had a lot of fun in the band. Frank and Lukie were also in the Grover Cleveland orchestra and dance band.

Somewhere along here, I bought a better set of drums that Mr. Kessler got for me; they were used by Jo Jones, a well-known drummer at that time. I paid $150. For that I got a bass with foot pedal, snare, and a floor tom-tom; a high hat with two twelve-inch cymbals; and a large Zildjian ride cymbal. The front of the bass drum was painted with a fancy-lettered *Jo Jones*. I meticulously scraped off the lettering and cleaned off the skin. Then my brother George designed and painted a very nice *Bill Lockwood*. The *Bill* was vertically elongated down the left size of the bass drum skin in black ink with a big red dot over the *i* and the *Lockwood* was printed horizontally across the lower section of the circle.

The set also came with a carrying case, which was a big army medicine box. I put rollers on the bottom and Pat made cloth cases for the snare drum and bass. She remembers how tough the cloth was by the number of needles she broke in the process. Everything else fit into the medicine box that included the cymbals, the high-hat mechanism, a collapsible seat, a cowbell, and a variety of sticks, etc.

During those high school years, I also worked in the local supermarket. It was called Dilbert's and was run by a little Jewish guy by the name of Abe. Abe and I got along just fine. I worked every day after school and all day Saturday. The store closed at about 6:00 p.m. so I had time to do my homework and go out. On the weekends, when I had band jobs, I would have to finish up at Dilbert's, rush home, change my clothes, and rush off to the gig. (We didn't call them "gigs" then. That term seemed to come out in the sixties or seventies, or maybe it was the word to use but we just didn't know it at the time. I can't say we were the coolest dudes around.) Somehow or other, I don't remember ever being tired. I just did it all.

At Dilbert's I was the stock boy, stocking shelves, bringing things up from the basement, helping to bag the groceries for the customers and cleaning up when things were spilled. Sometimes I had to deliver groceries home for the little old ladies. If I were lucky, I'd get a quarter tip. I can remember kidding with the other guys about the cheap ladies who would give you a nickel. We'd muse about telling them to keep it since they probably needed it more than us. I don't think anyone ever actually said it though.

High school was probably more than a quarter mile away, about eight or ten blocks, but it didn't seem to bother us. I would meet Don Thomas on the corner of Grove Street and Woodward Avenue in front of the Protestant church every morning for the walk to school. Don was the first trumpet player in the orchestra, that is, he was the best trumpet player. He only occasionally played with us. In fact, he used to laugh at us because we weren't as good as the band he played in.

The "Encores" had cardboard music stands with the "Encores" name on them, and we even went over to Canal Street in Manhattan and bought matching gray jackets. (The Grover Cleveland band had the same jackets in tan—the school colors were brown and white.) Canal Street was where all the garment industry stores were and where you could always get a bargain from the Jewish merchants. We paid fifteen dollars each for the jackets. Below is a picture of Patricia and me in the backyard with the band jacket. We also wore white shirts and very thin ties. Patricia reminded me after reading a draft of this that she worked very hard making all the ties for  the band, an important fact that I had forgotten. Thanks, Patricia!

We used to practice in my basement next to the furnace. We'd leave the cellar door open in the back if the weather permitted and everyone in the neighborhood could hear us. Mom thought we were great. We even recorded a song once, but I lost track of the tape. Our "gigs" varied around parties, weddings, and Friday or Saturday night dances at the school or the VFW or American Legion posts or the Knights of Columbus (KofC).[76] The old married couples loved going to these dances where they had pitchers of beer and pretzels on the tables and were able to dance from 9:00 p.m. to 1:00 a.m. There were many times when they were having such a good time that they'd chip in to pay us for another hour or two. We played all the "standards" of the day: "Red Sails in the Sunset," "Stardust," "Dream," "Sweet Georgia Brown," and oh so many more. It was a great time. I didn't have a care in the world; I had a few bucks in my pocket and a date whenever I wanted. What more could a fifteen- /sixteen-year-old boy ask for.

John Tromposh was a man who lived directly across the street from us with his mother, and as it turned out, he was a terrific guitar player with a five-piece combo, which he played in on weekends. One night he came over after hearing us play. (I think he worked in an insurance company during the day.) He offered to arrange some songs for us and give us some pointers. He even asked me to play with his band a couple of times when his regular drummer couldn't make it. I was thrilled. The money was also much better than we were getting, like $15 or $20 for the night. Unfortunately, one night I had gone to practice with his band and on the way home he asked me if I

---

76. K of C was a Catholic men's organization.

wanted to play some miniature golf. It turned out to be too crowded to play, but when we were in his car, ready to leave, he grabbed my crouch. I told him to get away, and he wound up driving me home without further incident. I was real shook up; I had never had an experience with a gay guy before. I never told my mother about it, and he stopped asking me to play with his band. But we got several great arrangements out of him prior to that.

The Encores stayed together until I graduated.

As I mentioned earlier, I played in the dance band as well as the orchestra in high school. Pete Delora was the leader of the dance band, and I became the drummer. Pete was an excellent drummer as well as a vibraphone[77] player. Here is a picture of the band. Pete is far right. Don Thomas is the trumpet player in the middle with the dark shirt and light tie. Next to him on his right with the "high hair" is Frank LaRosa who was the trumpet player in the Encores. I'm the guy with the snare drum. (Notice Pete's shawl-collared suit with the pegged pants? That was the style!)

We finally got a television set sometime in the late forties. It was a "pilot" television with a very small screen. Amazing technology to

---

[77]. *Vibraphone* was an electrified xylophone, which gave it a much smoother sound and extended tone. A beautiful instrument that I always wanted to play.

think we could see images on the screen as it happened. A lot of the shows were variety shows like *The Ed Sullivan Show*, *Sid Caesar Show*, and the *Arthur Godfrey Show*. Mystery and drama shows came along such as the *Twilight Zone*, *Mystery Theater*, *Hallmark Hall of Fame*. *Theater One* was a full-hour live drama every week. There were also cowboy and Indian shows and musical shows of every variety. In the last years of high school there was the *Air Force Hour*, every Wednesday night, which starred the First Air Force Band from Mitchell Field on Long Island. Some of the guys in the school band and I used to go to Manhattan to see the show live. Another show in the daytime was a combo that played every day for an hour from four to five. I used to rush home to see them: "The (something) Five." They played jazz, sang, and had guest performers. Actually, I only watched the drummer who usually played on one floor a tom-tom that was raised up to waist high and a high hat and ride cymbal.

In my final year or so in high school, I would go to Dick Roethel's house every night to watch the *Late Show*. It came on at eleven o'clock

every night and showed old movies. Dick's mom would make us giant liverwurst or ham sandwiches with a big glass of milk before she went to bed and we sat there watching the movie until one or two o'clock in the morning. Some nights I'd wake up to find the TV humming away with no programming (TV didn't stay on 24/7 then). Dick would be fast asleep too. I had to drag myself home, which was just around the corner from Dick's house so it wasn't a big walk. I guess it was our age, but I don't remember ever being tired. It seems that we only had about six hours of sleep every night. And then on the weekends we'd play until one or two in the morning and then go out for hamburgers after that and again not get home until the wee hours.

Dick's mother and father treated me like one of their own sons. Dick was the youngest in the family. He had a couple of much older sisters and one brother, all of whom were working or were married with grown children of their own. Dick's father was an old German guy who hardly spoke English, at least English that you could understand. He worked for the Schaffer Brewing Company on the East River in Long Island City, repairing the wooden boxes that they shipped beer bottles in. From other kids in the neighborhood whose fathers worked at the various breweries (there was a big Rheingold plant next to the Schaffer facility) and also from our next-door neighbor in Ozone Park when we lived there, we learned that the brewery workers had access to a fresh barrel of cold beer whenever they wanted it. For that reason I think Dick's father was perpetually zonked out on beer. Matter of fact, it was not unusual to see the brewery workers from the neighborhood weaving down the block as they came home from work. Dick's mother thought "Dicky" was God himself. He could do no wrong according to her. She waited on him hand and foot, she gave him whatever money he needed, she nursed him when he came home battered and bruised from his various sports endeavors. She was a saint. She made a totally different sauerbraten than Mom, however. We could never figure it out, but it had a totally different, unique flavor which must have come from what she put into the marinade. Her potato dumplings were also different, but good.

When we weren't playing a gig on Sunday, which was normally the case since most things happened on Saturday night, we'd go to the Miraculous Medal Church dance. It was the biggest thing around. They usually played records or they had an occasional live band. The Encores actually played there a few times too. Everyone got dressed up in a suit, shirt, and tie and the girls were dressed to the nines. It was a great place to meet girls. During my high school days I didn't see much of Connie. She was going to a different school and traveled a long way so she was never around or available. Occasionally, I'd see her at the confraternity dances or at the Miraculous Medal dance, but she wasn't a regular. Nor did she hang out with the girls I knew from school or the regulars at the MM dances.

The confraternity dances were on Wednesday nights at St. Brigid's. They were designed to give religious instructions to Catholic kids who were not going to Catholic high schools. So on Wednesday nights we had an hour of religious instructions and then an hour or two of dancing. It was also a good place to meet girls. But it was also a place where scores got settled or fights started. There were kids who came from different neighborhoods just to meet girls or who were invited by guys from the church who went to nonlocal high schools. Once I dated a girl who had been going out with one of the local tough guys. He confronted me at one of these dances, and we wound up going outside and I got my ass whipped but not before I closed one of his eyes. My friend Dick Roethel was supposed to be my sidekick that night, but he took off after seeing the ten-to-one odds I was facing. I wound up with a black eye and a sore head as everyone was pounding on it, but nothing too serious. I decided it wasn't in my best interest to continue to date that girl anyway.

That skirmish and the one I had with Henry Braido in the gym were actually the only two fights I ever had in my four years in high school. I occasionally got threatened, but they never amounted to anything. The threats usually came from someone who thought they were tougher than me and tried to act that way in front of some girls or in the gym or something. Red Schultz, who turned out to be a hardened criminal after high school, was an off-and-on-again menacing type. We were friends through grammar school, but in high school he tried to act tough in front of the girls. I think he actually had a few screws loose. He lived on Palmetto Street where his house was right under  the elevated trains. No kidding, you could almost reach out of his second-floor front-room window and touch the trains as they roared by. You literally couldn't talk or hear what anyone was saying when the trains passed. It was ten times louder than the low-flying jets coming in for a landing at JFK.

Dating was the number one pastime for me in high school. It was generally picking the girl up at her house so that her parents could give their approval then off to the movies where everyone tried to sit as far back in the theater as possible. Usually there was not much interest in the movie itself. There was a strong interest in necking and, if you were lucky, maybe a little petting. It really depended on whether it was the first date or not. After the movie, it was off to the ice cream parlor for a soda and then home where the necking resumed in the vestibule until curfew time, usually twelve or one o'clock. It was then the trip home which could take up to a couple of hours if the date was a bus ride or two away. That happened a lot because our high school covered several communities and the kids came to school mostly by public bus transportation. So if I dated a girl in Maspeth, for example, I had to take the Fresh Pond Road bus and then the Grand Avenue bus. At one o'clock in the morning, those buses usually ran maybe every hour if I was lucky. You could wait that long for the first one, get to the interchange, and have to wait another hour for the second leg of the journey home. But of course, who cared. It was fun, particularly if she was a nice girl. Time didn't seem to matter at that time of my life.

I never got into any real trouble in high school. Detention hall, as it was called, was not something I think I ever had to attend. I was not a troublemaker. I wasn't a wisenheimer making wisecracks in class or anything like that. I respected the teachers, and in those days the teachers earned everyone's respect. They were well dressed, studious, and authoritative, unlike today. I never had any problem with the police either. Once in a while, a bunch of us would get stopped by a patrol car just to check us out because there were roving gangs in the neighborhood from time to time. But it was never a big scene or anything.

I think the most daring thing I ever did was go over to Jersey City to the burlesque to watch the strippers. Another time a bunch of us from the HS band went to one guy's house to watch a porn movie he found hidden in his father's closets. His parents happened to be on vacation so the coast was clear. That was a real eye-opener for me and the most risqué thing around.[78] Remember, this was around 1949. There were no *Playboy* magazines, and I can't remember ever seeing a girlie magazine the way they are sold on every newsstand today. I guess I could be considered being much on the "straight and narrow," and that goes back to Mom. I couldn't even think of doing anything that would have gotten back to her and then what would I have done.

Dress was an issue in high school too. At left is a picture of me in 1951. I was sixteen and wearing George's neat topcoat which I borrowed when he was in Korea. He was upset when he saw how much it had been worn in his absence. Everyone was required to wear a shirt and tie to school; jackets were optional. The late forties and fifties was the era of the zoot suit. A real zoot suit was a very long suit jacket with matching baggy pegged pants (see Pete Delora's picture in the GCHS band photo for a good example). Pegged pants were pants where the bottom cuff was very narrow so that the pants legs bloused out. I had one gray suit that I bought at Mo Ginsburg's in NYC that everyone considered to be a zoot suit. It had a shawl collar (no points)

[78.] The priest hearing my confession that Saturday afternoon got an earful.

with pegged pants. Mom hated it. I think I bought it out of spite for something she wouldn't let me do. I also wore shirts with very wide collars and very thin ties. The zoot suit rage didn't last too long for me. I remember vividly in my senior year bucking the trend and going for modified pegged pants. It took a bit of courage because I had to fend off all the criticism from my friends, but I got through it unscathed.

As I write, the one thing that I can remember about dressing in those years was the fact that my socks always fell down and they would work their way down my heel so I'd always have to pull them up. Socks were all wool at that time too, and they wore through pretty quickly. So Mom was a spectacular "sock darner." But the socks still crept down to my heel, making walking very uncomfortable. I didn't start wearing "garters" until I went to work in the late fifties.

As I mentioned, throughout high school I dated a lot. The nights we weren't playing in the band meant there was time for dating. Sometimes we'd bring the girls to the gigs, but they'd have to go home by themselves since I had to schlep the drums home or leave them at the place until Jack could drive me the next day to pick them up. There was only one girl I really ever had a heavy crush on, and that was Leticia Antonetti. Unfortunately, she wouldn't give me the time of day. I think I managed to go out with her maybe once, but she seemed always to have a big Italian guy as a boyfriend. Lettie, as she was known, was close friends with Grace who was the bass drummer in the band. Grace was Cuban and very dynamic, funny, and talented, a load of fun. She was not my type, however, although we partied a lot over the years but always at her house with a lot of other kids.

In the last two years of high school, I was somewhat popular because I played in the dance band and occasionally performed at the high school assembly. The orchestra played at all assemblies. And kids liked drums so I was "the man" although they didn't use that term then. In fact, whether right or wrong, I was voted the class musician in my graduating class of '52. I've always been a bit disturbed by it because Gunter Schmidt, the other senior in the orchestra who was graduating at the same time, was a much better musician. Gunter came from Germany with his parents after the war and settled in

Ridgewood. He was a fantastic violinist but he hardly spoke English and the kids, not surprisingly, didn't go for the violin music as they did for the more popular stuff.

In my senior year I was dating Gloria, and I gave her my yearbook by mistake and never got it back. I would give anything to have it today to see my classmates. Gloria had my ring too, but that I got back. Mom didn't like Gloria; she was a bit too, shall we say "tough looking" for Mom. Gloria was a little Italian girl with a great body. She wore her hair on the top of her head and she also wore a lot of lipstick and tight skirts and sweaters. She was not what I would consider a girl you'd bring home to Momma. Mom and Patricia met her at the gala concert that was given at the end of the school year by the music department to honor the graduates. In honor of Gunter Schmidt, myself, and one other person I think a clarinet player whom I don't remember, Ms. Smith selected the overture to the *Sleeping Beauty* and that brings us to the most embarrassing event of my young life.[79]

Sleeping Beauty starts with a timpani role for forty or fifty bars while the violin plays a melody. The timpani and the violin gradually reach a crescendo before the rest of the orchestra joins in. Halfway through this opening crescendo, with a spotlight on me and another on Gunter and with the temperature up in the nineties because it was late June, one of the timpani sticks slipped from my fingers and flew end over end up into the balcony, riding up as it were on the beam of light shining on me. The heavy white felt end of the stick shown brightly in the beam of the floodlight. The audience roared, Ms. Smith laughed, and I reached for another stick which Grace, the bass drummer quickly handed me, and *Sleeping Beauty* went on as planned. It was embarrassing to say the least.

As I said, scholastically I was out of it. Spanish and math were my worst subjects. I don't think I was very good in English either. But I failed Spanish and math in my junior year and had to go to summer school. Again, I barely passed. But to my surprise, when it was over, my brother Jack invited me to go with him and his friend, Joe Dobbin, to "the farm" in Rhode Island. I was happy not because I was going away but because my older brother, nine years my senior,

---

[79]. Matter of fact, I can't remember any other event that was more embarrassing.

had thought of me. The farm became an important place in my life years later so I won't dwell on it now except to say it was a great week. Jack and Joe were great to be with. Joe remained a friend even when I got out of the service. He recommended that I get a job with an oil company, which I did. And at "the farm," I met a nice girl from Glendale and we dated a few times during the fall of '51.

In my senior year, my best friends were clearly Dick Roethel and Joe Brocco. Joe was a big broad, hairy Italian guy whose Uncle Angelo owned a fruit and vegetable store on the corner of Menahan Street and Woodward Avenue on the same block as Dilbert's. Joe worked in the store, in fact, he often had to go to the produce market with Angelo at three o'clock in the morning to pick up supplies for the day before he went to school. Unfortunately, Joe had a negative feeling about himself. Although he considered himself a pretty handsome guy, the girls didn't like his hairiness. Once, when we were at the beach, a girl said he looked like an ape. That got him all upset and he remained down on himself for quite a while. That didn't stop him from trying however; he managed to meet some girls and we'd regularly double-date. He was already eighteen, and Angelo let him use his black Chrysler New Yorker sedan with red leather seats. We thought we were hot stuff driving around in Angelo's big black sedan. Joe's dad had died when he was young, and he lived with his mother and two very noisy sisters. Boy, did they have big mouths. Actually, everyone in his family spoke at the highest decibel level they could in order to be heard. There was always a lot of screaming and arguing in the house. But Joseph, as his mother called him, was in command. What he said was law. He'd give you the shirt off his back.

Dick Roethel went to Bishop Laughlin High School in Brooklyn and was the school's star baseball catcher and basketball center. He was very athletic. He was also madly in love with Pat Cox, a girl from Jackson Heights whom he had met once at a dance. Pat was beautiful, and Dick and she were in love.[80] We didn't see much of him except when we had a gig. Pat often—no, always, came along. They were inseparable.

John Perry, who lived up the block from Dick on the corner of Grove Street and Woodward Avenue, was another good friend. When we were much younger, his mother would invite me for Sunday

---

[80]. They wound up getting married and having six kids.

dinner. One in particular I remember was on Easter Sunday. It was a feast. John was an only child. He went to St. John's Prep and he too was a good athlete. He was a star on the school's football and soccer teams. His mother was a very heavy lady with a heart of gold. His father was a little skinny guy who spoke out of one side of his mouth like a movie gangster with a thick Brooklyn accent. He worked in a bank; I think it was Manufacturer's Hanover. He and John loved to play pool, and they were both very good. (My mother wouldn't let me go to the pool hall because there were too many unsavory characters there. Most of the guys there were the local toughs.)

John did not drink primarily because of his sports, he claimed, but one night we got him to come to a wedding at which we were playing. He and Dick made a bet to see who could drink the most beer without getting drunk. To everyone's surprise, John drank several more pitchers of beer than Dick who wound up smashed out of his mind. We played at a catering hall on Fresh Pond Road (which is now an office for the Salvation Army), and when it was over, we had to carry Dick's accordion and my drums as well as Dick himself back to Grove Street, which was about a mile. We decided to first take a detour to the local diner for some food and coffee to sober him up, but as we were waiting to be served, Dick threw up all over the counter and we had to make a fast exit. John then got the bright idea of taking Dick to his house and letting his mother sober him up. We had concluded that we couldn't let Dick go home because he could hardly stand up and we would have had a difficult time just getting him into the house without waking his parents.

Up to John's house we went with Dick between us, barely able to keep his knees from folding up under him. As we got to the front door of John's apartment, Mrs. Perry opened the door and, seeing Dick hanging between us, promptly punched John squarely in the jaw, almost knocking him over. When she found out that John was all right and that it was Dick who was out of it, she quieted down and made some espresso for him. When Dick took the espresso, the only thing he could say was, "What is this shit?" He eventually sobered up enough for us to get him home without waking his parents. But I'll never forget that night. Years later, John and I talked about it and laughed hysterically.

While Dick Roethel and John Perry were star athletes, I could not have cared less about sports. I was more interested in music and girls. Even in gym, I rarely participated in any active sports. While other guys played basketball, there were several of us who basically stood around shooting the breeze unless there was a class contest or some sort of test we had to take, like climbing a rope or shooting basketballs. There was however one year in the fall football season when I played football on the Ridgewood Stealers, a sandlot team made up of guys from the neighborhood. We had real classy white and green jerseys. Getting teams to play us was the funniest. The Long Island Press was our local newspaper, and it carried a section called "Games Wanted," which was just that: other teams like ours put ads in this section to pick up games with like teams, i.e., teams with kids the same age or they would often refer to a team by the average weight of their front lines. So the ad would read something like "Game Wanted, 13- to 16-year-olds with 150# line, any Saturday morning, your field or ours, call HE-3-4398." We were never without a game on Saturday morning.

In the only year of our existence, the Ridgewood Stealers played probably seven or eight games in October and November and basically got trounced most of the time (except when we played much younger

lighter kids whom we rolled over). Dick Roethel was the fullback, and a guy he went to school with, John Norton, was quarterback. I was the center (see right, the only picture ever taken of me in a football uniform) and we had probably about fifteen guys in total on the team. Once we went to a game with just eleven and ended up having to play with nine or ten guys halfway through when some of the players got hurt. Another time we agreed to play a team from Baisley Park, "the Baisley Park Bombers" they were called. When we found out where Baisley Park was and whom we'd be playing, everyone wanted to chicken out. Baisley Park was an all-black neighborhood near Jamaica, Queens. We had never played any black teams. But we got brave and went. What a disaster. Not only were these guys black, they were also huge and real tough. They beat us to a pulp, the score was something like 73 to 0. That was in fact the last game of the year, and no one thought about playing the next year.

As most teenagers, I too had problems with acne. Patricia and I both had a number of zits from the time we were about twelve until we were eighteen or nineteen. Mine never got that bad. I think it was because of the good chiropractor I was going to. I don't remember his name; his office was on the other side of Myrtle Avenue on Catalpa Street. He was a little old man with a very old-looking office. His adjusting table was a straight bench with a little padding on it and nothing else. He also had some electronic-looking apparatus along the wall and that was about it. When I started developing zits, the first thing he did was take me over to one of those electronic machines. At first I was apprehensive, but he assured me it would be okay. He had me hold a chrome bar with both hands; the bar was attached by wires to the machine. He then turned on the apparatus and rubbed his fingers together before touching each of my zits with the tip of one of his fingers. As he touched each zit, a spark would fly from the contact point. That was it! The next day, miraculously the pimple would be pretty much dried up. I never found out what that machinery was but it worked. Patricia also went to him for the same treatment. He only charged us a couple of dollars, and Mom didn't seem to have any problem paying for it.

Other than playing in the band, working at Dilbert's, and dating whenever I could, there wasn't much time for doing anything else except going to the movies. There were two good movie houses on Myrtle Avenue—the RKO Madison and the Ridgewood Theater. The Parthenon which we went to every Saturday as a kid didn't really show the most recent releases, and it has turned into a really junky place. When I had time, Joe Brocco and I would go to the movies and then get a cup of coffee and a piece of pie next to the RKO Madison at the "Assembly." It was a large well-lighted cafeteria-type place where everybody congregated after they took their dates home. It was like the Horn & Hardart Automat restaurants, but it didn't have the little doors for the food. The last Automat just recently closed in NYC. It was noted for the way it served its food. The walls were covered with little glass doors and inside the little boxes were sandwiches or pieces of pie or a fruit cup, etc. Everything was labeled with a description of the contents and the price. I seem to remember 25¢ to 50¢ would get you just about anything. There was a coin slot for the nickels, dimes, or quarters. After inserting the proper amount, the door would automatically pop open so you could retrieve the contents.

The Assembly was just a cafeteria where you stood in line with your tray and picked out what you wanted as you went down the line. It wasn't the nicest place at night because all the drunks would congregate there to sober up or meet someone. There was always a cop stationed outside to break up fights. I really couldn't tell my mother that I went to the Assembly because it has such a bad reputation for unsavory guys hanging out there.

I was reminded recently that across the street from the RKO Madison and the Assembly was a live poultry store. The place was filled with live chickens and turkeys in cages. The customer was able to come in, select the chicken of their choice, and the owner would take the chicken into the back room, chop off its head, and defeather it with a large rotating drum with spikes sticking out all over it. As the drum turned, he'd hold the chicken over it and the spikes would rip out the feathers. I remember having to buy a chicken there once but don't remember doing it on a regular basis. We might have gotten our turkeys there too.

C. Mountain View Villa, Catskill, New York

Just before my graduation from high school in June 1952, Mr. Kessler, my drum teacher, asked me if I wanted to work at a resort that coming summer. He had gotten a request from one of his friends for a drummer. I jumped at the chance and met with two guys somewhere in Manhattan to audition for the resort owner, Nick James. The two guys were Walter, an accordion player about my age, and Frank, a tenor saxophonist who was probably in his thirties.  He was actually a tailor during the regular year but took off summers to play at resorts. We played a few tunes for Mr. James and were hired for $50 per week each, plus all meals for two months. We played six nights per week and had Mondays off.

The resort was Mountain View Villa near Palenville, New York, not far from Catskill on the west bank of the Hudson River. It was a cute little resort with a main building with rooms upstairs and a kitchen and dining room on the first floor. There were about a dozen individual cabins around the left side of the property as you look toward the main house from the road. Near the road was another larger building which was constructed as a dance hall with a small bar and pizza kitchen in the rear. The owner called it the "Casino." In the Casino, there was a small platform for the band with a piano. We were the entertainment six nights per weeks and we attracted not only the villa guests but also people came from other resorts in the area. One of the villa's cooks, a heavy Italian woman, sang practically every night and the owner played piano with us as well.

In front of the main building was a large beautiful pool with a high diving board, and in front of that stretching down to the road was a very well-manicured lawn. Behind the house were several bocce ball courts (it had predominantly Italian guests).

Nick James was a retired Italian American musician and bandleader who led his own band for several years and played around the world. His wife, Adrian, was a very proper English lady whom he met while playing the palladium in London. They were probably in their late fifties or so and were very nice. The only rule they gave us was "Don't mess with waitresses. They are off-limits." There were probably about four or five of them. Two were young cute local girls from Saugerties, a town about twenty miles south. Frank was married but apparently liked to "fool around." Before going to sleep every night, Walter and I were forced to hear all about Frank's many female conquests in the most graphic details. I can honestly say that I learned more about the birds and the bees that summer than at any time before.

Nick liked running the Casino every night and making pizza pies. We got a free pizza after the place closed every night but had to sit and listen to Nick's musical career and exploits with the ladies all around the world for at least an hour. I think Frank played in Nick's band for a period of time.

In spite of the admonition to "don't mess with the waitresses," it didn't take Walter and me very long to fall deeply in love with the two young ones. I liked Honey and actually dated her a few times after the summer when she came down to visit her aunt in New Jersey. (Talk about a long trip for a date. I had to take the subway into the port authority and then two buses to her aunt's house. I didn't get home until four in the morning because the buses only ran every hour.) Since we had to have our meetings on the q.t., as they say,

Honey and I would generally meet by the bocce ball courts after I was set free from listening to Nick's exploits at around one o'clock in the morning. It was tough on Honey because she had to get up to serve breakfast every morning while I could sleep in. But we had a great summer. On our day off, Honey's mother would pick her up and take her back to Saugerties. Sometimes we would go with her and the other waitress. The other girl's parents had a summer cabin not far from Saugerties, and we were invited for dinner there on several occasions. The toughest part was making up stories for Nick so he wouldn't know that we were fraternizing with the waitresses.

Walter was a kid who was constantly hurting himself, slipping and falling at the pool, tripping over something in the barn, etc. I really don't remember much about him. He was a decent guy but was awkward in many ways. When the summer ended, we never kept in touch.

The food was great at the villa. Sunday was roast chicken, Thursday was meatballs and spaghetti. Another night was chicken cacciatore while another was sausages and peppers, etc. You name it, we had it during the week. Since we slept in, we usually missed the official breakfast, but the chef always saw to it that we had a nice healthy start for the day; whether it was cereal or bacon and eggs, it was the best for us.

I used to spend most of the day sitting by the pool reading or fooling around with the guests. About halfway into the summer, I dove off the high board and snapped something in my lower back and wound up taking a bus home so I could see the chiropractor. It must have healed okay, but I do remember being very uncomfortable coming down the bus.

It was a great summer at Mountain View Villa; one I'll always cherish for the people I met and the experience of playing a summer gig.

D. Waiting for the Air Force

Working all summer was just a stall for me. The Korean War was in full swing, and if I didn't do anything for myself, I'd be drafted either into the army or the marine corps. The marines were losing a lot of men fighting the Chinese in the northern part of Korea, near the Chinese border (at the infamous Incheon Reservoir) and most of the draftees were being sent to the Marine Corps to replenish their losses. The marines were not the kind of service I thought of for myself. Remember, I wasn't a very muscular kid and the marines looked like too much of a challenge for me. I couldn't see myself doing fifty push-ups every morning before breakfast. It was much too strenuous for this lazy guy. Joe Brocco was in the same boat. We talked about it all the time. When I heard that two of my friends from high school signed up for the Air Force Band in Mitchell Field and wound up being home every weekend and playing in the dance band on television and elsewhere around Long Island and Queens, I made an appointment to audition for the First Air Force Band stationed at Mitchell Field in Garden City, Long Island. The warrant officer who auditioned me said I was a good drummer, but they didn't have any room at Mitchell Field so he gave me a letter that said that I would be assigned to an air force band somewhere in the United States upon completion of my basic training. That was good enough for me. Joe didn't have anything like my letter, but he still thought it was a good idea to enlist in the air force. So we went down to the recruitment office and signed up for the air force. It meant a four-year commitment, but we thought it would be worth it if we could stay away from Korea. And the air force, except for the fighters and bombers and their support teams, sent very few of its people to Korea, so we figured we had a good chance of surviving. From my standpoint, I figured I'd be playing the drums in some marching or dance band somewhere. So Joe and I committed ourselves sometime in September and sat back and waited to be called. Joe was called up sometime in January 1953. I got an order to report to the Whitehall Street induction center in Lower Manhattan in early February.

The wait in between was sort of boring. My brother George had been in the army and spent two years in Korea as an artist for a propaganda unit, drawing leaflets to drop over the North Korean and Chinese troops to persuade them to surrender. When he got out of the army, he did some kind of artwork and met a girl who was putting together catalogs for mail-order houses. One of them was a guy in Kew Gardens who was actually a court stenographer by day and ran a mail-order business out of his apartment at night. He sold a lot of junk items in the one-to-five-dollars price range, sort of an early version of today's Lillian Vernon. George learned from his girlfriend that this guy was looking for someone to operate the business during the day. It meant being at the storefront he rented all day to collect the products as they came from the manufacturers and organize them internally and eventually package them up and mail them out to the customers. He paid well, and it wasn't too far from home—somewhere in East New York on Atlantic Avenue. At first it was really an organizational project. Making shelves for each product, making sure the items arrived in good shape, getting the packaging ready with the proper labels, etc. Once that was done, it was a snap. He and his wife liked what I was doing so they didn't bother me. They in fact were thrilled at the job I was doing. I took on all the workload and finished all the orders generally without too much fuss during the day. He usually came after his day job to take all the packages I had packed up to the post office for shipping and leave me the mail to process for the next day. It got real hairy as Christmas approached. The orders came in droves. But I had it all organized in such a way that the stuff got collected, boxed, labeled and shipped, bingo, done! And everyone was happy.

About a week before Christmas, everything stopped. There was no way the customers could get anything from us in time at that point, so we stopped shipping and closed the place down. The funny thing about this was that this was 1952, long before today's mail-order rage was even conceived. This guy and his wife could have become a modern Lillian Vernon, L. L. Bean, or the Sharper Image or something had they known mail order would become such a big business. (Maybe they did since I never saw them again after that Christmas.) They did this with just a mailing list they bought and some planning and selection of products. How simple. Why didn't I follow up when I got out of the service? But that's just wishful dreaming on my part. I never gave it an ounce of thought at the time; I wasn't thinking about business or making money then.

During the time I worked for the mail-order guy, I was also playing every Friday, Saturday, and I think Sunday nights in a little bar/nightclub in Brooklyn with a small combo headed by Denny Cardella, a terrific piano player who lived in East New York. I don't remember how we met, but we became fast friends and had a nice little combo. The place we played in was a Mafia hangout and sometimes it was a little scary as known criminals got into fights with other customers. In fact, the bartender had a sawed-off shotgun clipped under the bar for quick use if needed. I saw him pull it out only once. But we had fun. Again, we didn't worry about how late it was and what time we got home or whether we had to get up the next morning. We played jazz which at the time was forties and fifties songs played in a cool, smooth rhythm. Denny was a master pianist who could play any song. He wrote his orchestrations and was indeed the center of the trio. The guitarist, I don't remember his name, was equally as good. Denny's younger brother also played the drums but was just learning. When I left for the air force, I sold him my drum set without the cymbals.

Denny's family was a close-knit Italian family. I used to have dinner with him before we went to the gig. His mother used to treat me like one of her own kids. The guitar player had a car so he would pick me up and then pick up Denny. I can still remember driving through Brooklyn on a Saturday night. It was maddening; the traffic was awful. But again, we were cool young guys without a care in the world. Nothing bothered us.

I was dating Connie a little bit during that period. (And she invited me to her high school prom at the Waldorf-Astoria Hotel in Manhattan. We made a good-looking couple, didn't we?)

I saw Joe Brocco and Dick Roethel regularly during this time, and we generally just hung out together. Dick was still in high school. He was about a year and a half younger than me. We would go to the movies or go for a sandwich and a beer; there was a bar a couple of blocks away that served great sandwiches. It seems as though we were there every night for a ham and swiss cheese on rye or a meatball sandwich. Pizza was around, but it wasn't as popular as it is today. We wouldn't think of "going for a pizza."

John Perry graduated from high school at the same time as Joe and I, but he went straight off to Niagara University in Buffalo, New York, a Catholic college run by the Vincentian Order of priests who also taught at St. John's Prep (and St. John's University, for that matter). I didn't see John Perry again probably until the late fifties or even the early sixties. (He claims he saw me at my mother's funeral.) He graduated with a degree in accounting and joined the Arthur Andersen accounting firm as a junior auditor and eventually became the chief financial officer for a major chicken producer in Delaware. He had five children and now lives in a suburb of Birmingham, Alabama.[81]

While I didn't realize it at the time, it has certainly become quite evident that this next chapter in my life would have a huge impact on me for the rest of my life. The people I met, the challenges I faced, and the places I visited would forever change my view of life in many important ways. It's for that reason I believe strongly that every young man coming out of high school should experience at least two years in the armed services—preferably right out of high school. I view it more like a ship on its shakedown cruise. The service is able to get the kinks out of young men, so to speak.[82] Here we have young foolish kids coming out of high school knowing not a wit of what they want to do in life and probably not really caring about it one way or another. What better recipe is there than a heaping dose of discipline and self-denial mixed with some real training and testing of one's leadership potential and ability to handle responsibility. I would never in my wildest dreams have received that kind of developmental training were it not for the air force (or any other service had I been drafted, for example). So now it's a new experience, a new horizon that will take me on a fascinating journey. Let's see how it works out.

[81.] I recently learned that his oldest daughter was killed in an auto accident in 1999.

[82.] Unfortunately, it sometimes adds a few kinks.

History of the Times—1950s

The early part of the **1950s** was marked by a sharp rise in economic activity, which had not been present in the United States since the late 1920s. The returning servicemen went back to school on the GI Bill and got married and built homes and families, the so-called baby boomers of the **1950s.** Television became the rage.

These good times were clouded by the rise of communism around the world. Russia had gobbled up Poland, Ukraine, the Baltic States, and other far-flung countries to become the dreaded Union of Soviet Socialist Republics or the Soviet Union (USSR), which in turn created the cold war. The spread of communism came through in Korea as the communist North Korea invaded South Korea and got the Unite States back into armed conflict involving the now-Communist China, which didn't end until the summer of 1953.

The threat of communism brought the McCarthy Hearings and the blacklisting of scores of writers, directors, and actors in Hollywood plus other notables for being communist sympathizers or supporters.

The Soviet Union launched the first man-made satellite, which caught the United States by surprise and caused a great deal of embarrassment both home and abroad.

In 1959, Fidel Castro overthrew the Batista government in Cuba and quickly raised the communist banner on an island only ninety miles from our coast. This would later lead to a major confrontation with the Soviet Union when they tried to install missile sites on that island during President John F. Kennedy's presidency.

The **1950s** had its greatest impact on America's culture with the introduction of rock 'n' roll music. Elvis Presley emerged as "the King" of rock 'n' roll. Other noteworthy participants were Chuck Berry, Bo Diddley, Buddy Holly, and Little Richard. Major performers in the movies and on television during this decade were Jack Benny, Humphrey Bogart, Marlon Brando, James Dean, Ava Gardner, Audrey Hepburn, Charlton Heston, Alfred Hitchcock, Marilyn Monroe (who married Joe DiMaggio), and John Wayne.

In sports, Rocky Marciano and Sugar Ray Robinson dominated boxing while Willie Mays and Yogi Berra were our baseball stars. Bill Russell showed everyone he was the greatest basketball player of the era.

CHAPTER IV

The U.S. Air Force—1953 to 1957

A. Sampson Air Force Base, Geneva, New York

February 1953 came around, and I finally got called up. In retrospect it was rather uneventful. I remember saying good-bye to my mom. I think Jack drove me into Whitehall Street in Lower Manhattan where I went through a cursory physical. Some of the things you don't forget easily, even though it was fifty-odd years ago, happened at the Whitehall Street induction center during this so-called physical. There had to be at least fifty to seventy-five inductees in the room, and we were told to take off all of our clothes including our underwear. The clothes were put in lockers, and we walked around with only our shorts in our hands and were poked and prodded here and there. One room was long and narrow with a naval officer sitting in a chair in the middle of the room down at one end and behind him a line of guys going into the next room to our left. As we entered the room, a single line was formed in front of this officer. He beckoned the first guy in line to step forward and stand in front of him. It was the "hernia test." "Turn your head and cough," was the command. After I went through and wound up on the line behind him going into the next room, we all watched the guys coming into the room for their "hernia test." Suddenly, everyone broke out laughing as this very tall black dude strode into the room. In one hand he held his white shorts and on his arm hung a traditional English umbrella, long and black and tightly wrapped with a curved wooden handle, and on his head was a traditional black English bowler. He looked so out of place. The

officer beckoned him forward and asked him what he was doing with the umbrella. "It might rain," he replied. That broke everyone up even more. It doesn't sound funny as I reread it. I guess you had to be there.

After that ordeal, we got dressed and piled onto a bus that took us upstate to Sampson Air Force Base outside of Geneva, New York, near Rochester on Lake Seneca, one of the Finger Lakes. Getting off the bus in what seemed like the middle of the night in a snowstorm was no fun, and the guys in charge made us stand around until we were almost frozen.

The next three months of "basic training" was a totally new experience for this New York kid. And it was indeed one of those turning points in my life. I learned to endure hardships: running long distances, getting very little sleep, taking a lot of crap from the drill instructor, being disciplined, taking orders, learning to live with others, making friends, etc. The guys were all pretty good. There  are always a few bad apples that cause trouble or who try to be the bullies in the crowd, at least that's what I found in high school. There was some of that in the air force too, but by and large, it was at a minimum. We were all equals here. We all had to endure the same tough treatment, the bad food, the cold, and the physical abuse so no one was really trying to stand out as the tough guy or the wise ass, probably because they really didn't want anyone to notice them for fear of being the brunt of the DI's (drill instructor) further abuse. What was noticeable was how guys from different parts of the country acted differently. There was one black kid who hadn't been in the practice of bathing regularly. The DI quickly made an example of him by getting several guys to "give him a blanket party," putting a blanket over his head and taking him into the shower and physically getting him wet. It led to a few fights, but the point was made. He showered regularly after that.

Other guys were very slow to get up in the morning or very slow in doing anything in spite of the fact that they were told to "move your asses." Wake up was at 4:30 a.m. The DI would come into the barracks room with a nightstick and walk down the length of the room running the nightstick against the iron uprights of the bunk beds. That woke most people up. But there were some guys who could sleep right through it.

The drill instructor was our god. When he said something, we jumped. There was no hesitation, no questions about what had to be done. At the beginning it was tough because sometimes you couldn't understand what he was saying—mostly shouting. And God forbid you had to have it told to you twice.

Our days were pretty much filled with marching, calisthenics, more marching, rifle training, KP (for kitchen police), gas mask training with tear gas, more marching, long runs, bivouac and classroom time, something that turned out to be quite helpful. For much of the three months, every afternoon we went to classes to learn military rules and regulations, rank markings so you could identify the colonels and generals, and also classes on what jobs were available to us in the air force. And while we were still fighting in Korea, and there was a possibility that many of us could wind up there, our training was not what one would call strenuous. The obstacle course was being renovated so we didn't have to go through that, and we heard it was really tough when it was open. But no one had any trouble with the training that I could tell. (If I could do it, anyone could.) They even had us stand guard duty a few times, I guess just to see what it was like. The first time was funny. I was told to stand guard on just one side of this plain concrete block building that was supposed to be filled with ammunition and to not move from that spot. Little did I know that there was someone else standing on the other side of that same building also not knowing that I was on the opposite side. Trying to keep warm and awake, I naturally started walking around. As I turned the corner, I bumped into the other guy and we both screamed with surprise.

The only other time I had guard duty we were put into a truck and hauled out to various sites. The DI would call out a name, and that guy would jump off the truck and relieve the guy who was there. The guy who was relieved would climb into the truck and off they'd go. This was at two or three o'clock in the morning. This time the truck stopped and my name was called. I jumped out and found myself in front of the Sampson AF Base Officers Club, a swank-looking low-slung building. The DI directed me to knock on the front door and take over for the guy inside, which I did. And there I was inside this plush building too afraid to sit down for fear someone would catch me and at the same time trying to stay awake by walking around. I might add I had an unloaded carbine rifle that probably hadn't been fired since World War II. The night was going by slowly, and there I was trying to be the officious guard when suddenly at probably four in the morning a light went on down on the next level and some guy strides in whistling a happy tune. I jump up and shout, "Stop, who goes there?" as I was instructed to do. He doesn't answer. I say it again louder, "Stop, who goes there?" He then looked up at me and explained that he is the early morning chef and comes in at this time every morning and "every morning some new recruit shits in his pants thinking the place is being burglarized." "Come on down and have a cup of coffee and a donut," he says, and that was the last time I had to do guard duty in the air force.

I also had duty once picking up ashes from the various barracks all of which were heated with coal. That was tough duty, but I only had to do it once. We hauled the barrels of ashes up and over the edge of the truck and dumped the contents. When we finished, we were covered head to toe with white ash.

KP was the roughest because it was the longest. We had to start at about 3:00 a.m. and go until dinner was completed which was about 9:00 p.m. There were choice jobs and there were really bad jobs, and

it was the luck of the draw. Pots and pans meant that you would be scrubbing those wretched things for practically the entire twenty or so hours. Working the tray line wasn't bad. As the metal food trays were turned in, they were scraped clean and put onto a rack that went through a huge tray washer with hot water and steam. It was hot, wet, and messy. Everybody took turns dishing out the food along the food line too. If there was a really bad job, it was skimming off the grease pit. This has to be described: It was a large outside open pit beside the mess hall. It was probably ten feet by ten feet in diameter with a wide board spanning the middle. Working the grease pit meant standing on that board and skimming off the grease with a big long-handled ladle and putting the grease into big garage pales. The smell rising from that pit was enough to make anyone sick. Almost everyone threw up while working it. Actually, only the real goofballs got that job. At the start of KP, when the cooks were picking people for various jobs, it was always wise to be a real nice, quiet, unassuming guy. If the cooks didn't like you, you got the lousy jobs.

Evenings were spent either writing letters or polishing shoes, which had to be spit-shined to a real gloss. So even if you had been knee-deep in mud all day or soaked through from being on KP, those shoes had to be like new the next morning.[83] There were also inspections just about every day to make sure you made your bed correctly—using the proper military corner folds—and the inspector could bounce a quarter off the top blanket to prove it was on tight enough. Everything in your locker had to be in the correct place; nothing could be out of position, otherwise it was twenty-five push-ups or cleaning the urinals for a week. By nine o'clock, everyone was so exhausted they couldn't wait to hit the sack; four thirty was coming around real fast. I don't remember getting too many nasty jobs during my time there. If they were, I've probably blocked them from my psyche.

I remember only once having a pass to go into town; that was Geneva, New York. It couldn't have been very much of anything. There were airmen recruits everywhere, and the bars were crowded. We just walked around looking at the sights and I guess looking for girls. I don't remember even seeing any on the memorable six-hour pass.

When I first got to Sampson, I was pretty homesick, but I started writing home on a regular basis and never got out of that habit. The best surprise was when Mom came up all the way from Ridgewood to see me on the one weekend we had off. We had a great day together talking about home and taking pictures. She was really something. She had come with Joe Brocco's mother on a bus. Also, Jack and Joe Dobbin came to visit at another time. They even visited with Joe. I'm thinking maybe they came up but weren't able to see me for some reason.

---

83. We actually had two pairs of boots, so the wet ones had time to dry out.

Looking back at the entire four years in the air force, Mom wound up with a whole drawer full of my letters, which I foolishly threw out when we cleaned out her apartment. Oh, how I wish I had those letters back to be able to relive those days in the service through my own letters. That would have been a real treat. But it was not to be.

At Sampson, I also learned something about disappointment. Something I had not had much of in my life, either then or even now, thank God. There weren't too many things I missed, and during my short life, I hadn't been denied many things (of course, a lot of girls said no, but that was to be expected). But looking back, what had I not had in life? I had a great family. My mother got my clothes for me when I was young. When I got older, I bought my own clothes with the money I earned. No one ever said to me "you can't have that." But I was in for a rude awakening and about to find out firsthand how rejection and disappointment felt.

In the last few days of basic training, every airman went before a placement officer to tell him what it was he wanted to do in the air force going forward. In that session, I learned that the warrant officer from Mitchell Field that gave me the letter saying I would be assigned to a band somewhere in the United States was all wet, and the letter he gave me meant absolutely nothing. What a letdown. I had basically slept during all the instructional classes I had had describing the different jobs available to me after basic training. Who needed to know that? I was going to an air force band somewhere in the United States. It wasn't over yet however; I was given a chance to take another audition this time at the drum school at the Sampson AF Music School. I didn't make it. The instructor was very nice, but he basically said there were a lot of better drummers coming into the air force and they didn't have any more room for guys like me. Now, what do I do? Who knew what else was even available? I certainly didn't. I had slept through it all!

In a fit of anger and total disappointment, I rolled the dice and said I'd like to be a radio operator. As a result, I was shipped to radio operator school at Kessler Air Force Base in Biloxi, Mississippi. But first I was able to spend some time at home with Mom, then it was a train ride to Biloxi.

B. Kessler Air Force Base, Biloxi, Mississippi

Kessler was a nine-month school to learn Morse code and how to type and how to operate a radio receiver and transmitter. It all went great until we got to the very end; I just couldn't take the code fast enough. In order to pass, you had to be able to receive code at twenty words per minute. The more I tried the harder it got. I finally passed, but it was tough. I was smoking three and four packs of cigarettes a day at that time and I was a nervous wreck. Flunking out of radio school meant either becoming a cook or a military policeman. Both were unacceptable alternatives to me.

Biloxi, Mississippi, was about one hundred miles east of New Orleans on the Gulf of Mexico. It was a small resort town with an air force base with over fifty thousand servicemen. For recreation (Sunday was our only day off), we played touch football or went to the beach to pick up girls. On a few occasions we drove to New Orleans for the weekend when we had enough money. There was also a USO where we could go to dance on Saturday night or just go to the local beer joint where there would be country and western music, waitresses with low-cut blouses and Falstaff beer. But most of the time, we just hung around the barracks.

We had a great bunch of guys in the barracks. When we didn't have enough money to go to town, we would chip in for pizzas from a pizza place right outside the gate. Someone would also get beer from the commissary and we would sit around and tell jokes the entire evening. In fact, one of the guys in our barracks, Frank Maura, was a gay dancer and singer from Brooklyn who had tried to make it on Broadway. He had a few bit parts in the chorus but nothing really big. Frank had a huge repertoire of jokes, some of which I still remember. It was nonstop the entire evening, joke after joke, laugh after laugh. Frank was several weeks ahead of me at school, but near the end of his term, there was a giant upheaval at Kessler. Evidently, a large contingent of gay airmen was discovered at the base, and since it was against the rules to be gay in the air force, the brass made a huge fuse about it and put literally several hundred potential gays on barrack arrest pending investigations. Frank was one of them and wound up getting discharged along with all the other gays they found. My roommate was, in fact, one of them although I never knew it until he was arrested and put under barrack arrest; I don't remember his name, but he was a nice guy.

One of the weekends I went to New Orleans with two friends. One had a car. We went in spite of the fact that we had very little money (I still don't understand why we did it). We wound up picking up three girls at Pontchartrain Lake, the local "Coney Island playland" for New Orleans. We took the girls to a Dixieland club, had a few beers, and drove them home about three in the morning. The problem was that we didn't have enough money nor did we know where to go to sleep. So we drove into a local park and changed from our street clothes into our khaki work overalls to sleep in the car. While we were changing our clothes however, a police car pulled up next to us and wanted to know what we were doing. After we told them who we were and why we were there, they kept asking us if we planned to go swimming. We assured them that we were not thinking about swimming. The next morning when we woke up, we realized why they had been asking us: we had parked right next to the park's public swimming pool complex.

That was a memorable trip in several ways: First, we totally ran out of money and almost didn't have enough gas to make it back to the base; second, we forgot that there was a toll bridge between New Orleans and Biloxi and wound up having to leave one of our watches with the bridge operator as collateral until payday then drive all the way back to pay the toll and retrieve the watch.

The third thing was the biggest surprise to me. I was still going to Mass every Sunday and had to find a Catholic church. My two friends were not Catholic. After driving around for a while, we found the Church of the Corpus Christi. My friends let me out and agreed to come back in an hour. I was a bit early but went into the almost empty church and sat near the back. I didn't notice anything different about the church until the parishioners began filing in. They were black! It was an entirely black parish in the heart of New Orleans. I didn't know there were so many black Catholics until that moment. Frankly, I was shocked. Why? I don't know. I guess I never thought about it before. I always assumed that black people were Baptists. In Ridgewood there were no blacks, nor did we actually know any black people. I can't remember even seeing a black serviceman in the Kessler base chapel.

At Kessler I managed to play drums in the dance band on base for a couple of months. The leader of the band was an entertainment officer who traveled around the world putting on shows at different air force bases. After a couple of months he left and the band unraveled although it was fun while it lasted. Matter of fact, the band leader was a hypnotist and entertained us constantly with tricks he played on some of his assistants who were actually "under his spell." He would "knock them out" in the middle of a dance and not wake them up until the dance was over. These guys couldn't remember what went on for the entire evening. About a month before he left the base, he hypnotized me to stop smoking. It worked beautifully until he left, then I went back to my two- to three-pack-a-day habit. He actually made my subconscious think that cigarettes tasted like garbage.

The one major drawback in Biloxi was the heat and humidity. Being on the Gulf, the weather was always hot and always very humid. We had no air-conditioning in the barracks so sleeping was a real problem on those very sultry nights where the temperature and the humidity were both up in the nineties. The sweat just poured off.

The radio operator school and all the other schools on base operated on three shifts—6:00 a.m. to noon; noon to 6:00 p.m.; and 6:00 p.m. to midnight. I was in the noon class the entire time. That meant we had to assemble every morning at about 11:30 a.m. and march to school, mostly in the blazing sun. But many days there were on and off rain showers. Noon to 6:00 p.m. was the hottest time of the day. Our classes were conducted in giant airplane hangars, and they tried very hard to keep them cool by leaving the ends open and having fans running all the time. Our dress for class was khakis with long-sleeved shirts but no tie. By the end of the day, everyone was soaked from perspiration (on rainy days, we started out soaked from marching to class in the rain).

Over Christmas 1953, I managed to get home for several days. It was crazy, but some airman in our barracks from New Jersey had a car and offered to drive a bunch of us to NYC. It took us a few days. I don't remember much of anything about the trip. Since I didn't know how to drive, I sat in the back and slept most of the time. I don't even remember going back. He drove us to the port authority bus terminal and I think Jack picked me up.

I graduated from Kessler in late February 1954 and got my orders to report to a security service squadron based at Sembach Air Force Base in Sembach, Germany. The security service to which I was now a part of was a top secret group that monitored Russia and other communist nations' air forces radio airwaves on a regular basis. I had several weeks off at home during March and then reported to Fort Dix in New Brunswick, New Jersey, where I was processed for overseas—i.e., shots, shots, and more shots. I can still see the line of medics on each side of the gauntlet, each holding an injection "gun." As you stepped up to them, one on each side, they simultaneously whacked you with a needle. There seemed to be three or four rows of those folks. Several guys going through the line collapsed and had to be carried away.

Eventually, we were bussed to a pier in the port of New Jersey and put aboard a troopship. The ship was a typical troop transport that was stacked to the gunnels with troops. The weather was stormy and the seas rough for almost the entire trip, and many of us got seasick. It convinced me that I was glad I hadn't joined the navy. There was absolutely nothing to do aboard the ship. Every day whether we wanted to or not, we had to go up on deck for an hour or two to allow the cleaning crew to clean the sleeping quarters. If it was storming or raining, we could stay just inside in an area that was meant for much fewer people. Even the deck was not big enough for everyone. Below decks, the bunks were so close together that I don't think you could turn over to your side; you essentially had to sleep on your back. Every morning, one of the sergeants in charge would walk through the area yelling, "Let go of your cocks and grab your socks!" That was the wake-up call. There were a few lasting memories of the voyage: one was the latrine. The sitting section consisted of a long row of toilet seats over a long trough. When everyone was getting seasick, that trough was overflowing with vomit and everything else. The other thing was the metal garbage cans sliding from one side of the ship to the other during the night as the ship tossed in heavy seas; no one ever tied them down. We landed at the port of Bremerhaven on the north coast of Germany and went by train to Kaiserslautern and then by bus to Sembach.

C. Sembach Air Base, Sembach, Germany

Sembach was a tactical air base that was the home of a tactical reconnaissance wing and my new home, the 85th RSM (Radio Squadron Mobile). We later became the 6914th RSM, part of the 6910th Radio Group Mobile. Our barracks were quite nice, far better than I had expected. This was a relatively new base so all of the facilities were in good shape. Our barracks were three-story concrete block buildings. We had no KP and no cleanup duty. Local German men, who

worked very cheaply, did everything. I think it cost everyone $2 to $4 per month to contribute to cleanup cost. On each end of the building were what we called "open bay" rooms—that is, they were the full depth of the building from front to back and where probably slept about twenty people, side by side. In the middle part of the building were smaller four, five, or six-men rooms that were assigned to noncommissioned officers. In the very middle of the floor was the bathroom with a large shower area, urinals, private commodes, and sinks. Each floor was identical except the first floor usually had an office or two for administrative work. The cleaning help took care of the bathroom each day and every so often mopped the sleeping rooms. Once a week was bed-linen time, which meant you had to strip your bed and pillowcase and exchange them for fresh ones. I think towels were included in that exchange. Personal laundry was taken care of by a separate laundry service that cost you a couple of bucks a week for getting your fatigues washed and ironed and dress uniforms dry-cleaned.

The base was out in the middle of farm country about fifteen miles west of the town of Kaiserslautern, which was the headquarters of the Rhine Ammunition Depot, the largest concentration of army and air force personnel in all of Europe. Near us, also bordering around Kaiserslautern, were two fighter air bases Ramstein and Landstuhl. Kaiserslautern itself was a rather large city that had been devastated by Allied bombs during the war (it was the headquarters of one of the main Germany army units and was bombed repeatedly). Part of the town had been rebuilt, but there were still large areas of rubble. Streets upon streets where houses once stood now contained just tall chimneys standing like sentinels watching over what had been a grand neighborhood. In 1954, it was a full nine or ten years since the war ended and much had been rebuilt. The shops, the main theater, the railroad station, the opera house were there to use. Apartment buildings were gradually being rebuilt. Scaffolding around buildings was everywhere to be seen as reconstruction was in full swing. The streets outside of the heart of the city were surprisingly quiet. The German people in general had not as yet recovered enough to be able to afford the luxury of automobiles; cars seen on the streets were typically driven by American soldiers, mostly the officer class. The dollar was very strong while the Germany economy was still very weak. The exchange rate was four deutsch marks to one U.S. dollar. A liter of beer was DM 1, U.S. 25¢. A full four-course meal with a local bottle of very nice local wine would set you back a whopping eight to ten deutsche marks ($2.00 to $2.50). When I first arrived in Germany, we were paid in "script," which was fake money that could only be used on base, but it could be exchanged for DMs if you wanted to go off base. The U.S. soldier was getting paid anywhere from $150 to $250 per month. That money was for the most part being pumped into the German economy at a very rapid pace. The restaurants were flourishing, the nightclubs and bars were packed with Americans, and the prostitutes were probably the only women who could afford to buy their own cars. At one point, to deter counterfeiting, the army had a recall of all script in exchange for new and different script. It happened literally overnight so if you were caught with old script beyond the exchange cutoff date, you were out of luck.

Rural Germany was a series of farms stretching from one village to the next. Farmhouses contained an attached barn for the cows. In the middle courtyard of the house complex was a large square well-like pit that went deep into the ground. The straw and cow manure taken from the barn would be dropped into this pit and allowed to ferment. In the spring, the fluids that accumulated in the bottom of that pit were siphoned out into a large wooden keglike container possibly fifteen or twenty foot long carried by a rubber-wheeled horse-drawn wagon. The wagon was called by the Americans the "honey wagon." The fluid was then sprayed over the vegetables in the field as a fertilizer. For that one reason, Americans were forbidden from eating fresh local vegetables.

The Eighty-fifth RSM work site was actually about twenty-five miles northeast of Sembach on top of a hill surrounded by vineyards. We needed to be on top of the hill because we were monitoring Russian Air Force radio networks in East Germany, Poland, and

Czechoslovakia and using giant "sloping V" antennas to pick up their signals. We were also supposed to be "mobile" so we worked in giant trailer vans that were backed up to specially made buildings with doors at the right height to accommodate the vans' back doors. Before the special buildings were built, we actually worked right in the vans themselves, but they weren't attached to any type of building structure. In fact, very early on, the vans were rather primitive little vans that were much smaller stuffy, un-air-conditioned backs of trucks. Once the new buildings went up, the new eight-wheel trailers arrived.

The base contained our full operations headquarters, a mess hall, and a motor pool. There was a full complement of military police guarding the place. (We called them "air police" or "APs" in the air force, in case you're interested in the proper terminology of the military.)

I started out as a radio operator, monitoring a whole bunch of "target" frequencies on a regular basis. That meant tuning in to those frequencies at a scheduled time and copying down by typewriter everything I heard coming over that frequency in Morse code. Sometimes the traffic—as they called the data that came over the frequency—got very busy and things were missed, but it was mostly just routine messages to establish contact between one group or base or station and another.

Within about three/six months of working as a radio operator, I learned that the operations people were looking for guys to become "traffic analysts." TAs were the guys who actually analyzed the material that the radio operators copied down (radio operators actually sat at a typewriter with two very high-powered radio receivers and listened to the Morse code as it was being transmitted by, in our case, Russian Air Force personnel sitting at bases mostly in East Germany, Poland, and Czechoslovakia. The operators immediately converted everything they transmitted into letters and numbers. Much of their transmissions were standard Q signals such as QRX, QOW, etc. Each one of these Q signals has, under international Morse code standards, a specific meaning, such as "How do you hear me?" "How strong is my radio signal?" etc. The idea of not having to listen to Morse code for the next three years appealed to me, so I asked for the TA job and got it.

When I first arrived at Sembach, we were restricted to the base for the first thirty days. After that, we were allowed off base but only in uniform. That lasted about six months. The rules changed after that and military personnel were then allowed to wear civilian clothes. But after that first thirty-day restriction, a few of us took a bus into town to see what it was like. What we weren't prepared for was the strength of the beer, the first thing we went for. One large stein of beer was about my limit; I was totally knocked out from it. It was much stronger than American beer (and I wasn't a big beer drinker to start with). We all got back to base eventually but not under our own control; we were all totally drunk. It didn't take long for me to realize that I couldn't drink beer without getting inebriated. I also realized that I didn't like not having control of my faculties, so I limited my drinking then and throughout the rest of my life. I can only remember a few times that I dropped my guard and allowed myself to drink too much, and I didn't like it.

My three years and a couple of months in Germany were terrific. I was able to take all kinds of trips around Europe. I went to Bavaria in the German Alps a number of times; other cities in Germany such as Heidelberg, Frankfurt, Essen, Cologne, Munich; in Switzerland, Bern, Basel, Zurich, Interlaken, Geneva; in France, Paris; and many smaller cities on the way. We also went to Amsterdam, Holland, and Copenhagen, Denmark.

What made most of those trips possible was my ability to buy a car. I had never driven a car before, but I knew that if I was ever going to see any part of Europe, I needed to have my own wheels. I wrote to Mom and got her to send me what little savings I had in the bank, probably $200-$300. I then talked to the Volkswagen people in town, and they had  a deal for servicemen, which was quite attractive: a low interest rate and low monthly payments over a two-year period. The Volkswagen was DM 4,400 or U.S. $1,100.

That was only the beginning. First I had to order the car. They said it would take a couple of months to actually be delivered. I then had to frantically search for someone who would teach me how to drive. A friend who ran the motor pool offered to show me how to drive a Jeep after work or on my lunch hour at our work site. We actually had a driving range for training drivers who were assigned to drive the semi-tracker trailers that we worked in. That driving range had simulated loading docks, street crossings, etc. So it was ideal for me, particularly since no one was around when I went out on the range. Once he showed me how to shift, the rest was up to me.

The fun began when I picked up the car at the dealership in downtown Kaiserslautern. Bernie Welsh and Jack Lynch came with me since both knew how to drive and I'd need some help getting started. Driving out of the showroom was frightening. I stalled out probably a dozen times before I turned the car over to Jack so we could get out of the traffic of downtown Kaiserslautern. That evening we started on the midnight shift—twelve to eight in the morning. I invited three of my roommates to come with me on my maiden voyage to our work site in my new car. It was September, and the fog rolled in[84] to the point that we couldn't see our hands in front of our faces and I wound up putting the brand-new black Volkswagen into a ditch beside the road in a little town of Eisenstadt, not more than five miles from our home base at Sembach. Fortunately, there were three big strong guys with me; they merely lifted the car back onto the road, and Jack Lynch drove the rest of the way to work because I was too shaken by the experience. Gradually, I caught on and gained confidence behind the wheel. Of course, I had to take a huge ribbing for months for not knowing how to drive and putting the car in the ditch on its maiden voyage.

1. Travelling around Europe

Our first overnight trip in my new Volkswagen was on a three-day pass to Amsterdam. It was a three-day trip. After arriving in town,

---

[84.] Heavy fog was commonplace at that time of year. We often would have to literally have someone walk in front of the car to be able to know where the road was.

we got a hotel room and then roamed the nightspots. At about three that morning, as we were barhopping in a noisy nightclub full of Americans, whom do I run into but Dick Lockhart, a guy from St. Brigid's who was in Connie's class. He also went to Grover Cleveland a year behind me. Dick was in the army stationed in Kaiserslautern. I had tried to pick up some bottles of beer at the bar, but a large hulk of a man was blocking the way. I pushed ever so gently and the hulk turned around ready to break my jaw. Fortunately, we recognized each other before any (or I should say his) fists were thrown. We made arrangements to see each other when we got back to base. His barracks were just outside Kaiserslautern in the opposite direction from Sembach and we did get together from time to time. We later met again back in the States when we both went to St. John's.

Amsterdam was followed by numerous trips to Nuremberg, Paris, back to Paris again, etc. We also took two- and three-week leaves to Italy, the Riviera, Spain, and Southern France. My closest friends in Germany were Bernie Welch from Maryland; John Lynch from Upstate New York; Wendy Groff from Iowa; and Bill Mannion from El Dorado, Kansas. Bill and I were very close for about two years before he rotated back to the States and out of the service. He was a great guy. Bill is on the left: quick-witted, honest, and very religious. He hated the air force and couldn't wait to get out. I guess we all felt somewhat that same way, but we enjoyed it while we were there as did he. But when he left, he assured us that we would not be hearing from him ever again because he didn't want to be reminded of the air force by staying in touch. I wrote to him several times after he left, but never got a response.

Bernie Welch and John Lynch, Bill and I all slept in the same room along with a couple of other guys. Originally we all worked on the same shift and had great fun playing hearts or pinochle, going out to bars, drinking, going to the base movie theater, or just hanging out or planning our next trip over a cheeseburger at the base diner. We had a good arrangement; I had the car and paid for the gas, they paid for my hotel room and my food. Often we would just drive down to Bern,

Switzerland, for a couple of days and tour around the countryside or go sixty miles to Heidelberg and hang out for the weekend.

We went to Paris a few times, but the only thing I can remember was the Moulin Rouge and the cancan dances. We saw the Eifel Tower and Napoleon's tomb and we walked along the Seine and saw all the artists painting Parisian scenes. But it was not a friendly place. The people appeared to speak no English, and as much as we tried, we couldn't get through to many of them.

One trip was to the Neuerburg Rink, which is the famous race car track near Cologne and Essen. We watched gull-winged Mercedes and Porsches scream around the track. The funny part was that the track was a couple of miles long and most of it was hidden from sight except for a split second when the cars sped by. I think that's when I made up my mind that I didn't like watching auto racing. And that's true today!

We had time off to travel because we worked around the clock in three shifts. We worked six days on and three days off always rotating the shifts. The hardest was the so-called midnight (or graveyard) shift. That first night on was really tough trying to stay awake. By eight in the morning, everyone was so tied that nothing really got accomplished. But after six days on the midnight shift, we had a full three-day pass. After the other two shifts, it was slightly shorter.

We were also entitled to a month's leave every year, which I found hard to use up because I didn't have enough money to spend on vacations.[85] But I had two great ones. One was when Bernie Welch, Jack Lynch, and I took two weeks in Italy during April 1956. We drove down through Switzerland where we had to put the car on a train to get through the Goddard Pass because the snow was still too heavy to drive over the mountain. From there we continued down past Lake Como in Northern Italy to Milan

---

[85]   I was paying off the car with a good chunk of my monthly paycheck.

and east over to Venice. We then drove to Florence and on to Rome where we spent a couple of days. We visited the Vatican and actually got a glimpse of Pope Pius as he blessed the crowd outside of the St. Peter's Basilica. While in Rome we hired a guide to show us the major sights. We specifically told him that we did not want to see a lot of churches. The guide was a young man who had been brought up in Atlanta, Georgia, so he spoke perfect English. When his father died, his mother moved back to her native country. He drove like a madman and pinched all the girls as they walked next to his car in heavy traffic. We definitely saw a lot that day and he scored big-time by making dates with at least three young American girls whom we couldn't get to first base with.

From Rome we drove down to Sorrento, took a boat over to Capri, and finally wound up in Pompeii, which I found fascinating. We then drove up the coast past Rome and on to Pisa. I managed to hit a bicyclist in a rainstorm in Livorno, just south of Pisa. The old man was riding the bike and had gone through a red light in crossing the main thoroughfare. We

took him to the hospital and had to report the accident to the military police in Livorno the next day. That put us behind schedule so we hightailed it over the mountains surrounding Genoa and then onto the Italian and French Riviera and back north into Switzerland and up to Germany. It was a great trip that we all enjoyed; however, Jack and Bernie were annoyed with me most of the time since I insisted on smoking. Both of them were nonsmokers. My smoke bothered a lot of people in my life for which I'm terribly sorry. I wish I had come to my senses long before I did. It would have been much more pleasant and healthy for a lot of my friends and family.

Sometime in my final year in Germany, I was promoted to staff sergeant in charge of the traffic analysts, which meant I worked only the day shift—eight to four. That separated me from Bernie and Jack and the rest of the shift. I actually moved to a different room, which housed only guys who worked days so we would all be sleeping at the same time. But I managed to stay close to my friends as much as I possible. Staff sergeant was a prestigious title. It is the first step of a noncommissioned officer rank, and it carries with it certain perquisites and a nice pay increase. It also meant that as a S.Sgt. I received a food allowance instead of just eating in the mess for free. I now had to pay for my food, which was fine because it gave me the choice of eating in the mess and paying $1 for lunch or going to the base diner and buying perhaps a better lunch for $1.50 or something like that. The money was mine to do with as I wished.

In that last full year in Germany, 1956, I was able to visit the Lourdes in the Pyrenees Mountains of Southern France and Spain. Having the car made all the difference in the world and enabled my friends and I to see all of these areas. That last trip to Spain was what I would call the economy-class way to travel. I had enough gas to get us to Madrid and maybe halfway back. I also had only about $100 to spend. The guy I went with had more money but not much more. We decided to camp out on the trip to save our cash. That lasted just two nights. On the first night, we camped out on the shore of Lake Geneva and it poured rain. The next and last time was outside Barcelona (after the tent dried out from our night on Lake Geneva). All we had was a little pup tent, no sleeping bags, just army blankets. In Spain, lodging was extremely cheap, so we decided to stay at a few "pensions" which cost us about $1 per night, including a continental breakfast of coffee and a roll. One pension was actually a woman's apartment in Madrid that had been advertised as a pension. We had a small bedroom with two beds, again, for $1 per night. We stayed in Madrid about four nights. We toured the city and went out to some of the landmarks such as Toledo and Esperanza and spent most of one day at the museum El Prado, viewing the magnificent Spanish painters.

On our last night in Madrid, as we were barhopping we ran into three guys who were putting in the pipeline from northern Spain to Madrid for the U.S. Air Force. They happened to be Englishmen and Canadians working for this pipeline company. We traded a few drinks, and when they found out we were in the air force, they wouldn't let us buy them any more drinks. Their reasoning was sound. They made about $1,000 per week and we made $250 per month. (That was 1956, mind you). They also had bank accounts set up for them at home with $10,000 per year as bonuses for getting the job done on time and on budget. Any way, we had a ball. They took us all around Madrid's nightlife. They knew it pretty well since the pipeline was about fifty miles north of Madrid and they had been coming in every Saturday night for a little R & R for many weeks. On our way north, we passed the pipeline operation and stopped to thank them for their hospitality. We gave them a two-thirds filled bottle of Johnny Walker Black that we had with us. From Madrid we headed north into France and on to Lourdes, which was terribly disappointing because of its commercialism. There were trinket stalls all along the path leading to the grotto with people hawking rosary beads, crosses, and other religious things. I found it offensive; certainly nothing I had expected to find in such a holy place. It made me think differently about the Catholic church for the first time.

Then there were the "morale flights." Sometime in early '56, our squadron fell on hard times, emotionally. Morale was at an all-time low; promotions were not being awarded, and things were basically stagnant. To counter this, the commander initiated "morale flights." I'm not sure how it was done, but guys would be randomly selected to go to various countries or just other cities in Germany for the weekend aboard air force cargo planes that were essentially being used by flight officers who needed the flights to maintain their required flying time. I was lucky enough to be selected for a flight to Copenhagen. We left Friday afternoon and came back on Sunday evening. I don't remember the details of how our hotels were booked, but we ended up in the middle of Copenhagen with two full days and nights to enjoy ourselves. We went to several jazz clubs for which Copenhagen was noted for: Tivoli Gardens, a beautiful park with rides and other attractions, including pretty women, and the Copenhagen Zoo, of all places.

While we were visiting the zoo, we had a funny incident. As we passed the zebra enclosure, a male zebra mounted a female and began to do what comes naturally. One of my friends, Steve Blackwood, was able to catch the entire exercise frame by frame on his 34mm camera. When we returned to base, he promptly had the film developed and made up a poster, which he put in the main operations room at our field base. The poster was covered with scenes of the zebra mating. The final orgasm scene was enlarged and centered in the middle of the poster with the heading: "It's hard to make a strip in this outfit." It was promptly taken down by the officer of the day, but we all had a big laugh over it. But the morale flight accomplished its goal; it livened up the troops and everyone had a good laugh. Promotions came soon thereafter, but I don't think it was because of the zebra poster.

Besides the traveling, we toured the local wine country, visiting little towns around us, eating in great little inns, and having meals of venison, grouse, trout, everything caught locally. We traveled up and down the Rhine River with vineyards on both sides. We also drove along the Moselle River which was just northwest of Sembach. And we spent a lot of time in Heidelberg. It was headquarters for one of the main army units, and they had taken over the best hotels and even a beautiful pool complex that was right on the Neckar River that flowed through the center of Heidelberg. The bars and restaurants were exquisitely old, dating back hundreds of years. The streets were dark and narrow and cobblestoned. We hated to leave when our three-day passes were up. Bernie liked it so much that when his girlfriend from Scotland came over to visit him in the summer of '56, they stayed in Heidelberg the entire time. In fact, I joined him since Bea, his girlfriend, brought a friend and I dated her for the entire two weeks. The rub was that I couldn't get the time off for the entire two weeks so I had to finagle time by promising to make up for it at a later date. I was working days so I wound up working from 8:00 a.m. until 3:00 p.m. and then driving sixty miles to Heidelberg for the rest of the day. I drove back about eleven or twelve each night, slept at the work site and then did the same thing the next day. At the end of those two weeks I was exhausted. Oh, what you do when you're young.

I never told anyone this before, but during those two weeks of driving back to our base at eleven to twelve each night, I almost killed myself a couple of times after falling asleep at the wheel going sixty miles per hour on the autobahn. I actually woke up one night, driving through a field several hundred feet off the highway. Someone was watching over me.

I also dated a young German girl by the name of Josie. She looked a lot like Connie. I met her at the American Express office and tried to date her for months, but she wasn't interested. I eventually found out that she liked opera so I got two tickets to *Madame Butterfly* and that changed her mind. We had a nice relationship for about a year until I went home.

I never got into any real trouble except once when I was promoted to staff sergeant. One of the duties I had to perform was sergeant at arms which meant I was in charge of the squadron's office for twenty-four hours. My duties started at 6:00 p.m. one evening and I had to stay in the squadron's offices to be checked in by the base security people. I was told to expect a telephone call and to stay on the line. The call came; the person asked me to identify myself and give the password, which I did, and again I was told to stay on the line. I did—for about two hours—all the time wondering, "Did I miss something? Why am I holding on this line?" Finally I hung up and hung around for the rest of the night as I was told to do. Well, did I catch hell the next morning. The colonel was trying to get someone from the motor pool to pick him up at the officers club and take him home, or some such story, but I was on the phone for two hours and he couldn't get through. He found out who the jerk was holding on to the phone and had me in his office for a good old "ass chewing" as it's commonly called. Today if something like that happened, I'd be so upset over my stupidity and the chewing out that I'd be beside myself. But then, it just rolled off my back and we actually joked about it for several days. The rest of the time I was a model airman minding my own business and doing my job.

The guys in the squadron were generally great guys. I remember in '55 we decided to do something for the German people around us. Our boss found out that there was a sanitarium for kids with tuberculosis located in the mountains about thirty miles from us. We took up a collection and raised a fair amount of money, which we then used to buy tons of toys for kids of all ages. We actually had a list of the children, their names and ages and their sex so we could be very selective in the toys we bought. I was selected to be Santa Claus and we rented a suit to fit. We then  rented a bus and made arrangements to visit the hospital just before Christmas. I'll never forget that day. The kids were all seated in a double row of tables in a room sort of like a classroom. The nuns and the guys from the unit stood in the front of the room and I sat in front of them in full Santa costume. I knew only a few words: *Freulicher Weinauchten* or "Merry Christmas" in German. The guys and the nuns identified the appropriate toys for each child and each was called up to meet Santa. They all bowed or curtsied in front of me and took their toy with a "danke schein" (thank you). Everyone got a toy. They were thrilled. The saddest part was visiting the children who were too sick to get out of bed. Some were actually not going to make it. Seeing the joy on their faces will last me a lifetime.

When all the toys were given out and we had finished visiting all of the bedridden children, the nuns surprised us by having the children in the classroom serenade us with a half hour of traditional Christmas carols: "Silent Night," "O Holy Night," etc. All thirty hard-crusted GIs broke down and cried.

Bavaria was my favorite spot. Here I am (right) at one of the castles in Garmisch-Partenkirchen, which is a little town south of Munich right smack in the middle of the Alps. In addition to being the site of many great castles, Garmisch-Partenkirchen is a gorgeous ski area. The army had confiscated several of the swankiest ski resorts for use by the U.S. military. All told,

it was under five dollars per day for a room and three meals at the Eib See Resort. Breakfast was $0.50; lunch was $75.00; and dinner was $1.50. The room was $1.00 per night. You could borrow ice skates, old Army Ski Patrol skis and ski parkas and anything you needed to enjoy yourself. At left is a picture of a bunch of us that where at Eib See for a long weekend. This is the first time that most of us were ever on skis. (We all fell down right after that picture was taken.) Next to me are Wendy Groff and then Bernie Welch. On the far right is Bill Mannion.

Not far from Eib See was the town of Oberammergau. In the sixteenth century, the town was hit with the bubonic plague. The villagers prayed to God to save them from this awful plague and promised that if He saved the townspeople from the plague they would forever honor Him by putting on a Passion play in his name every year. The town was spared and an outdoor stage was constructed, and throughout history, the play has been preformed. It was later rescheduled for every ten years and has continued to be performed to this day. Sometime in the twentieth century, it was decided to stage the Passion play only once each decade, I believe starting in 1920. The townspeople do all the acting and make all the scenery and costumes. We were there in 1955 and already there were several townspeople sporting long beards like Jesus Christ for the 1960 showing. Seats to the play are sold out more than ten years in advance.

Oberammergau was and still is a center for wood carving in Bavaria. Storefronts after storefronts were filled with wood-carvers and their work, mostly religious objects. Wood carving friends who have visited Oberammergau recently have told me that it continues to be a major wood carving mecca with schools for the craft right in town. I took this picture in 1955, and it has been an inspiration to me since. I keep it on my workbench. Isn't it strange, it was fifteen years before I even thought about taking up wood carving and here I was fascinated by this carver of the Crucifixion in Germany.

In the Eighty-fifth RSM, life was not like the real military. We had no extraneous duties other than our work at intercepting Russian Air networks. Three incidents bring that home more than any others. In the three years that I was there, we had only two—yes, two—military-type activities. One was a five-mile hike in which everyone who was not on duty had to participate. The march was in full gear, i.e., backpacks and helmets, no guns.[86] We marched in formation to Eisenstadt, that small village about five miles from our base where I drove the Volks into a ditch on its maiden voyage. It was the morning of what turned out to be a hot summer day and everyone worked up a good sweat. But in true AF tradition of the time, we

---

86. We were never issued guns.

were met in Eisenstadt by a full mess truck which treated everyone to a wonderful breakfast out in the field with scrambled eggs, bacon, sausages, toast, pancakes, and coffee. I think they also had SOS,[87] which was a staple of every military breakfast menu. What topped the march was that our commander also had trucks come to pick us up so we didn't have to walk back to base.

The second incident was a forced bivouac that was held over a Saturday night in and around our work site. We pitched our tents in various comfortable areas and bedded down for the night. But no one went off to sleep until a small group of guys made it back from town with several cases of the town's finest local wines. The partying went into the night and everyone had a ball.

A year later the bivouac was scheduled again, but wouldn't you know it, it began to rain so they called it off. That was the third incident and the last bivouac held while I was there.

Several guys I worked with had their wives in Germany with them. Sid Smith from Seattle was one of them with whom I worked closely. He actually sat right next to me. He brought his wife who immediately had a baby and they were having a hard time making ends meet. They had a small two-room apartment above a barn in a small town not too far from the base. I don't remember her name, but Sid's wife was real cute and we used to go out together with several of the guys and perhaps one or two other wives. Sid was sent off to Wiesbaden for a week of training and his wife couldn't drive so I volunteered to help her out. I delivered milk every morning on my way to work and took her shopping once. When Sid returned from Wiesbaden, his wife told him she was in love with me. When he confronted me with the news, I was shocked. I had no idea of her feelings. I hadn't made a pass at her or anything. That really cooled my relationship with Sid even though we worked side by side in a crowded van. Eventually, things changed and we became friends again. I guess it's true: the girls just couldn't keep their hands off me. What a cross to bear. Oh well.

The base also had a large recreational building where they had talent shows, paid USO entertainment brought in from the States or

---

87. This was chopped beef in a cream sauce poured over a biscuit, commonly referred to as "shit on a shingle."

some good European talent. They had dance lessons, card games, etc. At one point early on, we actually formed a band and played at a few talent contests. They had a terrible set of drums with no cymbals so I wrote home and had Jack box up my good ride cymbal and the two high-hat cymbals and send them over. Unfortunately, the ride cymbal was bolted to a piece of plywood too tightly and it arrived with a crack in its crown. But it served me well. The musicians at the base changed almost daily as assignments changed and guys worked different shifts. After a while, all my musical interests seemed to fade away.

D. Incirlik Air Base, Adana, Turkey

In about September 1956, I was selected to be part of a group to test the mobility of our unit by going on a mission to an unknown Middle East country. It was supposed to happen quickly; however, in the true tradition of the U.S. Air Force, it dragged on throughout the fall with planning, meetings, checklists, etc. We actually didn't leave Sembach until sometime in November or December 1956. The plan was that we would go by convoy of about twenty trucks to Frankfurt, get loaded on big cargo planes, and take off for a destination that turned out to be Adana, Turkey. This occurred with a great deal of fanfare, generals waving good-bye to their troops yelling "godspeed," photographers recording every step, etc. The letdown came when we arrived at Frankfurt only to find that the cargo planes that were supposed to fly us to Turkey were being rotated back to the States and we would have to wait for another squadron to be assigned to this mission. That literally took about two months during which time we sat and did absolutely nothing at Frankfurt Air Base. Since we were not part of any unit, we had to buy our own food at the mess hall; this quickly exhausted most of our funds and left everyone scrounging around for money. I had to write home to Mom for a loan as did most other guys. The air force had paid us three months in advance when we started out and wouldn't give us another penny until we returned.

When we finally took off, the trip was also a complete disaster. First, instead of flying those big C190s that we had hoped for, we wound up in small C119 rattletraps. The one I was on broke down and we had to stop in Marseilles and again in Rome where it broke down and we had to stay overnight. Then it broke down again nearing Athens and we had to spend another night there again with no money. We actually stole cans of Campbell's baked beans and heated them on the hotel radiator (the AF paid for our hotel rooms only).

Eventually we landed at our destination: Incirlik Air Base, Adana, Turkey. It turned out to be a small oasis run by the Turkish Air Force and was the home of the U-2 planes that were being flown over the USSR for spying purposes. In 1958, Gary Powers, one of the U-2 pilots was shot down over Russia and was held captive for quite a while. The Russians made a big thing out of it, and it was a major spying incident between our two countries. The United States didn't think the Russians were capable of shooting down a plane that flew that high—I believe the U-2 flew above forty thousand feet.

In Turkey, we slept in a Quonset hut and worked out of our own vans that we brought with us, which were situated near the end of the flight line. It turned out to be a lot of fun and excitement. We were involved with tracking ferret missions—flights of U.S. planes flying straight into Russian territory across the Black Sea to test their (the Russian's) radar tracking capabilities and how rapidly they would send up their pursuit MIG fighters. We tracked the flights by intercepting the Russian radio operators transmissions, sending the coordinates of the plane's path back to headquarters as picked up by their radar. It was fascinating to track the planes on a big chart (by marking the coordinates) and then also seeing the tracks of the intercept planes taking off from various bases inside Russia and going in pursuit. There never was an actual meeting of the ferret planes and the Russian MIGs; everyone would chicken out and hightail it back to their respective bases. The excitement often came from the Russian fighter pilots conversations, which were translated

for us by our own Russian linguists. They would be shouting into their microphones to quickly pursue and shoot down the "arrogant Americans" and things like that. It was exciting to be part of that.

We also listened to Syrian, Egyptian, and Israeli networks because there had been the famous Six-Day War between Israel and Egypt sometime in September/October 1956 and there was a lot of friction around the entire Middle East. In fact, when we first found out that we were going to a mystery location in September, we thought it was to participate in that conflict. But the timing was a mere coincidence.

Turkish soldiers were housed almost next door to our Quonset hut, and their lives were difficult by comparison. Besides having regular jobs on base, there was a whole contingent of perimeter guards. The Turkish Army was noted for having very hard-fighting soldiers. At night the guards would be deployed around the outside perimeter of the base, sometimes a few miles out into often desolate fields where they would stand unflinching all night until they were relieved. They were actually scary, standing there in their long capes and tasseled hats, not moving, not making a sound, just holding their long rifles with fixed bayonets on them. In fact, the Turkish soldiers were renowned for being excellent sentries, and Turkish bases boasted of having no fences around them, mainly because of their sentries. The regular soldiers we came in contact with were also fascinated with our Zippo lighters. It was against regulations, but several guys would buy Zippos at the PX and resell them to the Turkish soldiers for four times the price they paid for them in the PX. The price to the Turkish soldiers represented more than a month's salary to them.

The Turks didn't have a mess hall like we did. They cooked their own meals over an open fire outside their barracks. What bothered us most was the chanting every evening as the Moslems were called to prayer from the top of the mosque. We kiddingly suggested that someone may want to do some target practice on those guys.

Our mess was in a large airplane hangar and was opened, as they say, 24-7 (twenty-four hours a day, seven days a week). What turned me on the first day I went for breakfast was this huge grill covered with frying eggs. You could have as many as you liked. I've never seen that anywhere else in the service. What I didn't know that first day was that the base's supply plane or ship had just come in so there was plenty of everything. Three weeks later when the eggs were gone, we were eating the powdered eggs variety.

There wasn't much to do in Turkey, but we managed a few trips. One was a bus ride to the port city of Aleppo, right inside the Syrian border on the Mediterranean Sea. Another time we took a truck and a few cases of beer and drove into the countryside. Someone had gotten directions to the ancient ruins from the Crusades that were built high on a hill overlooking the valley. We were told that one of the Crusades landed on the coast near Adana and traveled up the river and into this valley where they built this fort. It was tough getting to the top because the hill was so steep. I could only imagine troops laden with armor and bows and arrows and spears and swords fighting their way up this steep embankment in the siege of the fort. Joining us on this trek up the hill were a bunch of local children that I guess ran up and down these slopes on a regular basis. They had no trouble at all. We made fast friends, and they were particularly interested in our beer cans; I don't think they had ever seen an aluminum can before. They cherished the empties.

Adana, Turkey, was rather primitive in many ways. In fact, Adana was quite old and lacked many of what I would call basic necessities of life. There were hardly any cars. Everyone rode around on donkeys or in horse-drawn wagons. The women, of course, were Moslems and covered their faces, and few were actually seen walking the streets. A couple of the hornier guys actually went to the local jail, which doubled as houses of prostitution. In Turkey, wives who were unfaithful wound up in this prison for a specified term. They could get out early by buying their way out. Since most of them had been abandoned by their husbands and their families, there was only one way out and  that was prostitution. Needless to say, the place was a pigpen and the women were awful. (Out of curiosity, two of my friends and I went in to see the inside of the prison. We were physically searched, and our cameras were taken from us before being allowed in.) As an epilogue to this story, the horny guys all came down with the worst cases of venereal diseases with which to remember the place.

Besides analyzing the "traffic" being intercepted, I was the group's draftsman. The leader of our contingent was Captain Blanchard, and he wanted to impress everyone back at headquarters in spite of the screwups that had occurred—none of which were really his, so he prepared this elaborate report. One page of the report was a scaled-down drawing of our setup out at the edge of the flight line. So I was assigned that job: mapping the site. I had never done anything like that before but learned quickly. I got a long tape measure and measured off every piece of equipment, the site itself, the trucks, vans, water tanks, and jeeps where our antennas were located and everything else connected with it. Captain Blanchard actually pulled some strings and got me a drawing desk at the base headquarters. The draftsmen there gave me all the tools I needed and even supplied the paper, pencils, pens, and erasers. Unfortunately, my copy of the report with all the pictures was destroyed in a flood in our basement when we lived in Ozone Park.

Captain Blanchard was a guy probably in his late thirties or younger who was single and a career officer specializing in intelligence operations. He was also a regular-type guy. One day when we were off duty, he invited a few of us enlisted men to his trailer for some freshly cooked pistachio nuts. Turkey is a major grower of pistachios, and you could buy them by the pound real cheap at the local market. Blanchard loved pistachios so he bought what appeared to be about ten pounds of the raw nuts. He then borrowed a large pot from the mess hall and proceeded to boil the nuts in heavy brine. When we arrived at his trailer, the nuts had cooled and were ready for eating. To wash them down, Blanchard broke out a bottle of Irish whiskey. The afternoon ran into the evening, and we ate practically the entire ten pounds of pistachios and naturally finished the Irish whiskey. We were all very sick that night.

The trip back to Germany from Adana was on a par with the trip down. We packed up the equipment and moved it to the flight line to be loaded aboard our planes, but they didn't arrive for two days. We literally sat on the runway waiting for them for those two days. When they finally arrived, we spent another two days loading them up. One incident was terrible. We were loading the trucks, jeeps, and vans into huge C190 cargo planes where the whole front of the plane opened up to reveal its entire empty belly. In order to get those large vans up into the belly, they used a large cable system. One end of the cable was attached to the van being loaded while the other end of the cable was then threaded through a pulley attached to the back end of the plane inside the belly and then out of the plane and attached to a funny-shaped vehicle that looked like two huge truck cabs welded together back-to-back. That double truck cab was used to pull the equipment up into the plane's belly. During the loading of one of our vans, a jeep filled with Turkish fighter pilots returning to the control tower from the flight line (where they had parked their jets) apparently were all watching this big van being loaded and didn't see the stretched-out cable running across the loading area in front of the C190. The jeep hit the cable at probably fifteen or twenty miles per hour, dumping all its passengers onto the concrete with many broken bones and scrapes and bruises. The damage was quite serious, but watching it was hilarious.

After taking off with our load of equipment, we wound up getting into a major thunderstorm and were forced to land at Rome's airport. Knowing the plight of the men—i.e., no money—Captain Blanchard frantically radioed the U.S. Embassy in Rome to get us lodging for the night and some spending money. The embassy came through with $50 for each of us. They also arranged for us to stay at a mountain resort south of Rome that had not yet opened for the season. Remember, this was in late April. A bus picked us up at the plane and sped us to the resort. The workers greeted us with open arms and put out a spread of food fit for a king. We feasted on cheeses and pasta and chicken and meats and also drank many bottles of their finest wines. The cost was something like $25 per person and a good final meal for a troubled trip. We left the next day for Germany, arriving without further incident. But I've got to say had we been in a real serious military situation, we would have lost the war considering the inefficiencies and screwups we saw from MATS (Military Air Transport Service) which was responsible for the cargo planes and the scheduling. They were incredibly inept.

Timing of my trip to Turkey was coordinated to end just at the time my four years with the air force was up, but because of the delays, I officially had to extend my service by three months otherwise I would not have been able to go on the mission. So when I returned to Germany, I almost immediately flew back to the States for discharge. Wendy Groff had to take my car up to Bremerhaven and put it on the ship back to the States for me because I wasn't going to be there to do it myself. I had spent a total of four years and three months in the air force and had attained the rank of staff sergeant.

My days in Germany were over in April 1957. I returned to the States by plane and was taken to Manhattan Beach in Brooklyn for processing. I didn't mind the eight-hour flight back to the States. I don't even remember where we landed. It was like returning to a strange land. Once, I had known this place like the back of my hand, but now I wasn't sure what street came next—was it Gates Avenue then Linden Street? Now, it's all coming back to me. Connie lived on Onderdonk Avenue and I around the corner. Now I remember.

E. Lessons Learned

What did the service do for me? An awful lot! First, I think it was the best thing that could have happened to me at that particular time. My disappointment in not becoming an air force drummer never bothered me once I was in Germany. How could I have ever seen what I saw while playing drums in some insignificant air force band somewhere? Yea, maybe I could have been shipped overseas with a band, but that was a remote possibility.

Secondly, the guys I met in the service, particularly the ones I lived with for three years in Germany, were some of the finest people I have ever known. They were bright, articulate, giving, and so much more. Our squadron had guys who were Russian linguists, and most of them had some college education or had actually graduated from college and had signed up for the air force to avoid the draft. I was among a unique bunch of guys who taught me that there was more to life than playing drums. I realized during those three years that I had to do something with my life, and college was one sure way of achieving something more than drumming (unless I wanted to go to Julliard or something like that but frankly, I wasn't good enough for that).

Thirdly, I was able to see a large part of Europe that I had never even heard about before. Venice, Florence, Rome, Capri, Pompeii, Genoa, the Riviera, Barcelona, Madrid, Lourdes, Paris, Amsterdam, Copenhagen—they were all great and I got to see them.

Fourthly, I was able to mature into what I believe is a man. That's why I think every young man should have the opportunity to go into the service for at least two years. It would teach them discipline, responsibility, and so much more. Here I was, a twenty-year-old kid without a college degree and I was responsible for breaking the Russian

Air Network's secret code on New Year's Eve on January 1, 1956, in a matter of two minutes, something that had never been done before. How about that! I would have never experienced anything like that sitting behind a set of drums in some air force band anywhere in the world. I am so thankful for that warrant officer's faux pas. It made a man of me, and for that I am eternally grateful.

The service gave me self-esteem. I was able to accomplish something! I realized that I had a head on my shoulders and could think for myself. I probably also realized—but would not admit it right away—that I wasn't really a very good drummer. The service was a cleansing for me. It was a rebirth. I had seen a different aspect of life that I had not experienced in Ridgewood, Queens, and it would take me to a new plateau that eventually allowed me to reach beyond the ordinary. (It sounds corny, but it's true.)

I actually liked the service too. There was a routine in my life. If I had been married and an officer, I probably would have considered staying in, as crazy as that may sound. But my thoughts at that time might have viewed things differently only because it was an uplifting experience. I didn't realize it then, but my whole life even now is an organized life. I like organization. I like to have things in their proper places. Perhaps had I stayed in however, I would have quickly realized that the bureaucracy was something I could not take for the rest of my life.

CHAPTER V

Life as an Adult—1957 to 20__

A. Returning to Civilization

I didn't have a problem coming back into civilization life after spending four years away from home. But what do I know; I was swaying in the breeze, taking what came along. So I wasn't in the air force anymore. I was happy to be home and out of the service. No more military bullshit. In fact, it was a very happy time, seeing Mom and old friends and being free of the regimen of the service (that I professed to like). The hardest part was trying to decide what I wanted to do from that point forward. I hadn't the foggiest idea. I didn't even know what kinds of jobs were available. At least when I was in basic training in the air force, they made us sit in classes every afternoon and learn about the various jobs that were available. No one does that for you in civilian life although it would be a great idea to start something like that at the high school level. However, the air force did try to help by giving me a two-day aptitude test, which consisted of testing plus interviews and then a final counseling session with an advisor. In the combined sessions, most of which I don't remember, my advisor told me one thing that stuck with me. He said that I had a definite aptitude for numbers but not math. That didn't help me much at the time because I didn't know how I could apply that "skill" in the job market. The aptitude for numbers, I'm sure, came from working with the codes every day. Numbers came easy. But only years later, when I worked with closely held businesses, did I realize what it meant. I was very comfortable working with numbers, such as those that I had to work with from balance sheets and income statements of corporations, knowing relationships with different columns of numbers, calculating percentages and rates of return on investments, etc. But I clearly would not have made a good accountant because I didn't have the discipline of an accountant to sit and run through columns and columns of numbers day in and day out and then have to make sure they are all balanced. I was more suited to dealing with numbers in a variety of different ways where it was not monotonous and repetitive.

Right out of the air force, the first thing I did was spend some time with Mom—she was thrilled to see me after more than three years. And while we had kept up on everything with hundreds of letters, there were little things we found to talk about and feasting on some home-cooked meals that I missed so much. At first I couldn't get over what a heavy "Brooklyn" accent she and many of my friends had; I actually hadn't heard a Brooklyn accent for three years. Most of the guys I worked with came from outside New York. They were from California, Louisiana, Indiana, Iowa, Kansas. I visited my two old friends, Joe Brocco and Dick Roethel, then spent some time with Jack and George and Uncle Will and Harry and Beatrice and Tommy. I had been writing to a girl who lived next door on Linden Street, Pat Buscemi; we really talked seriously in letters over that three-year period. Some of it was pretty hot and heavy in fact. She had moved next door during the time I was in Mississippi and we met just before I shipped out for Germany and we wrote to each other for the entire three years I was away. It was great having that connection. She was really young, like sixteen. When I got back, we dated a few times and it was quite clear that we were not meant for each other.

I was also interested in seeing Connie, even though she had written to me only a few times during those four years. Having been away that long, I was certain she didn't really want to have anything

to do with me. She was graduating from college and here I was with no education; what would she want with me? But I went to see her anyway. (I actually kept this picture of her in my locker for four years.) Her parents had recently moved to Glendale, a community not too far away in Queens. She was as beautiful as ever and just about to graduate from Saint Joseph's College. I was immediately in love with her all over again and didn't want to let her out of my sight. When she invited me to her graduation ceremonies, I rushed out and bought a new suit for the occasion. (It was a light blue summer cord suit.) But back to that first meeting: Connie always talks about what I looked like that first time I went to see her. I had on air force khaki pants, loafers, and a neat dark green long-sleeved crew neck Vellore shirt that I brought back from Germany. (George borrowed it once and spilled paint all over the front so that was the end of that shirt.) My lack of college was overshadowed by the great green crew neck shirt I wore because it was as though I had never left. I think we saw each other every day after that.

Another thing I had to do when I got home was pick up my car, which the government graciously shipped back to the States for me (a fringe benefit of being a staff sergeant). I had to go to the docks in New Jersey. Once I got my car, I also drove out to Long Island and visited my dad who was living in a trailer park in Bay Shore. I had dinner with him at his favorite steak house, Bronco Charlie's, and had a nice visit. I brought him an authentic pair of lederhosen (size 40). He lived in a rather small trailer. It had a small living room area, kitchen, and in the back, a bedroom. He was very proud of the fact that he had a place for everything and everything in its place. He was glad to see me. I guess I also brought news of other family members that he wouldn't otherwise have gotten. (here's Connie at age 10)

Mom and I also drove up to Litchfield to visit Patricia. Mom got a big charge out of driving with me in my little Beetle. It was unique to the States because it had been a domestic car in Germany. It didn't have the same emission standards as U.S. cars and it had funny little directional arms located on the support bars behind the front doors, one on each side. They were actually little lighted arms shaped like an arrow that popped up when you hit the directional lever. They were called "Mack nix  sticks" roughly translated as "makes no difference" because—like drivers everywhere—the directional signal often goes on for one direction and the car goes in the opposite direction or straight ahead. Anyway, they drew a lot of attention from everyone who saw them. As a matter of fact, there were so few VWs in New York that every time you passed one, both cars honked.

In retrospect, everyone was happy to see me as I was to see them after three years. Much had changed since I was away: Jack had gotten married to Eileen; Dick Roethel had married Pat Cox, the girl of his dreams; George was in graduate school at Yale; etc. The world had changed too during those three years. *Playboy* had become one of the most popular men's magazines on the newsstand, Elvis Presley had become the rage in music, General Dwight Eisenhower had become president of the United States, and the cold war had gotten colder.

The summer of 1957, I was twenty-three with no education, a half-assed job, and in love with a beautiful woman. Connie and I saw each other practically every day. She had a summer job at a Catholic day camp in Whitestone, and I worked at the helicopter service at LaGuardia Airport in the afternoon. We managed to get to the beach in the early afternoon somehow, that's all I remember. On weekends I had to work, but we went to the beach in the morning. We went out dancing or we went to the movies on my days off. Connie remembers our going over to the city one day when we were both off. We wound up at the Cloisters in the Bronx, driving around the city and topping it off with drinks at the Whaler Bar in some hotel in Manhattan. (My brother George had taken Patricia and I there when we graduated from high school and I remembered the place. Connie loved it.)

I tried to teach Connie how to drive the Volkswagen which had a stick shift, but she had learned on her father's big automatic Chevy and couldn't get the hang of shifting with a clutch. Since she was out of school and needed a car to get to her new teaching assignment in East Meadows, she wound up buying a 1957 two-tone green Chevy sedan.

Jack was living in an apartment in White Plains and working for Royal McBee Typewriter Company on Park Avenue in Manhattan. He and Eileen had had a son, John William, sometime in the late fifties and I was his godfather.

George was teaching at Amherst College and getting his MFA (master of fine arts) at Yale. I didn't see much of him during that time, but he dropped in every so often to see Mom. Patricia was still in Litchfield, and we drove up to see her whenever we could. It was usually three times a year.

Mom was working as a secretary at Coyne and Delanney, a plumbing supply business on Myrtle Avenue. She loved her job, and the owners loved her. In addition to being the secretary, she also answered the phones so she always had funny stories to tell about the people who called in. She took this job when Dad left and was thrilled when she found out that her typing skills had not deserted her after all those years.

Connie was the first daughter of Walter and Sophie Runkle who originally lived in Elmhurst, Queens, in a two-family house with Sophie's sister, Helen, and her family. They moved to Ridgewood when Walter and his brother-in-law couldn't get along, and they never spoke after that. Connie had two younger sisters, Janet, who was only about a year younger, and MaryAnn, who was nine years younger.

As we found out many years later, Walter's family actually changed its name to Runkle from the original Italian name of Roncoli. Remember, the twenties was a time when the influx of Italians to New York was causing many problems of overcrowding and crime.[88] Italians were not looked upon very favorably. We know that Walter's sister Alice was still using Roncoli in 1918 when she married Ed Flug. But in 1924 when Walter's father died, he was reported as John Runkle on the death certificate.[89] Interestingly, his (John's) father was Louis and shown as being born in Germany, according to John's death certificate. His mother's name was Teresa Peretta, and she was reported to have been born in Italy.

John Henry (or Andrew)[90] Runkle was married to Margaret Sullivan and they had three boys Walter, Henry, and Robert and four girls, Alice, Hazel, Grace, and Anna.[91] John was a glass cutter and probably worked in Brooklyn. Apparently, Margaret had left John and moved upstate, leaving John to care for the kids. John died in 1924 of an infection of the middle finger of the right hand, which he got while working. It's been told that Alice and her husband, Ed, took Walter and his siblings under their wing. (Walter was actually twenty years of age at that time, but his brothers may have been younger.) Alice was married to Ed Flug who had a good job as a court stenographer in the Queens courthouse

---

88. Actually, Walter's father was born in the USA as was his mother, Margaret Sullivan.

89. John died from an infection in his finger from a metal splinter.

90. We see it both ways: on daughter's birth certificate it was Andrew in 1900 and Henry on Grace's marriage certificate in May 1927.

91. Anna Teresa was born January 22, 1900, but apparently died at a young age.

on Suphtin Boulevard in Jamaica.[92] They had one daughter, Eileen, who was a science teacher in a Catholic high school in Brooklyn and never married. Eileen died of cancer in February 2008 at the age of eighty-six. Aunt Alice lived in Jamaica, Queens, and died of cancer in 1995. I don't know the timing, but Hazel was married to Axel, an antique dealer. Aunt Grace married George Parris and had three children—Patricia, Sally, and one other. Henry eventually got married to Ida and lived in Brooklyn and worked in a factory for most of his life. They had no children. Robert was married to Aunt May; he died before I knew Connie. I don't believe they had any children either.

For many years, Walter had a good job as a stationary engineer at the Brooklyn Navy Yard. It was a government job; he was responsible for all the boilers at the BNY, which was a huge facility. He often worked different shifts so he wasn't around all the time. In the sixties however, he pretty much worked the four-to-twelve shift, which allowed him to be home during most of the day. Walter died Sunday morning June 5, 1983, while taking a bath before going to church. He had had a heart problem in the seventies and had a pacemaker inserted in his chest which never seemed to work properly. It was eventually removed.

There is very little known about Sophie's family. Her parents were Alexander and Mary Anna (nee Polak) Markowski.[93] The Markowskis had three daughters—Sophie, Helen, and Stella—and two

---

[92.] From his records, Ed spent twelve years in the U.S. Navy. He enlisted at the age of eighteen and spent time on the USS *Maui* in 1918 and as a recruiter for the rest of his time on active duty. His parents, August and Matilda, were born in Germany. They had three children: Frank, Margaret, and Edward.

[93.] Some papers show the last name as Markowsk*a*.

brothers whose name we don't know. The girls all lived in Elmhurst. Stella had two children, Edmond and Claudia. She died of cancer sometime in the sixties or seventies. Helen had two sons and one daughter—Victor and another boy whose name we don't know and Susan. Helen died in 2004. Because of the strained relationship with Walter, we had no contact with that faction of the family. Sophie died in June 1996 while Connie and I were celebrating Robin's second birthday in Alaska with Mark and Sharon and the baby. She had no air-conditioning, and the weather was reported to be extremely hot and humid for several days. She apparently died while getting dressed that morning.

Beside Connie, Walter and Sophie had two other daughters, Janet and MaryAnn. Janet graduated from Bishop McDonald's High School and studied English Literature at St. John's University. She wound up getting her PhD from Oxford University and while there she met, fell in love with and married a Czech mathematician by the name of Vaskou Panuska. They moved to Montreal, Canada where he worked at one of the Universities. Janet taught English at a school also in Montreal. The marriage didn't last and after their divorce Janet moved to Saskatchewan and then to Red Deer, a small town outside of Edmonton, Alberta where, in addition to teaching school, she took on the awesome task of raising several dozen sheep on her small ranch. She's now back in Montreal and retired. We rarely see her but Connie talks with her sporadically. Connie and Janet have never really been that close as sisters. I don't expect that will ever change.

MaryAnn grew up in front of our eyes during the sixties and has always been an important person in our lives. After graduating from High School she worked in NYC as a secretary at Christian Brothers Winery and eventually married her high school sweetheart, Fred Gebert, Jr. MaryAnn and Fred bought Fred's parent's home in Woodhaven and lived there until the seventies when they moved to Glen Head, Long Island. Big Fred worked as a switchman for the New York Telephone Company in Nassau County. MaryAnn and Fred had three children; Stephanie, Jacqueline and Frederick (Little Freddie or Fred III, as he's called).[94]

Connie has always been close to her sister and to Stephanie who is her Godchild. Sometime in the early nineties, after he retired from the telephone company Fred and MaryAnn bought a small farm house with several acres in up-state New York, ironically in the town of Lockwood. They've made it their weekend retreat and travel there whenever they can. Holiday celebrations, which had traditionally been at either their house or at ours, have not included Fred and MaryAnn in recent years as they have chosen to spend their time in Lockwood—not at the Lockwood's.

Stephanie is the oldest girl and attended Fredonia College in Western New York where she received her master's degree in speech therapy. She now works as a contract therapist for the Glen Head school district. While in college she met and fell in love with Rob Bottie from Northport. They now live together in a beautiful house they bought in the early 2000s. Rob is a very successful dealer in military collectibles which he sells primarily on EBAY and at a few large shows. Rob's business is the most fascinating I have come upon. He has been able to become a major player in the collection of military collectables by going after items from WWII and even earlier wars and other conflicts. He buys from estates, people who just want to clean out their attics and other collectors and then creates descriptive write-ups and pictures of each item up for auction on EBAY generally for a period of ten days ending on Sunday nights. At any one time he may have as many as twenty items up for auction at the same time. The task of cataloging and keeping track of literally thousands of articles of clothing, helmets, insignias, German swastikas. SS headgear, rifles, swords, daggers, etc. is awesome. I give him a great deal of credit for finding something he truly enjoys and then making a business with it from which he can actually earn a good living.

Stephanie is a beautiful girl with big blue eyes, blond hair and a winning smile for everyone. She has a great sense of humor and a warm heart which is evident to everyone with whom she comes in contact. She reminds me so much of her mother. Her interest in

---

[94.] As of January 15, 2008 there is now a Little Little Freddie (the Fourth).

collectibles also fits appropriately with those of Rob. Together they spend the "yard—and tag-sale season"[95] roaming the country-side searching for hidden treasures and those special "finds." The result of their efforts has evolved into a quaint antique shop in Kings Park. They make a wonderful supporting couple. And while they haven't married there is every indication that they are a very happy couple together.

Little Fred graduated from York College and has become one of the top salesmen for a dental supply company, Benco out of New Jersey. Fred consistently ranks right up at the top of the list for outstanding Benco sales people. In 2007 Fred met and married Jennifer Ewald, a school teacher from Brightwaters. To the delight of everyone Freddie the Fourth arrived January 15, 2008 and to my shock and delight Fred and Jen asked me to be his Godfather. I actually thought he had made a mistake. Who makes an old man the Godfather to a new baby? Well, for one, the Fred III family. It is a real honor and the little tyke is adorable. I'm looking forward to seeing him grow up. His parents are a wonderful young couple. They are both dedicated, hard working, family oriented people with a great work ethic and attitude. Connie and I love them as our own children. We've enjoyed meeting Jen's family. Her father, Warren has done a magnificent job of renovating the newly-weds house despite suffering a severe stomach problem in the midst of the work.

Stories about the family wouldn't be complete without my relating how Fred met Jen. Fred called us for dinner so we could meet his new girl friend, Jennifer Ewald. We met for dinner and in the course of the evening the question came up as to where they had met. Fred told us that at one of his dental customers' office the receptionist and other staff mentioned that there was a great patient of this one dentist that they thought he should meet. A blind date was set up and they met and the rest is history. It was such a heart warming story we naturally went around telling everyone how our nephew met his girl friend and how it seemed to be love at first sight. But that's not the end of the story. When they decided to get engaged they invited us to dinner, again. This time we took them to

---

[95]. I think it starts some time in April/May and ends in October/November depending on the weather.

St. James, a little pub in Mineola. In the booth, probably over the salad, Fred and Jen announced that they were going to get married. We were thrilled and totally delighted for both of them. "What was the reaction of the women in the dental office who set up the whole thing, originally?" The question was like giving Novocain to one of the dentist's patients. Fred and Jen both stared at us and said nothing. With a slight red face Fred then told us that the dentist office scenario was made up. They hadn't met that way at all. Actually they were embarrassed to tell us that they had met over the internet. Fred got the idea when he told Stephanie that he had met someone and she came out with something like "Were you set up with a dentist's patient?" So they took that story as their own. It certainly sounds better than the internet connection.

While we've become close to Fred in his adult life—after college—we really never saw too much of him or his sisters as they were growing up. Sure, we saw them at Thanksgiving or Christmas and the occasional other outings here and there but they were busy doing their thing. But they've all turned out to be great individuals.

I'll never forget Little Freddie sloshing around in our back yard as I was putting in a brick patio. We were at the point of having leveled off the dirt and about to fill in the area with a layer of sand when the Geberts arrived for a visit. Little Freddie found the muddy dirt and dove in. MaryAnn was furious but realized that he was a real boy and the dirt washes off, eventually. Fred was always a good looking blue-eyed typical boy who wound up playing all the requisite sports throughout grammar school and high school.

Jacqueline is the traveler in the family. Unhappy at home, she wound up getting married and moving to Colorado probably sometime in the nineties where she got into the real estate sales business. Her marriage didn't last and eventually she got tired of the cold Colorado winters and moved to Los Angeles. That didn't work too well, so she tried Portland, Oregon but somehow or other that wasn't right, so now she's settled on Stowe, Vermont where she continues to try her real estate salesperson skills in a big new development which at last look was not doing well. Jackie is a warm beautiful girl who has been blessed with a large dose of self confidence which has enabled her to travel across the country in search of her nirvana. I certainly hope she finds it. In the meantime, Connie and I will continue to give her whatever spiritual support we can.

This picture of the three Gebert kids shows their personalities up front. Jackie on the left is the pixie wanting to have fun; Stephanie is the oldest and in charge while Little Freddie is looking to get into trouble. That was one of the best pictures I have ever taken simply because it reflected each of them perfectly. Connie and I love all of them and hopefully we will continue to stay close.

B. Job Hunting

The one major thing I learned in the service was that college was essential to building a solid future. My mother and father had never pushed college; in fact, it was never even discussed, so it wasn't something I anticipated having to do when I graduated from high school. It was only when I met the guys in the air force who encouraged me to not miss the opportunity did it strike home. Connie also encouraged me since she had just graduated; that was another incentive for me. So I applied for and was accepted as a provisional[96] student in the undergraduate business program at St. John's University School of Commerce under the GI Bill at night. The GI Bill was the greatest. It paid me something like $125 per month while I was going to school based on the number of credits I was taking. (The money was raised when I got married and again when Mark was born. I think it was as much as $240 per month for ten months of the school year.) All I had to do was submit my program from St. John's and the checks were mailed every month. If I completed the whole program, which would normally take about six years going nights, I could expect to graduate with a bachelor of business administration or BBA degree. I could probably have

---

96. My grades in high school were not that great, but St. John's gave me a chance to show them I could hack college.

done it quicker if I wanted to go to school every night throughout the summer; I chose not to.

Since I was going to school at night, I needed to get a daytime job. I checked around for various jobs and found nothing that was of interest. (Actually I didn't know what I was actually interested in.) Everyone had different ideas of where the good jobs were. I was looking for something more enlightening. Here I was, a kid of twenty-two with no experience, four years of service that meant absolutely nothing, and no idea of what I wanted to do. There were millions of guys getting out of the service from their two- or four-year commitments, like me, who had all gone in at the same time to avoid the draft.

Sometime in mid-July 1957 through an employment agency on Hillside Avenue in Jamaica, I wound up taking a job with the New York Helicopter Service, which ferried people and cargo between LaGuardia, JFK, and Newark airports. (I figure I was offered the job because they thought since I was in the air force I must know something about helicopters, who knows.) I worked from 4:00 p.m. to midnight, basically loading cargo and luggage at the same time as the copter was loading passengers. It was a boring job. How much cargo could a little helicopter take? It would take a few minutes to complete the unloading of cargo coming in and loading of outgoing pieces, then you'd wait for the next scheduled flight in about half an hour or so. The oddest cargo we handled were crates of laboratory mice coming from or going to research laboratories either in New Jersey or Massachusetts. We had to fumigate the inside of the cabins once they were unloaded. In the meantime, the passenger guy and I sat around and bullshitted with each other. I had taken the job on the promise that my hours could be flexible to accommodate my school schedule. But when I told my boss that I needed to work days once school began in September, he disavowed any knowledge of the fact that he had agreed to that kind of flexibility. So I quit, but not before I took Connie on a round-trip from LaGuardia to Newark on the helicopter (which I was allowed to do because I had worked for the company for more than a month). I can still remember it. It was sundown in August, about eight thirty, with a beautiful sunset developing in the western sky. The helicopter went right over Central Park at about one thousand feet. It was a great experience for both of us. Coming home, we saw Manhattan light up as only it could be. We saw all the lights and the rows of streets from one end of the island to the other. I left the job the next day.

Dick Roethel, who worked for a meat company, Hoffman Bros. Purveyors of Meats, told me they needed a delivery driver for a few weeks and he talked me into taking the job. So for a couple of weeks I delivered meat and poultry to mostly Chinese restaurants in Midtown Manhattan. This was in August, the hottest time in the city. Traffic was bad and the job miserable. Dick understood that I was just trying it out and probably wouldn't stay once school started. I think someone was on vacation so having me there meant that Dick didn't have to make the deliveries himself. I actually stayed for the two weeks. It was a tough job. I guess I learned something from the experience: *Never work as a truck driver. Get an education so you will never have to do that kind of work again.*

Poor Dick, he was studying engineering at Manhattan College but couldn't wait to marry beautiful Pat Cox. She got pregnant immediately, and Dick had to find a job to support the family. What prompted him to get into meat cutting I'll never know, but there he was stuck in the job whether he liked it or not. In fact, soon after I left that two weeks in hell, Hoffman Brothers filed for bankruptcy because the Chinese restaurants they served were notoriously bad payers and the Hoffmans had extended credit to many of them and they didn't get paid. Dick, to his credit, saw a way to beat the system. He borrowed from his parents and other members of his family and bought the Hoffmans' equipment and took over their lease. The good news is that he succeeded in becoming one of the top meat purveyors in New York City.[97] He also wound up with six kids. He always complained that Pat got pregnant every time he put his hand on the bedroom doorknob.

C. Sinclair Refining Company

I next took advice from Jack's friend, Joe Dobbin, who suggested that I get a job with an oil company because, according to Joe, they paid well and oil companies were getting bigger and bigger and he thought I would have a good future with a big firm like that. With

---

[97.] He refused to sell to the Chinese restaurants.

no experience and no college, the best I could do was to become a mail boy. It didn't pay very well, but it was a start. I was still single and figured I'd move fast. It was worth a try. I was hired by Sinclair Refining Company at $70 per week and became literally the office mail boy for the Purchasing Department. It was my first office job and the people were nice, but it was clear that any move up the ladder would be a very slow process as everyone was there forever and they were all waiting for the guy above them to move up to the next notch. In any event, a college degree would be essential. I also wasn't thrilled with the purchasing process of a big oil company. The purchasing department bought everything from toilet paper to giant refineries, and it was just huge volumes of paperwork. The top purchasing agents, about a dozen guys, were the kingpins and everyone else worked for them. They were high-priced executives who for the most part couldn't bother to say hello. On top of that, most of them were actually Texas oilmen types.

At the same time that I took the job at Sinclair, I was also admitted to St. John's School of Commerce. The way it worked I usually took three courses, two three-credit and one two-credit. That way I went to school three nights per week; two nights were from six until ten. The two-credit course met once per week from six until eight. In the beginning, the two-credit courses were business law and were only held on Friday nights. When they were completed, then the schedule was changed to Mondays, Tuesdays, and Thursdays.

Sinclair's office was at the corner of Fifth Avenue and Forty-eighth Street, the southeast corner of the Rockefeller Center complex of office buildings. We were on the third, basically looking down over Fifth Avenue. On St. Patrick's Day, the parade came right under our window. Not much work was done that day as everyone flocked around to two large windows waving down at people walking on the sidewalk or cheering for the marchers going by.

Just below us on the street level was a great men's haberdasher whose name I can't remember. It's no longer in business. The regular suits were very expensive, but in the rear they had their "university shop" where they had moderately priced suits that looked very expensive but were mainly for young men like myself. My favorite suit at the time was a black-and-white herringbone heavy wool tweed suit. The wool was very thick, and because of that, the knees had silk linings in them to help prevent the wool from stretching out and losing its shape. But despite the silk linings, which by the way was a sensation in itself because the silk was always cold, the knees still bulged out and lost the crease. I had to keep steaming the legs every night to keep the creases. The sad story was that I ironed off the pants once too often; the iron burned the wool on one side of the crease and when I looked in the mirror you could see one side was brownish while the other side wasn't. I was crushed. My favorite suit and it was gone. But I learned a lesson: never to press off pants without putting down a cloth on top of the pants to protect the fabric from the burn.

There was also a certain amount of peer pressure back then as everyone tried to outdo the next person with the nicest suit, the classiest tie, or spiffiest shoes or even in the summer a straw hat with a madras plaid band. I tried it for one summer, but the subway was so hot that I couldn't stand having to wear a hat.

In 1957, there was no air-conditioning in the subways. Some of the subway cars had overhead fans which moved the dank, damp air a few feet one way or another, but that was it. On those three *H* days (hazy, hot, and humid), there was no relief to be had on the street or in the subway. One just had to endure. Nor was our home air-conditioned. We may have had a fan in the window to pull out the stale air out of the room, but that was the extent of it. The wiring in the old house was used to the reason there were no air-conditioning units. I don't even remember finding out what a window air-conditioner cost. They were big and noisy as well.

My favorite hot subway story was when I was traveling home in the middle of the summer standing by a pole under a ceiling fan wearing a light tan Haspel summer suit. Standing next to me was a rather endowed blond woman wearing a light pink dress. At Bridge and Jay Street Station, the doors opened and in walked a guy with a fishing pole straight up. When he reached to pole under the fan, there was a *pling, pling, pling* as the fan blades hit the fishing pole. When I looked at the blond, I saw soot on her shoulders and on the top of her protruding breasts and also on my extended-out arm holding on to the pole. Realizing his error, the fisherman retreated to the next car before the doors closed. The fishing pole had loosened up years of soot attached to the fan blades and we were sprayed black. The suit survived to live another day in the subway, but I don't know about the pink dress on the full-breasted woman.

D. Marriage

One thing that was good about Sinclair was that the staff people with whom I worked every day were great. Gordon Howath, who wound up marrying Judy Roach, one of the secretaries in the department, and Connie and I became close friends. I actually became godfather for their first child, Bob. Gordon and Judy lived in Forest Hills and gave great parties. Gordon's father was a publisher or editor of something and always gave parties where there were a lot of young people. There was also Roy Heaney and his wife Sue, a nurse, who wound up years later unknowingly living only a few blocks from us in Garden City. Unfortunately, Roy died of a heart attack in his early fifties. Another friend was John Flatley and his wife. One of the other secretaries, Clair, married Ken Blair and years later they too lived not more than a couple of blocks from us in Garden City. Ken became the national sales manager for Heineken Beer. But at Sinclair, I realized very early on that I did not like doing this sort of mindless paperwork, and on top of that there were a lot of people ahead of me on the so-called succession ladder. Where could I go? There were guys who had been there for ten years who were just invoice clerks or something like that. The top jobs seemed to go to the Texans or Oklahomans who came up from the field operations outside of New York City.

Connie and I got engaged at Christmas 1957. Mom liked Connie a lot; Dad liked her too. When I first told Jack that I was dating Connie, his comment was that she looked too skinny, but he came around to like her anyway. Mom gave me her engagement ring, and we went to a jeweler in the city that someone recommended and had the stone reset into a more modern setting. I don't remember what I was thinking about in those days. Getting married was just the thing to do. Everyone was doing it. It was like the next step to adulthood; perhaps the step *into* adulthood. I don't remember when we set the date for the actual wedding, but it was done with the idea that Connie would be off from school so we could have a one-week honeymoon. So it was set for December 27, 1958.

We hadn't really started looking for a place to live during the early part of 1958, but then tragically, Uncle Will died suddenly from a massive heart attack in July. Mom offered us his apartment, which was the entire second floor, and she said we didn't have to pay the $50-a-month rent until we actually moved in. The summer of 1958 turned into a working summer of fixing up the apartment. The place had not been painted or taken care of for many years. We also decided to do some renovating. We closed up a door between the kitchen and living room, redid the bathroom, wallpapered the living room, painted the bedroom, wallpapered the kitchen, and made a really neat entrance hallway using red burlap glued onto the walls and I made a Japanese-style rice paper screen which was used as a drop ceiling and gave off a nice fused light. We worked like dogs. Joe Brocco helped us with the plastering since he had worked on his uncle's new house in New Jersey and learned how to plaster from the Hungarian laborers his uncle hired. Joe had gotten out of the service just before me and was looking around for a job when his uncle started building this house. He hired Joe to work on the house along with the Hungarians ostensibly to keep an eye on them when his uncle wasn't there.

In the middle of the summer prior to our marriage, Connie and I drove down to Washington DC to visit Bernie Welch and his new Scottish wife Bea, whom he had met on a trip to Edinburgh, Scotland, while he was stationed in Germany. We took two rooms in a hotel in downtown DC and visited with Bernie and Bea for the entire weekend. Unlike today, here we were away from home, single and very much in love, but we didn't dare sleep together. It was just one of those things you didn't do before marriage—although God knows we really wanted to very much so. When we got home, Connie caught hell from her father who definitely believed we must have slept together since we were away from home in a hotel. He didn't actually speak to us for the rest of the year until the wedding, even though Connie swore to him that nothing had happened.[98]

I wound up getting shingles[99] in September that year. That put me out of commission for several weeks. It was extremely painful and uncomfortable because there was no way to get relief from the pain and itching of the sores that broke out on one side of my back and around my right side to my stomach area. The chiropractor actually helped to speed up the healing process, and it went away in a couple of weeks instead of months estimated by the doctor.

[98.] And nothing did happen.

[99.] An inflammation of the nerve endings in my back and around to my stomach.

The wedding went off without a hitch. All our respective family members showed up along with selected friends and colleagues. From  Sinclair there were Gordon and Judy Howath, Sue and Roy Heaney, John Flatley and his wife (I don't remember her name), and Dick Huewitter and his girlfriend. Jack Lynch who was my roommate in the air force and his wife, Fran, came down from Amenia, New York. Joe Brocco and Dick Roethel were in the wedding party with their spouses. My brother Jack was my best man. Connie's sister Janet was maid of honor. MaryAnn had the flu and missed the entire wedding and reception. George was there with Margo. The only ones who didn't come to the reception were Patricia and Dad. Dad did show up at the church and left by a side door. Bea and Tommy were there as were Aunt Peg and Uncle Ted, Little Peggy, and her new husband Jim Daley (who had gotten married during the summer of '58 in Southampton, which we had attended).

All of Connie's relatives were there including Uncle Axel and Hazel, Uncle Henry and his wife Ida, Aunt Alice and Uncle Ed, their daughter Eileen, Aunt May (Uncle Robert's wife); and others whom I don't remember. We were married in St. Pangrias Roman Catholic Church in Glendale, Queens, where the Runkles had moved in 1957. The reception was at a restaurant not far away called the Welcome Inn. (I believe it's still there on Forest Avenue across the street from the cemetery.)

Connie and I left after the reception and drove to the city where we spent the night at the Biltmore Hotel. The next morning, we drove to the Poconos and stayed at Strickland's Resort until New Year's Day. Strickland's is best described as a 'honeymoon haven." Probably 95 percent of all guests were on their honeymoon; the rest were celebrating anniversaries, having celebrated their honeymoons at Strickland's in past years.

The weather was actually balmy for December; there was no snow until New Year's Day. We went to dance lessons, toured around the countryside, and generally amused ourselves. We met a real nice couple from New Jersey, Audrey and Charlie, who visited us in Ridgewood one weekend that following summer. Then nine months later, they asked us to be godparents to their daughter. That relationship turned sour after the christening because of our lack of knowledge of the traditions in the Armenian religion. Connie had gotten a beautiful gift for the baby but forgot to bring it with us when we went to the ceremony. We told Audrey and Chuck that we would send it down once we got home. A few days later, they called us all upset over the fact that we did not give their daughter a certain item for her christening. Chuck was Armenian, and under the Armenian tradition, the godparents were supposed to give a certain gift—I don't even remember what it was, but they were outraged. We apologized for not knowing their traditions, but it didn't seem to help. We couldn't believe that someone would be so upset over a gift particularly when we had no way of knowing their traditions. They cooled down after that and wrote us a nice note apologizing for being so upset with us. But the relationship never warmed after that.

We settled into the life of a married couple. We had to get furniture, lamps, carpeting, everything. Some of it we did before the wedding. I don't remember there being a wedding shower for the bride. I'm not sure that tradition was alive at that time. Connie was teaching second grade in the East Meadow school system on Long Island and I was still at Sinclair. We socialized a lot with the guys from Sinclair, and Connie had a good friend in Virginia Hoey with whom she taught. Ginny's husband, Ed, was a brand-new chiropractor practicing on Long Island. It was a real struggle because chiropractics was not licensed in New York State as yet. Actually, Ginny and Ed were championing the chiropractic cause in many different ways. Ginny was the president of the New York State Women's Auxiliary of the Chiropractic Association. Ginny and Ed loved to throw parties. Eventually they bought a big house in Wantagh, Long Island. At the time in 1960, it was $50,000—an incredibly expensive house that Eddie thought would be perfect for attracting more patients since he would appear to be a successful chiropractor.

It worked. However, Ginny and Ed's marriage fell apart after they had three children. Their first child was a boy born with a deformed hip and short leg. The third child was a girl born with deformed arms. The middle child was a beautiful girl with no deformities.

Ginny and Ed spent years trying to find out why their kids were born deformed, and they came to the unfortunate conclusion that it was each other's fault and that in fact they were both descended from the same Irish family and should never have married in the first place. (Ed's mother was a Murphy and Ginny's father was a Murtha—a name that was changed from Murphy when they emigrated from Ireland in order to be different from all the other "Murphys" coming to this country.) They both became bitter alcoholics and eventually divorced. Sadly, Ginny contracted cancer and died before she reached thirty-five. Ed died several years later of a bad heart.

Our newly decorated apartment was just as we wanted it. We were very comfortable with the rooms. I even built a stereo cabinet that fit in a certain spot in the living room. I made it from birch plywood with sliding doors covered with wallpaper that matched our living room walls. I was quite proud of that—my first big piece of furniture. In fact, we still have it and surprisingly it is still in perfect shape. It was put together almost entirely with Elmer's glue and no nails. In those days we had a turntable and we listened to a lot of jazz and some Frank Sinatra and the like. We also had a television in the living room, but I can't remember what shows we actually watched. At that time I was at St. John's and studying most of the time. We also visited with Mom downstairs and with Connie's mom and dad in Glendale. They invited us for dinner practically every week.

We also visited Jack and Fran Lynch in Amenia, New York. Jack and I were in the same room overseas (along with Bernie Welch). Jack's father owned the local grocery store/butcher shop in Amenia, and Jack worked with his dad until they decided to sell the place when the large supermarket chain encroached on the small town of Amenia and ruined their business. Jack wound up working as the athletic director at the nearby state mental hospital as an athletic director. We were also godparents to one of their children, but I don't remember which one. Matter of fact, we were godparents to a lot of little babies and we probably were not very good godparents. We didn't take the honor very seriously as we probably should have. In some nationalities as was the case with Audrey and Chuck, godparents are very important.

We never followed through with annual gifts, birthday cards, etc. I think had we done more following through, we probably would have stayed more in touch with these people. Instead, our relationships seem to have faded away with the very people we wanted to stay close to. I know with Jack and Fran I got annoyed with them because Jack's sister lived in Glen Cove and he would say how he was down visiting his sister but he never stopped in even though I gave him a standing invitation. With Bernie, it was a little harder because he lived so much farther away. In fact, we haven't seen Bernie and Bea since that weekend in 1958 although we have spoken by telephone.

E. Holland-Columbo Trading Co.

In early 1958, I decided to leave Sinclair and started looking around but really didn't know what I wanted to do. I went on a couple of interviews for sales positions but realized that I didn't want to be a glad-hand salesperson or a life insurance salesman; I didn't want to have to talk people into buying something from me. So in May, I took a job with Holland-Columbo Trading Co. (HC), a Dutch importer of cocoa, cocoa beans, essential oils, rubber, and spices. HC was a subsidiary of Internatio-Rotterdam Inc. I don't even remember how I came across this company, it may have been a newspaper ad. Holland-Columbo was basically a commodity trading company importing commodities mostly from the Far East and hedging their future delivery commitments by trading on the commodity exchanges. It was a pressure cooker job that I soon realized didn't appeal to me. I worked with the cocoa trader and later with the spice trader who imported pepper, cassia, nutmeg, and a lot of different spices. Again, there were a lot of nice people. Bill Lankaster was my first boss. He was a Dutchman and founded HC which he eventually sold to Internatio-Rotterdam. Bill had lived in Ceylon for many years buying commodities that were shipped to Great Britain, Europe, and the States. When World War II broke out, Bill and his family moved to London and stayed there until the late forties when he came to New York to operate on the import side of the business. He was a very smart businessman. One of his businesses was importing essential oils, so we had hundreds of little sample bottles in the office (the office had a nice aroma all the time). Lankaster had to identify the quality and essence of the oils. He also was a tea taster and had to sample and grade the tea that companies wanted to sell us.

I learned a lot at HC, but it was a purely business environment, one that I was not familiar with. It was cutthroat: make a profit or get out. All the officers were Dutch. I also worked for Ari Nugterin who was only about thirty when I was there (I was twenty-four). Ari had been trained in Rotterdam to be a commodities trader from the time he was fifteen. His entire existence was trading. He was also brilliant, but tough to work for. I didn't grasp the nuances of commodities trading, buying deliveries for June and hedging them by selling deliveries in September and that sort of thing. It was a very fast-paced, frantic trading environment. Ari would stay at his desk and trade through a "floor broker" or he'd go to the floor of the Cocoa Exchange and do the trading there himself. He'd come back to the office after a few hours of trading and practically collapse from exhaustion. He had the capacity to come back to the office and only then write down in his trading book all the trades he had made. Sometimes he would be trading all day and never miss a trade in the book. That kind of stuff convinced me that I was not cut out to do that work.

F. Mark Is Born

Talk about a life-changing event. That came when we learned that Connie was pregnant. We were thrilled and overjoyed by the prospect, but what was it going to be? We decided we wanted to be surprised. It didn't matter; boy or girl was fine with us. We thought of names and eventual decided on Mark Steven if it was a boy. I don't remember what name we picked for a girl. Connie carried well. During the first

. . a child, more than all the other gifts that earth can offer man brings hope with it, and forward looking thoughts, . . .
Wordsworth

Mark Steven Lockwood

first child and first son of

Mr. & Mrs. William Lockwood

was born on

Sunday, August 7, 1960

at 8:25 a. m.

and weighed

5 pounds - 15 ounces

couple of months, she had some sickness but came through it beautifully. As she grew bigger, she got more radiant, more beautiful, and more loving.

We cleaned out the room next to our bedroom, put down new flooring, painted the woodwork and ceiling, and since we didn't know what we were having, we put up neutral yellow wallpaper with little baby things on it. Then waited.

While Connie was pregnant, we spent a wonderful week in June 1960 at Bea and Tom's house in Southold where we sat on the beach, fished, and just had a great time. Little did we know that all those many years later we would own a house on that same beach. It was at that beach that we were surprised to learn that there were blowfishes being caught. I rushed to the bait store for some squid and ran back to the beach. Just casting out with a flounder hook spreader, I caught a dozen blowfish in no time. We had them for dinner that night and I broke out into a rash from eating so many.

Connie's pregnancy went well, no complications. Her doctor was pleased with her progress. I was actually going to summer night school four and five nights each week to finish up some accounting and management courses and then studying all weekend hoping to finish up before the baby arrived. On Saturday, August 6, we invited Ginny and Ed Hoey for dinner. Connie had felt great all day and actually scrubbed the kitchen floor Saturday morning. We were having a grand old time Saturday night after dinner when Connie suddenly

started to go into labor. Eddie said not to worry and we began to time the intervals. Around midnight, the intervals got to the critical stage. Connie was already packed and ready to go. We excused ourselves from our guests and off we went to the hospital.

What a joy Mark was, a perfect little human being in every way. Connie knew exactly what had to be done. I was all thumbs. I know I carried him and played with him regularly, but I can't remember ever changing his diaper (unlike Mark who always changed his daughters' diapers). In fact, Connie decided to breast-feed Mark from the beginning, and the first night he was home I bravely

agreed to get up when he awoke and carry him in to his mother for his nightly feeding. The next morning when I awoke, I was surprised that he had slept through the night. Connie laughed and told me how I snored through the night, never hearing Mark's cries. I was such a heavy sleeper that I rarely heard him.

Before the big day, we scanned through the typical baby-names books but we both liked Mark and for his middle name we both also liked Stephen, so it wasn't a big decision where we couldn't agree and had to compromise with some name. Not at all. The name Mark had become fairly popular, and we liked how it sounded with Lockwood and also with Stephen. So there he was—Mark Stephen Lockwood, our pride and joy.

Mark grew up fast. On his first birthday, with Mary Ann, Janet, and Mom and Mom and Pop Runkle on the porch in Linden Street, Mark took his first steps for Mary Ann on the grass in the backyard. He never stopped walking after that.

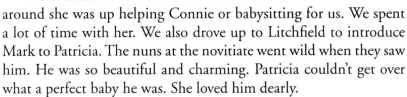

Mom and Pop Runkle and Mom Lockwood were thrilled to have a grandson. Dad was also thrilled, I think more so because he never saw Jack and George's children.

We lived above Mom so whenever she was around she was up helping Connie or babysitting for us. We spent a lot of time with her. We also drove up to Litchfield to introduce Mark to Patricia. The nuns at the novitiate went wild when they saw him. He was so beautiful and charming. Patricia couldn't get over what a perfect baby he was. She loved him dearly.

This whole parent thing was new to both of us, but somehow we got through it. Connie did everything. I basically had nothing to do with it. It was Connie who took charge and did a magnificent job of raising the little guy. I liked to take pictures of him: his first bath! sitting in the crib, sleeping in the carriage, playing in the backyard or at the playground. I think I got them all.

It was around Mark's first birthday when I decided to leave Holland-Columbo and join U.S. Trust. At that time of my life, I was consumed with both school and work. The family was there and I participated but not to the extent that I now see fathers doing. I know I took Mark for walks, spent time with him playing and things like that, but he was little and needed attention and at that time I had little to give.

When he was a bit older, I remember so fondly Mark sitting on my lap in the dining room (where the television was) watching cartoons together every Saturday morning. And when I got home at night while we were waiting for supper, we often played together. When Mark was six or seven, wrestling was one thing Mark liked to do with me. That sometimes wound up badly if I pushed too hard or muscled him a bit too much. But he loved it and I loved it more than that. There is nothing more precious than having your son hug and kiss you. And I might add that is true at any age.

But it was because of Mark that I decided I had to do something different from what I was doing at HC. I still wasn't sure what would thrill me in life, but I felt I had to keep searching. Friends I had made at St. John's had a variety of jobs and worked for companies with different benefits. Benefits seemed to be something we didn't have at HC. My friends all had good benefits such as bonuses, pension, and health care and they even paid for schooling. One evening as we sat around the school lounge, waiting for class to start, I casually mentioned to everyone at the table that I was unhappy at HC. Not long after that, Tom Lavan, Pete Arrighetti, and Howie Arnheim[100] all offered to get me an interview at U.S. Trust. They were all in different departments but felt they could get me in somewhere. U.S. Trust didn't hire just anyone; you had to be introduced by a present employee or be recruited from one of the Ivy League colleges. Actually I had no idea what U.S. Trust was or what it actually did. I did not know what a *trust* was or what banks did behind their marble columns and big heavy brass doors. But I would soon find out.

G. U. S. Trust Company of New York Inc.

I was a bit reluctant and nervous walking into Bill Miller's office at UST. Miller was a vice president in charge of the tax department.

[100.] About four years after I joined UST, Howie was caught with his hand in the cookie jar, stealing funds out of unsuspecting trust accounts and we never heard from him again. Ironically, when people heard what he had done, everyone's response was the same: "I wouldn't put it past him."

As I walked into his office, he came around from behind his desk with his hand extended. His first words were puzzling; he said, "Hi, Bill, any relation to Luke?" I had no idea what he was talking about so I responded, "Well, maybe if you go all the way back." He was actually referring to Luke Lockwood, one of the senior partners at the law firm of Carter, Ledyard and Milburn, the chief law firm for UST.[101] I, of course, didn't know that. But anyway, I must have made a favorable impression because he offered me a job as a tax person, essentially preparing fiduciary tax returns.

U.S. Trust was an entirely different world for me. It was a world of finance and truly unbelievable wealth. U.S. Trust's clients were some of the wealthiest people in the United States. I learned about personal and fiduciary income taxes, and this was the basis for my career. I learned about trusts and estates. I started out in the tax department, a subject I wasn't at all familiar with but I was willing to learn. Unfortunately, the learning was more rote than anything else. Put these numbers into these boxes and add up the columns. It was purely a "clerk" job. What I didn't like about it was that it was much like the Sinclair environment. People had been doing the same job for decades. Most of the people in the department were not college graduates either and weren't even going to school at night to get their degrees as I was. But I was told that this job could be used as a platform for going into other departments of the company that might be more suited to me. At that point I still had no idea what I wanted to do, but it was a job. What was really great was that the company paid 100 percent of my college even though I was getting $240 or so per month from the GI Bill. So financially it was a good add-on benefit. In fact, at age sixty, having spent twenty-one years at UST, I was able to receive an annual pension for the rest of my life of about six thousand dollars.

I started at U.S. Trust in September 1961. At that point, I had been going to St. John's at night for four years and had a good amount of credits built up toward a six-year undergraduate degree. Besides the requisite religion and ethics-type courses, I took a lot of marketing, management, and accounting courses, which I truly believe helped

---

[101.] I was referring jokingly to the first "Luke" in the Bible (in case you didn't catch that).

me years later. My worst subject was law—so-called business law which everyone was required to take in the first year. It was the only course given on Friday night, and it was from 7:00 to 8:00 p.m. The teacher was Mr. Duncan Frazer, a practicing attorney with offices in downtown Brooklyn—actually around the corner from the school. He was dry and boring as only law could be and I inevitably fell asleep. In spite of that I managed to eke out a D. Sixteen years after taking that class we moved to Garden City, and on one of my first days riding the LIRR, a guy walked by me in the aisle and I thought, "I know that guy" but I didn't know from where. Then one day perhaps a year or two later going to work with my neighbor Harry Blair, he suggested that we sit in the seats that face each other because he was meeting a friend getting on at Nassau Boulevard stop. Who walks in but the mystery man whom I couldn't identify. Harry introduced me and I mentioned that I had recognized him but couldn't remember from where. He shrugged his shoulders and said, "You must have taken my law classes at St. John's." Sure enough, it was Duncan Frazer, the guy who gave me my only Ds in St. John's. I didn't hold a grudge. Connie actually got his wife a teaching job in the NYC school system a few years later.

H. Mom Dies

Then the first and biggest tragedy of my life occurred in November 1961 when Mom woke up one morning feeling terrible. I had left for work, but Connie heard her calling out and called for an ambulance. She was rushed to Bethany Deaconess Hospital, a small local hospital on St. Nicholas Avenue. I was called at work and rushed home. We called Patricia, Jack, and George and they all made arrangements to come to see her. Mom was hooked up to several monitors and in an oxygen tent, but she didn't look that bad. I figured she would come out of it. When they made all the visitors leave the building that night, I kissed her good night and left. Never did I think that that kiss would be my last.

The call came in the middle of the night. Connie took it and passed the phone to me. It was the doctor on duty. His only words were "Your mother died, I'm sorry." I was stunned. I didn't cry. I was too shocked to realize the finality of what that doctor had just told me. "Your mother died, I'm sorry," he said. You will never see her again. It was days later after the funeral that I woke up to the reality of that statement. At the time, one of the only things going through my mind was that she would never see Mark grow up. She would never hear him say, "Grandma." She would never be there to celebrate another of his birthdays. That hurt me more than anything else. I so wanted her to enjoy him and see him grow and for him to know and love his grandma as we loved her. What a tragic loss. That was also true for all of her other grandchildren. She had enjoyed seeing Jimmy at Chappaquiddick earlier that summer but would never see him again. Nor would she see John, Patty, and Susan or Jonathan, Juliet, and Jennifer.

It shattered me. Not right away. It actually took a few weeks after I returned to work from the funeral. UST was very nice about it. They gave me as much time as I needed to get back to work. I wound up getting severely ill in early December for about two weeks. Mom's death at such a young age has hung over me to this day. Mom was just sixty-one years old. By today's standards she should not have died. I would have thought that cardiology was much further along in its ability to save people from heart attacks. An aspirin would have saved her life in 1961, but it didn't. She was taken from us much too soon. She would never see Mark grow up. She would never have all the kids over for sauerbraten dinners or see her daughter when she left the convent and begin to live a normal, happy life. It was truly tragic because she deserved to enjoy the fruits of her labor of love, what she worked so hard to build despite the hardships she had to experience throughout her adult life. She has been sorely missed.

And Mom's death would be a turning point in my life because it transformed Connie's and my way of life and sent us into new territories that we may never had traveled otherwise.

The sharing of Mom's possessions was somewhat unpleasant as we tried to take the items that we wanted to remember Mom by—a vase, a broach, etc. It was the big stuff, the furniture and dishes and other things that became difficult. Then there was the matter of the house itself. What was to happen to it? At this point, I think the house was owned by Uncle Harry, Joe Donitz, and Mom.

Connie and I thought about buying it. It was appraised at about $20,000; and as we figured it, we could make it with the rents from the other two apartments if we could get it for that price. But because there were other owners, everyone felt that we should put it on the market to see what we could get. It proved to be more valuable. I think it sold for $23,500 or something like that. In any case, it was more than we thought we could afford.

I'm still not sure what the crux of the problem was, but with Mom's death came a total disconnect with Jack and Eileen. There were certain accusations made by Jack over what Connie and I were doing with regard to Mom's remaining possessions, which were nothing more than a few pieces of furniture and a bed that no one wanted.

Since we lived in the house, we took on the job of disposing everything that no one wanted and also clean up the apartment to start showing the house to prospective buyers. But for some reason, Jack got his noise out of joint over what we were doing. Connie and I have never been able to figure it out. So we basically drifted apart. It wasn't that we were terribly close to begin with, but we now had a reason not to call. Jack and Eileen must have felt the same way because they never called either. And that's the way it stayed, unfortunately, until 1983.

I. Ozone Park

We had actually engaged two realtors to try to sell the Ridgewood house. When one of them found the buyer, the other was naturally disappointed. Since we needed a place to live, we asked the unsuccessful realtor to find us an apartment. I was making about $70 per week and had been paying Mom $55-a-month rent and we didn't want to stray too far from that level, but we soon found out that rent was much higher in the real world, more like $100 to $150 per month. But as luck would have it, the realtor had a sister whose house was for sale in Ozone Park, an area we didn't know at all. We found the house to be nice, clean, located in what appeared to be a nice neighborhood, near a church, and importantly, near to transportation into the city and the price was $17,500. With an FHA mortgage and some cash under the table, we were able to swing it. We moved in August 1962. That was the start of eleven great years in Ozone Park.[102] It was a new beginning for Connie, Mark, and I. Mark was just two, Connie was still at home taking care of him, and I had been at U.S. Trust for just about one year.

[102.] From 1962 to 1973.

We did a lot of work on the Ozone Park house. I cleaned up the basement, painted the floor and the walls, and made it more accommodating for both work and play. My shop was at the front of the house, and we had a washing machine and even a basement toilet. As the years went by and we accumulated some money, we also had the house resided with dark gray shingles and expanded the living room by taking down the wall between the porch and the living room. We also built a vestibule-type area to block the cold when the front door was opened. My father came in from Bay Shore and helped me paint and wallpaper the interior.

We referred to the house as an "Archie Bunker" house from the TV show that was so popular in the seventies. In the opening credits of the show, they pan a street with houses very similar to those in our neighborhood. The houses were on small twenty-five-by-one-hundred-feet lots with a garage in the back. The driveway was the only thing separating each house. The kitchen was in the rear followed by the dining room and then the living room and closed-in porch (which we eliminated). A staircase in the living room led up to three bedrooms and a bathroom on the second floor. Mark's room was the front bedroom, and ours was the back bedroom. The middle room was made into an office/den.

The garage was actually an old two-car model but one side had been closed in and a conventional door replaced the large garage door. That meant that we could get into the garage from the little door without having to open the overhead garage door each time. After I bought the Sunfish, it worked out even better since I was able to roll the Sunfish into the garage and then, equipped with dollies I made especially for the wheels of the boat trailer, I was able to slide the boat and trailer sideways over to that closed side for storage when it was not being used. Between the garage and the house was a small plot of grass and some flowers and a small concrete patio. For privacy, I made a four-by-eight-feet privacy screen on wheels that we would slide into the driveway, blocking off any view of the backyard from the street.

We had a few good friends in Ozone Park. The Segesis across the street had two boys, Frankie and Glenn. Frank Senior worked for ADT, the burglar and fire alarm company. Then there were our next-door neighbors. On one side was Gene Corcoran who was the service manager for Rheingold Beer. He was in charge of seeing that all the beer dispensers at Shea Stadium and other sports arenas in New York were in good working order. He always had a little buzz on since he drank beer all day long. He also had a collection of beer glasses and other Rheingold Beer marketing paraphernalia like the neon signs in bars, comb holders, coasters, etc. One summer we had a "beer party" in our backyard. He went crazy, bringing out every sign he owned, which we hung on our chain-link fence. He also saw to it that we had a keg of beer and a beer dispenser right from the plant in Brooklyn. I can remember people remarking at how delicious the beer tasted. In fact, we had gotten in a few cases of soda "for the women" and once they tasted the beer, they didn't want soda. To our surprise and Gene's, who was an authority on how much beer one needed for a party, we wound up running out of it. It was a great party.

Next to Gene was an old Dutch couple, the Bauers. Mr. Bauer had been a ship's carpenter in Holland before moving to the States. His house was immaculate, the outside was wood clapboard, and every five years he would take the siding down to the raw wood and prime and paint all over again. It actually gave him something to do. He would visit with me or I would go over to talk with him practically weekly. Inside, his house looked more like the inside of a ship: everything was sparkling, varnished, the brass all polished.

Ozone Park was convenient for work and school; the A train ended at Lefferts Boulevard. It was an elevated subway that went underground in East New York, which was near Woodhaven. The ride was a little under an hour, and the train left me right in front of U.S. Trust's building at 45 Wall Street. That same train went through Brooklyn a few blocks from St. John's so it was an easy transfer. The only scary part was coming home at eleven o'clock at night through Brooklyn. There were bands of young black kids roaming the trains at that hour and while they were probably harmless they were nevertheless menacing to say the least.

I remember Ozone Park as a nice place to grow up. There were plenty of kids around, a good school, and nice people. Mark became a Cub Scout and Connie became a den mother. I wound up becoming the scoutmaster for the troop. We had a great following of parents, and the kids had a good time. Our pinewood derby contest each year was special. I remember making the track for the race and helped Mark in making the cars.

 The Cub Scouts also played softball and went on trips. I remember one softball game in the schoolyard of PS 108 where Mark was the mop-up hitter in a game we were losing. He was not that good of a ballplayer at that young age, which was the case with all of the kids, but he kept his eye on the ball and when the right pitch came he hit a home run and his team won. I doubt if he remembers that game, but I was so proud of him and never forgot it because it showed me that he would stick in there and try his hardest with just about anything he was doing.

It would be two winters—or as they referred to the period between January 1 and April 15 of each year—"two tax seasons" before I was able to transfer to the Estate and Trust Administration Department in May 1963. The tax seasons were brutal. All the work of the tax department was essentially squeezed into those four and one half months. Everyone was required to work every night and every Saturday. (The nice part was that you got overtime pay for it too.) But it was still brutal. I was going to school at night and so I could not spend as much time working as everyone else, but that was acceptable.

The Estate and Trust Administration Department administered the trusts and estates of the trust company's clients. When people died and named the Trust Company as executor of their estate, the estate administrators took charge of the decedent's assets. If their furniture or other personal effects were not bequeathed to someone in the family, we would see that they were sold or auctioned off. We sold their homes or apartments, disposed of other belongings, and in every way took care of what they owned at the time of their death. If they had a surviving spouse, then we'd basically turn everything over to him or her. In many cases the decedent's will called for setting up trusts for the benefit of their spouse and perhaps some children. The estate administrator would set up those trusts and turn over the job to the trust administrator; most of the time it was one and the same person.

J. Dad Dies

Early in 1963, my father was admitted to Good Samaritan Hospital in Bay Shore ostensibly with a slight heart attack. Good Sam was a relatively new hospital operated by the Daughters of Wisdom, Patricia's order, and Dad had a real affinity for that hospital plus it was close to his trailer. In fact, I think he felt as though he got preferential treatment because everyone knew he was the father of a Daughter of Wisdom. When he was released from the hospital, the doctor told me that Dad had heart disease and also cancer of the esophagus. Coming from a doctor then sounds strange today because he said, "Let's hope the heart disease gets him before the cancer gets worse." Not "we'll do everything we can to stop the cancer and improve his chances of living with the heart disease," which would probably be the response today. Dad did not seem to be in any discomfort from either of his ailments. From the time I was quite young, Dad was known as a cougher. He was always coughing. I can remember noticing the dark brown wallpaper in our living room in Ridgewood where he wound up sleeping on the couch when he and Mom broke up—before he moved out for good, it had all kinds of splatter marks from his coughing. Well, in 1963, he continued to cough and now we knew what it was coming from.

In late August of that year we received a call from one of Dad's close friends in the trailer park saying that he had found Dad dead in his trailer. He had apparently gotten out of bed but fell down dead on the trailer floor. I was glad he went the way he did. He was a lonely man who had disenfranchised his entire family except for Patricia and I. Just before he died, he converted to Catholicism at Good Samaritan Hospital with the nuns of the DW. They were thrilled and so were Patricia and I. We had gone to his first communion and that was really the last memory I have of him. I sure wish it had been better. I would have loved to have had a father that I could really love and respect, but the memory of him and my mother has burned an indelible picture that will never be erased. My brothers showed no emotion on the news of his death and neither one came to the funeral. We sold the trailer and disposed of his meager possessions, and that was the end of John Charles Lockwood Sr.

K. Maple Lake Farm

In 1964, we decided to find a place to go away to for a few weeks of vacation. We hadn't taken a vacation with Mark before other than the awful trip to Chappaquiddick. Instead of a full-fledged vacation, we would trailer the Sunfish to the Center Island Beach in Bayville on most Sundays. Mark was now four years old, and we were looking for a place to go, but where? I remembered the great time I had had at the farm in Rhode Island when Jack took me in 1951. The farm was started by a Finnish family back in the thirties, having moved up to Rhode Island from Brooklyn. The story has it that their friends from Brooklyn kept coming up to visit so they decided to build a few cabins and a communal toilet and charge them for room and board. The father and son basically took care of the farm while the mother, daughter-in-law, and daughter took care of the guests. The daughter was a schoolteacher and was off all summer to help out. Her husband was the butcher and took care of the kitchen, etc.

We tracked it down by telephone, and it turned into a great idea and actually became an annual ritual for us for the next eleven years. Going to the farm was something we looked forward to each year. We went at different times for the first couple of summers and eventually settled on the first two weeks in August because of the friends we made one year and then continued to see them every year thereafter.

The daily routine was simple: breakfast at eight then either hang out at the lake or run down to the ocean for a few hours, which was a few miles away. Back at the farm we would rinse off the saltwater in the lake before lunch. The afternoons were mostly filled with activities at the lake—i.e., sailing, fishing, diving off the dock for the kids, hiking around the lake, or playing tennis. We took the kids horseback

riding a few times too. Every so often someone would organize a softball game for an afternoon. Connie proved to be a pretty good underhand softball pitcher one year. Many of the kids liked to help out in the barn; that meant getting up at the crack of dawn to help with the milking, leading the cows out to pasture, and then bringing them back in the evening and helping with the evening milking.

The food was wonderful considering it was boardinghouse style. Breakfast was bacon and eggs, cereal, pancakes; lunch was hamburgers, sandwiches, soup, salads; dinner was chicken, steak, chops, etc. There were always a few complaints about it, but overall it was okay. Costwise, the farm was a real bargain. When we started, I think the cost for Connie and I was $35 per week each and for Mark it was $18 per week and was scheduled to go up each year by one dollar until age eighteen.

The addition of tennis came one year when a few guests who knew how to play started teaching the rest of us the basics of the game. As the years progressed, everyone brought up their new tennis rackets and we found ourselves playing competitively with practically the entire population of the farm turning out to root for their favorite players.

Usually on the middle Saturday afternoon and night (most people stayed for the same two weeks), there was a theme party where everyone dressed up appropriately. One year it was Hawaiian, another was hippie, and so on. There were games and a barbeque and dancing and everyone had a great time. On rainy days it was off to the town of Warwick to go window-shopping or drive over to Narragansett to look at the mansions and the boat docks.

Every day before dinner someone had happy hour. Some folks had elaborate setups of munchies and mixed drinks. After dinner we had a choice of activities that included poker, bingo, or other card games. I organized bingo one year, and that turned out to be a lot of fun, something everyone participated in. The dancing on Saturday night was a highlight for the kids and the adults because the owners brought out their Finnish folk dance records and taught everyone the steps.

The lake was also stocked with fish so the kids and some adults had wonderful times fishing either early

in the morning or at dusk. One year we discovered that the lake had several huge snapping turtles and people were concerned about letting the kids swim, so a snapping turtle hunt was organized and we actually caught two of these prehistoric monsters.

The lake itself was glorious. The water was silky clean and refreshing. In an old Finnish tradition, the farm sported a wonderful hot rock sauna at the edge of the lake. It was actually a sauna building with a dock leading out over the water. The rocks were heated with a fire which was started every morning by one of the farmhands. By nightfall they were red-hot. After cooking in the sauna for several minutes we would run out onto the dock and jump into the cool water. That was so refreshing. Because the body was so hot, it was not a shock when you hit the cool water of the lake. We usually used the sauna just before going to bed; it really made everyone sleep well. But the after-dinner crowd was usually the old Finnish people's turn. It was segregated by gender; women went from seven to eight and men from eight to nine. During the women's session, no one was allowed down at the lake or out in boats because the women (and men during their turn) went nude. Going with the old Finnish men was an experience in itself because they liked the sauna unbearably hot. In fact, most of the Finnish guys sat on the top step where it was the hottest. The few times I went with the Finns I had to crawl in on my stomach and lay on the floor where it was at least somewhat bearable.

For a few years, I even brought my Sunfish, but the lake was a bit too small for serious sailing; it was fun nevertheless. The boat proved to be useful in other ways. Once we transported a large load of cow manure back to Ozone Park for Connie's flower bed. We loaded one or two large plastic garbage bags with brand-new hot manure into the cockpit of the Sunfish for the trip home. Our garden flourished, but the boat wasn't the same for several years because the plastic bags broke and the manure stained the inside of the cockpit. Eventually the stain wore off and the smell went away.

It was several years before Mark moved up to the Boy Scouts from the Cub Scouts and then we had a dilemma when Boy Scout camp came on the same two weeks in August that we reserved for the farm. Mark really wanted to go to the BS camp, and we realized that going to the farm at a different time, if they even had room for us since we reserved our cabin a year in advance, would not be as much fun for any of us. In those years, when there was a conflict and I think there

were two years like that, Mark opted for the BS camp and Connie and I went to the farm without him. But we visited him on the middle weekend each year and it turned out okay for all of us. I don't think Mark minded not going to the farm in those years. I must admit though that I felt really bad that he did not go with us.

Our trips to the farm lasted for eleven years—1964 to 1974. The families that ran it decided it was too much work, particularly since the main driver, the daughter's husband, who had done a majority of the work died in 1972 or 1973. The brother and his wife who remained couldn't handle the chores by themselves any longer. It was a sad day when we discovered that they would no longer take reservations. I even wrote a long letter outlining how they could hire a team of people to manage the resort, but they didn't have the heart for it any longer. The farm will stay in our memories as having been a wonderful summer retreat with good friends and lots of fun.

Back to U.S. Trust, I thought I had found a reasonably interesting and challenging job and I put everything into it. In June 1963, I graduated from St. John's with a bachelor of business administration (BBA) degree and decided to go on for my master's degree in finance (MBA). It was understood generally that to get anywhere you had to have an MBA degree. We lived in Ozone Park then and it was convenient to take the A train to St. John's from Wall Street and then hop back on the same subway line to Ozone Park. So I decided to stay at St. John's rather than go to another school such as NYU or Fordham. St. John's had a fairly new MBA program that suited me just fine, but it wasn't considered a great MBA program as compared to NYU, Columbia, Fordham, and all the other top business schools around the country. But I was only interested in getting the degree. I didn't care where it was from, and being the lazy guy that I am, I opted for what I figured would be the easiest program.

Then my so-called "big break" came. I didn't realize it then, but it turned out to be just that. Sometime in 1965, the Trust Company was audited by the Federal Reserve Bank, which controls state banks, like UST. The audit proved to be a blow to the bank. The auditors found that the trust and estate administrators were doing a poor job of managing the closely held business assets held in most trusts and estates. Bam! What a shock for so prestigious a bank. The order came down from on high (the board of directors): "Get someone to take charge of those assets! NOW." Since I was the only guy in the department going for my MBA in finance, I was asked to help Ed Black, a guy in the securities research department, to work on identifying all the closely held business interests held by the bank in trust and estate accounts. Looking back, it was the single most important event in my career. It opened up a whole new vista for me and for the first time allowed me to utilize the "numbers" skills that the aptitude test revealed about me back in 1957 when I was discharged from the air force.

The work was fascinating. I had to analyze the financial statements of a large number of businesses in all different industries. Learning how to do it was most of the fun. Ed Black[103] was a big help because he was a security analyst and he showed me what to look for and how to analyze balance sheets and income statements (to a greater degree than I was learning in graduate school). Eventually I started studying closely held business valuations because we also had to value the stocks of those companies that we held in various accounts, either for commission purposes or for estate purposes (generally everything has to be valued for tax purposes). So that's what led me to start learning about valuations. In fact, by 1966 when I was in graduate school I had already started working on research for my master's thesis on the topic of business valuations. I received my MBA in June of 1968.

L. Connie Goes Back to Work

Just after Mark started kindergarten in 1965, Connie had a chance to work as a substitute teacher in PS 108, which was directly across the street from where we lived. Mark went to half-day kindergarten in that school so it was no problem for him to go to the Collinses'

---

103. Ed left UST in 1966 and I was given full responsibility for all closely held business assets in trusts and estates.

in the afternoon when Connie was working. Then when he actually started at Our Lady of Perpetual Help (OLPH) full-time, he left for school at around 8:00 a.m. and returned at 3:30 p.m. Connie didn't start until 8:30 a.m. and was generally home at 2:30 p.m., so Mark actually never knew she was working until many years later. The only problem came when there was a Catholic holiday. On those days, Connie arranged to have Mark stay with Joan Collins whose son, Timmy, was Mark's friend and playmate.

That substitute-teaching job at PS 108 actually led to Connie's new career in special education in the NYC Board of Education. She was asked to fill in for a special ed teacher who was scheduled to be out for several months with a mastectomy. Connie became intrigued with the special ed program and the kids involved and decided to stay in the program and get the required additional teaching credits from Hofstra at night.

Eventually the special ed class that Connie worked in moved to a school in Woodside, which was a relatively short drive from Ozone Park. Connie stayed there for several years, earned her master's degree in special ed and was eventually asked to become a coordinator of special ed at the board of ed headquarters in downtown Brooklyn.

From there Connie went on to earn another master's degree, this time in school administration from C. W. Post in Westbury. That led to her becoming a supervisor in special ed where she was assigned to the Bronx. Years later, she transferred to a similar position in Queens.

In 1969, I was promoted to assistant secretary, the first-level officer rank within the bank. (That's my official corporate picture) That promotion gave me five weeks' vacation each year and a great deal of individual prestige. It also gave me entrance to the officers' dining room and the opportunity to meet every important person at the bank. But the vacation time was much more important to me. It was at that time that we started taking Easter vacations. Unfortunately, Mark missed the first one in Jamaica, but after that, we wouldn't think of leaving him home. To our  dismay, however, his first trip turned out to be a disaster. Little did we know that late March in Bermuda was still a bit too early for the good weather. It stormed practically the entire week we were there, but Mark was a good sport. We did a lot of different things: we toured the island, we went to the aquarium, we shopped in the stores, etc. By late in the week, we even went into the water—in the rain. I'll never forget Mark and I swimming out to a reef just offshore (actually it was pretty far out). The waves were high, but we got to the reef and even managed to break off a piece of coral and take it back with us. Mark was excited and I think flabbergasted at being able to see the beautifully colored tropical fish below the surface of the water while we snorkeled.

Easter vacations followed every year after that. There were the Cayman Islands, St. Croix, Barbados, Antigua, and Martinique. It was great seeing Mark grow every year. He loved to snorkel, and it was on Barbados that we went scuba diving for the first time. What a thrill!

During those years in Ozone Park, several things happened:

- Mark made his first Holy Communion in 1967 and eventually became a Boy Scout.
- Patricia left the Daughters of Wisdom in 1968 and spent some time with us before deciding to move to Boston. She later moved to Texas, then back to Boston.
- My brother George died suddenly of a heart attack in 1969, leaving Margo and four small children. Margo eventually sold his print shop in Boston and the farm in Pembroke and moved to Ireland where Margo felt the children could receive a good education in an area where the cost of living was much lower. They eventually moved back to Boston where Margo opened a rare bookstore and the kids finished their education.

* * *

Back to work: I could go on forever relating stories and events that I experienced in those many years at the Trust Company. It was not a boring job by any sense of the word. I was responsible for ownership interests in hundreds of closely held businesses. That meant that I sat on several boards of director. I also was a corporate officer for many of those companies. In 1967, I encountered my first real challenge. It was Red Raven Rubber Co., a manufacturer of rubber bands with two operating plants in the heart of Newark, New Jersey. It was an awful place: dirty, smelly, hot, and the employees were mostly black and either ex-cons or cons hiding from the authorities. It was in such bad shape that I was literally required to spend at least two to three days a week there supervising the management people on basic business techniques. My clothing was covered with talcum powder.[104] But I learned a great business lesson from that two-year experience: don't trust anyone.

Red Raven was especially new to me. I had never run a company, nor had I any idea of how a company should be run. They don't teach you that in school, even in graduate school. So here I was thrust in with a group of lying, cheating people who were basically looking out for their own skins and their own jobs. It's a long story that doesn't get any better. Suffice it to say that we eventually got rid of the business at a very large loss to the Trust Company (in my time) and the estate of the man who had owned it. It had been his greed that had shaped the course of the company long before we got involved however so I don't feel that we failed in not keeping the company alive and well. It hadn't been well for a long time before the owner died because he had been taking the cash for himself and neglecting the machinery and equipment, letting it run down to a point where much of it could not be repaired. But I also learned a lot that I hadn't learned in school: such things as the intricacies of inventory control, cash flow, union negotiations, supply and demand, marketing, etc., it covered everything. Red Raven was in fact my introduction into the business world.

As UST took on more and more estates and trusts with closely held businesses in them, my involvement in those businesses grew. With that growth came the need for more help and I was fortunate to have some swell people to work with. Margie Johnson was the first person I hired. She was great—a tall, attractive girl from Walnut Creek, California. Peter Becket was next and he was probably the smartest guy I worked with at UST. Unfortunately, Peter, as bright as he was, had no common sense. He couldn't see the difference between a really

---

[104.] Used to keep the inside walls of the unvulcanized rubber tubing from sticking together.

simple, quick assignment and a long complicated one. He'd wind up spending the same amount of time on each and then wonder why everyone was upset, he was just doing his job. Peter was the son of a very prominent Connecticut attorney. He went to the best schools: Hotchkiss, Yale, and Columbia Graduate School of Business. He was an excellent tennis player, a pilot, and a talented woodworker, and he was married to an heiress to one of the McGraw-Hill Publishing families.[105] But as things turned out, he wasn't happy and wound up running off with a nineteen-year-old blond he met on the commuter railroad coming down from Westchester.[106] There were several others in those early years as we took on responsibility for oil and gas interests. In all, I can remember about four guys passing through the department at one time or another.

[105.] In 1972, when I was making probably $21,000 per year, his wife was receiving $40,000 from her family trust fund.

[106.] The marriage has lasted and they now live in Lakeville, Connecticut, with three kids. He actually started a valuation business there and now specializes in matrimonial valuations.

History of the Times—1960s

The 1960s can be said to have been the beginnings of a social revolution in a global sense. The decolonization of European empires abroad, civil rights at home, human rights, antiwar movements, and the counterculture movement are some of the characteristics of the 1960s. The Stonewall riots in NYC gave birth to the gay rights movement in 1969 and the rise of radical feminism.

Technically, the United States put a man (Buzz Aldrin) on the moon. But the Soviet Union was first in putting Yuri Gagarin in space. Solar power was being pioneered by Farrington Daniels in 1964. Compact audiocassettes were introduced.

The Cuban Missile Crisis and the Bay of Pigs Invasion of Cuba scared everyone in 1961. During that same year, the Berlin Wall was erected. The Vietnam War began and with it came the protesting. Huge protests against the draft.

The hippies' counterculture movement evolved in the late 1960s with Summer of Love in San Francisco in 1967 and Woodstock in 1969. The rise of the drug culture influenced bands such as the Beatles, Jefferson Airplane, and the Doors, and the radical folk tradition pioneered by Bob Dylan.

Our new president John F. Kennedy was assassinated in Dallas, Texas, in 1963; his brother Robert in 1968. Martin Luther King Jr. was assassinated on April 4, 1968. Malcolm X assassinated in 1965. Lyndon B. Johnson becomes president from 1963 to 1969. The failure of the Johnson presidency changed the country around Richard Nixon, a Republican, who was elected in 1969.

Crime in the United States was on the upswing; widespread availability of birth control pills for women—the sexual revolution—had begun. The "baby boomers" reached adulthood.

The number of celebrities and notables in the fields of sports and entertainment expanded tenfold during this era and are just too numerous to mention.

M. Garden City

In the ten years between 1970 and 1980, we watched Mark mature into an adult. We had moved to Garden City in 1973 essentially on the strength of a visit to a friend's (Tom Curran) in-law's house for a barbeque and some advice and hospitality from Bill and  Sue Moyer, one of my other friends at UST and his wife who also lived in Garden City. Bill and Sue showed us around town, and that was good enough for us. We started looking in the papers and went around with realtors. Ozone Park at the time was getting a bit seedy, and our income had increased to a point where we could afford a better house, more garden, etc. The tough part was Mark; how would he react? What effect would it have on his life and his newfound friends from OLPH?[107] Mark was getting ready to graduate from OLPH, and the question was where would he go to high school. Certainly, the local public schools were out. That left the Catholic high schools. There were none locally so he would have to travel great distances each day to attend. Leaving his friends was going to be hard, but it had to be done then in 1973; otherwise, we would have to wait another year. Connie and I decided to take that chance and hoped Mark would be able to make new friends in the middle school in GC.

Garden City was a lot different from Ozone Park. Our house was much larger; our garden was considerably larger and much more beautiful and we loved it. Affording it was not going to be a big problem although we felt that we were stretched to the limit of our finances. It wouldn't be long, however, before we realized that we could well afford the house and had money left over.

Mark made friends at the middle school and managed to do well although we still believe the school system was lacking in the amount

---

107. Our Lady of Perpetual Help Roman Catholic Church and School where he attended.

of attention he was given versus the kids who were on the fast track to big colleges. Mark was smart, but he needed to be pushed more than he was.

Sportswise, Mark tried everything and picked his friends and his hobbies carefully. He tried wrestling, he tried lacrosse, and other organized sports and decided they weren't for him. Instead, he chose skiing and mountain climbing. This was in no small way because of his participation in the Boy Scouts in Garden City, which he joined almost immediately. John VanTyl and Bruce Woodward, the duel scoutmasters at Troop 80, would be a large influence on his life. In fact, at the first Boy Scout meeting that Mark (and I) attended, the troop was given a slideshow presentation by one of the troops' graduates who had just climbed Mount McKinley in Alaska. I believe that presentation was indelibly etched in Mark's memory and was a major impetus in his pursuit of mountain climbing and skiing in the years that followed.

My position at U.S. Trust continued to be exciting and challenging. Connie was growing as well. She had gotten her master's from Hofstra and was recognized by several people at the board of education as someone who could do the job and do it well. She eventually was asked to be a coordinator for special ed at 110 Livingston Street in Brooklyn and she actually commuted in with me in the morning on the Long Island Railroad. That led eventually to a supervisory position in the Bronx. She also went on to get a second master's degree in school administration from C. W. Post College.

*   *   *

One estate that I was responsible of in the early seventies involved a fascinating business that had men stationed around the world to inspect and measure the quantity and quality of crude oil being shipped in supertankers out of the ports in the Middle East and into the refineries in the United States. The decedent, let's call him Jim Smith, who was seventy-two when he died, had lost his first wife and in his loneliness wound up marrying a thirty-year-old exiled Cuban manicurist working at the Waldorf-Astoria in Manhattan by the name of Adele. Jim owned the business and had several million dollars in securities. Adele was working on spending the several million dollars in the brokerage account just about the time Jim passed away.

As coexecutors of Jim's estate, the Trust Company was responsible for preserving the assets in the estate. I was assigned to sit on the board of directors and essentially work with her to keep the business going. Her appetite for spending money was insatiable, and her demands for more salary for herself and dividends from the company had to be handled with kid gloves.

As it turned out, she had a Latin lover in Florida, Juan, whom she quickly married and got pregnant with. He was the classic gigolo who spent his day looking out at the ocean from their luxury apartment in Key Biscayne, Florida, and hanging out with his buddies at one of the nightclubs in the Cuban section of Miami. I once brought Connie with me for extended weekends in Miami Beach and Adele and Juan invited us for dinner at one of the Cuban nightclubs. Juan reassured me personally that we would be safe with him as he revealed the small caliber automatic he had in his waistband. Juan boasted that he was Fidel Castro's roommate at Havana Law School but rejected his Marxist leanings.

Keeping the business viable had me visiting several offices in Tampico, Mexico, to discuss the bribes being paid to Pemex[108] officials; Venezuela to discuss new business opportunities; Rotterdam, Holland, to acquire a similar business that would allow our company to service customers in Holland and domestic locations like San Pedro, California, Houston, Texas, and New Orleans, Louisiana; not to

---

[108.] Petroleos Mexicanos, the state-run oil company.

mention monthly trips to Miami where we moved the headquarters in order to placate Adele.

After three years of struggling to find the right executives, which we never did, and fighting with Adele over her spending habits which seemed to be working, the straw that broke the camel's back came when she announced that she had just purchased a $750,000-waterfront house and needed $350,000 for the downpayment, money the company did not have. We finally got her to agree to sell the business, and we were done with it. It was a fascinating company and challenge for me and the others involved. One I'll never forget. The interplay of personalities and politics in trying to keep everyone placated was an education in itself.

Another interesting situation involved the owner of the NY Mets baseball team who died in the mid-1970s and which I had the job of valuing the team for estate tax purposes. That was probably the most interesting situation I had run into up to that time. We scurried around to find potential experts to help us, but there were none. I wound up valuing the team and negotiating with the Internal Revenue Service to settle the tax value and not too long after the family sold the team to Mr. Doubleday for around $35 million, substantially more than our tax settlement value.

*　　*　　*

Mark's interest in mountain and rock climbing reached a point in 1975 when he needed to get some professional help before we'd let him go any further with that sport. It was too dangerous to pursue without some professional training. With the closing of Maple Lake Farm at the end of the 1974 season, we saw a perfect opportunity to give him a neat birthday present with a one-week class at the Equinox Climbing School in Grand Teton National Park in Wyoming. It was a great trip for all of us. We flew to Salt Lake City and drove up through Utah and crossed over into the southwest corner of Wyoming and then up to Jackson Hole and the Alpenhof Hotel. After dropping Mark off at Equinox every morning, Connie and I hiked the beautiful trails in the park. One trail was more beautiful than the next. The wildflowers were in full bloom, and we soaked up the beauty as something we had never seen before. The separate fields of red, blue, and yellow blanketed the mountainsides and we looked down on exquisite, tranquil blue lakes and colorful valleys. We walked for the entire week; some days were exhausting like the day we climbed to Crystal Lake, which was at ten thousand feet, it took our breath away. At night we would spend with Mark talking about the hike and about Mark's experience in climbing school. He really enjoyed it and learned an awful lot about rock climbing, all of which came in handy in later years when he climbed the Gunk and out west in Colorado with his friends. Our memorable evenings having cheeseburgers at the Mangy Moose will forever stay with me. We also had other adventures: rafting down the Snake River and getting a good soaking, horseback riding up into the woods, and taking a gondola to the top of ski slopes overlooking Jackson Hole. It was on the top of that mountain with clouds running swiftly by as I took Mark's picture with the clouds behind him that I thought to myself, "He's on top of the world, the king of the mountain." I so remember that trip and the good times we all had. Mark was in his element, the mountains, which he continues to love passionately to this very day. After Jackson Hole, we drove to Yellowstone Park for another week, and again the sheer beauty was overwhelming; we had never seen anything like this.

We were actually sad to have to give it all up and drive back to Salt Lake City. Mark's plan from there was an extended trip traveling by himself to Edmonton, Canada, to visit his aunt Janet for another week or two. That trip was a turning point for Mark in his ability to handle rock climbing. On our last night in SLC, before he went north and we went east (since it was his birthday), we found a restaurant in a mall that served fresh Maine lobsters—Mark's favorite. Mark said it was a great fifteenth birthday for him. Mark was growing up too fast.

Sometime in the seventies, Mark started guitar lessons but ironically I seem to remember that it wasn't until he went away to college that his interest in music blossomed thanks to his roommate who taught him the "hip" tunes in contrast to the dull stuff he was getting from his guitar teacher in Garden City.

The following summer, 1976, Mark got into surfing with Mike Dwyer, Al Cacamo, and several other guys. Al had a little four-wheel drive Subaru that got him onto the beach so they spent a lot of time at Long Beach "catchin' the waves." Mark persuaded us to spend our vacation at Montauk Point for two weeks that next summer. We rented a house on Ditch Plains Road just up from the ocean. It was great. Mark loved the waves, and the weather was good. We had rented the place from the Kowalskis, a funny old couple who lived in the other half of the attached house. They lived there all-year round, having moved out to Montauk many years ago when Mr. Kowalski retired as a machinist in Long Island City. We rented the Kowalski place for two years. Mark actually came out for only that first year, then he was off doing something else. Connie and I loved Montauk, but at that time we could not see our way clear to buy a summer place of our own.

While in Montauk, that second year George and Celia Perla came out for a few days and we had a lot of fun playing tennis every morning and barbequing the meat George brought with him from his store in the evening. At that same time I was running regularly about two to three miles per day. George used to kid me because I'd come home after a run and wolf down some Entenmann's crumb cake. So what's wrong with that?

One of the proudest moments that Connie and I experienced was when Mark earned his Eagle Scout designation in 1978 just before he graduated from high school. In that last year, it was touch-and-go as to whether he would actually earn the badge because he seemed to have lost interest in scouting and I think his nonscouting friends applied a bit of peer pressure on him because of the uniform and all. But he hung in there and showed his true mettle. And it proved to be a significant asset when he was selected for his first geological summer job in the Brooks Range of Alaska partially on the fact shown on his resume that he had earned his Eagle Scout designation.

In June 1978, Mark graduated from GC High School and went on to college at St. Michael's in Winooski, Vermont. I can't fault him for being taken in by the social life of school and the availability of the ski slopes of northern Vermont. He did not do well scholastically at St. Michael's and was not invited back. He had to learn about life and failure. What happened after that materially affected the rest of his life. Jimmy Nothel, who was attending Clarkson College in Upstate New York, invited Mark to go to Vail, Colorado, with him to work in construction on the basis of an ad an alumni had placed on the bulletin board at his school. Jimmy and Mark rounded up some of their friends and together they all went out to Vail, rented a three-bedroom trailer, and worked in a variety of construction jobs for the Clarkson alumni. They actually did it for three summers straight during the massive development of the Vail ski area.

Mark was pretty much on his own at that juncture. Where he was going no one knew. Even Mark. But he was no doubt searching during the time between St. Michael's and his three years summering in Vail. A couple of those years he stayed in Vail for a few months after the summer job ended to get in some skiing. After his first year following St. Michael's, he came home and worked as a stable boy in Old Westbury. It required him to get up very early to take the horses out, clean their stalls, and feed them. He didn't talk much about it, but I think he really liked the unusual nature of the job and the discipline it required. He also had the opportunity to ride horses all afternoon when his chores were completed.

He eventually met some guys in Vail who introduced him to geology and the University of Alaska. On one hand, Connie and I were concerned, having no idea what Fairbanks was like and how Mark would manage up there; but on the other hand, we were delighted that he had committed himself to a plan of action. The rest is history, and I could not be happier for him because he found something he really liked and was able to make a living doing it.

*   *   *

At this same time, the late seventies, the Trust Company ran into difficulties with the retirement of its executive officers all within a few years. The board brought in an executive from Chrysler Corporation who was a complete disaster. But then around 1980 or 1981, they hired Danny Davison, formally a senior officer of J. P. Morgan Bank. He proved to be a driving force, but unfortunately he had people around him who were mean-spirited, ineffectual businessmen who broke the morale of the company and its people and sent everyone scurrying for safety. It was a difficult time for everyone because every system, every decision, every step anyone took was questioned and doubted and criticized. It was an unhappy time for me. I went into a deep depression, questioning my own abilities and sensibilities.

Prior to when the new folks arrived, I had been given responsibility for not only the closely held business group but also the entire real estate and insurance departments, a total of about thirty-five people. My assessment of those departments was that they were overstaffed with a bunch of do-nothings and it needed to be weeded out. The people who needed to be weeded out, however, were employees with a great deal of longevity and I was looking for other places where they could be utilized. Younger employees were clearly destined to be laid off. My boss at the time didn't want to ruffle feathers and cause any problems for the bank and himself. But the new regime came in and in one day ordered me to lay off eleven people, some that were the very best and not on my list of do-nothings. I was given no choice but to "fire them."

From that moment my life changed. I no longer felt secure as an employee. If they could do it to those people, they could do it to me. In fact, my responsibilities were cut back; I was rumored by this new regime to be incompetent because I had not done anything with the real estate people more quickly, and thus, for me everything looked bleak.

I started talking about having only so many more years to go when I could retire early and get out of this rat race. My new bosses, some of whom had been friends for years before, all became enemies. They didn't like me was my thinking. Fred Moriarty called me "imperious" with my employees, and raises weren't coming as I thought they should although I had been promoted to vice president in 1979 and still enjoyed the prestige of that title. But work wasn't the same. Pressure mounted to get more work done, bring in new accounts, cut back on employees, etc. I actually lost the responsibility for the real estate and insurance group and went back to having only the closely held business assets.

I then had only one assistant, Marian White, who turned out to be quite good but unreliable. She had an MBA from the University of Chicago and was married to a guy working in Marketing at Chase Manhattan. She was the one that made me look at hiring women in a much different light. I interviewed her in the beginning of June and hired her on the spot. And for three months she picked up everything quite well. But then the day after returning from our Labor Day weekend, she announced to me that she was three months pregnant. My comment to her was, "Did you conceive the night after I hired you?" and her response was, "Yes, I wanted to make sure I had medical coverage." My fear was that she'd be out for several months or forever and I wouldn't be able to hire a replacement because of the freeze on new hires. That turned out to be partially true. The real problem was that her doctor prescribed a regimen of every afternoon of swimming. The results were that not only would she be leaving me to have the baby, but for the five or six months that she would be with me, she only worked about a half day because the rest of the time she was off swimming. It was a difficult time. The work continued to mount, she was working half days, so to speak, so I wound up working long hours and again not feeling very good about it. I looked upon hiring women of childbearing age differently after that.

History of the Times—1970s

Many of the trends that are associated widely with the 1960s, from the "sexual revolution" to radical left-wing activism, reached fruition during this decade.

Technology was coming faster and faster: microprocessors were developed, pocket calculators made the slide rule obsolete, computer revolution began, Microsoft was founded in 1975, touch-tone telephones began to replace rotary dials, and digital watches and clocks reached the market.

Politically, the cold war began to thaw as relations improve between the United States and the Soviet Union, but terrorism and guerrilla warfare continued to increase. The Soviet Union invaded Afghanistan in 1979. Diplomatic recognition extended to China. Israel invaded Egypt in 1973.

The Watergate break-in doomed the Nixon administration, and he was forced to resign as president.

The long post-World War II period of economic growth came to an end in the 1970s. By contrast, Japan emerged as an economic power through the use of new technologies and a highly skilled and productive workforce. In the United States there was high inflation, interest rates, and unemployment. OPEC oil embargo and the Iranian Revolution sparked the first petroleum crises.

The government deregulated the airline industry and created Conrail and Amtrak.

Such great movie hits as *Star Wars*, *Superman*, *Jaws*, and *Rocky* came out in the 1970s. Crime was noted in films like *The Godfather* and *Taxi Driver*.

In the early 1970s, Jimi Hendrix, Janis Joplin, and Jim Morrison died. They were followed by Elvis Presley and Keith Moon later in that decade. Jamaican reggae music begins to gain an international audience.

The 1970s was to become known as the "Me Decade." And the wide use of marijuana and the introduction of harder drugs like cocaine became more popular.

Jimmy Carter became president and will go down as one of the worst in history (George W. Bush may take the grand prize, but that's yet to be determined).

The number of bands, singers, and famous actors are too numerous to list here. But some of the most notable are the Grateful Dead; Aerosmith; Earth, Wind and Fire; Fleetwood Mac; Jethro Tull; Billy Joel; Lynyrd Skynyrd; Bob Marley and the Wailers; Willie Nelson; UFO; the Who; Sex Pistols; and on and on.

As the Trust Company changed during this period, I thought that if we could get into the valuation business ourselves, this would add to my importance and credibility within the company and also bring in some profits. With a hiring freeze on, the only way I could pull this off would be if I took on the task myself, got the business, did the valuations and also handle the overwhelming in-house work that I was laboring under. There was no way I could find time to do both, so the out side valuation business would have to wait. But a wonderful turn of events happened that would change all of that. Keep turning the page.

N. The Chase Manhattan Bank, N.A.

November 1982 will forever be a month to remember in my personal calendar. I received a telephone call from John Nash, my counterpart at Chase Manhattan. He and I were roughly the same age and had similar jobs at our respective banks. He wanted to meet with me about something. At lunch he announced that he was leaving Chase to take over the presidency of one of the companies with which he had worked in his role at Chase. It was an opportunity he couldn't pass up. His job at Chase was open, and he thought I would do a great job there and asked me to meet with his bosses, Hans Ziegler and Dick Vartebedian, and some guy from Human Resources. I was apprehensive. How would I work out at a big bank like Chase? What was involved? How much money would I make? Why would I want to change now? A thousand questions ran through my head as John talked about Chase and his operation. But hey, why not check it out. That can't hurt.

John set up a meeting for me with Hans and Dick and the HR guy and it went surprisingly well. They appeared to like what they saw. We discussed what I was doing at U.S. Trust and my desire to want to start a valuation business. Hans indicated that he was receptive to a separate unit that would eventually stand on its own as a profit center within the Private Banking Division. It was beginning to look quite attractive from my point of view. John called me after the meeting and said that "I had them eating out of my hand." "They are very anxious to hire you immediately," John reported. That's when I had second thoughts. I was forty-eight years old, seven years away from early retirement. What did I need with this new challenge and all the headaches and hard work it would entail? What if I couldn't do the job? I could be laid off and then have no place to go. But I credit Connie for waking me up. "You're only forty-eight years old, not fifty-eight, not sixty-eight. You have a bunch of years ahead of you. Don't give up now. Take the opportunity and run with it," she counseled me. "Don't be a dope, try it out. What can you lose?"

So I agreed to take the job. It's funny recalling what went through my mind as I contemplated the offer I would get. Remembering what Nash had said, "You had them eating out of your hand!" I figured I'd demand (and get) $100,000, maybe a sign-up bonus, longer vacations and an expense account, and maybe they'd throw in a Mercedes-Benz for good measure. Fat chance!

The meeting was actually with the HR guy. He made me the official offer: a vice presidency, $75,000 plus an annual bonus (I was making $54,000 at the time with a small potential bonus—and it was indeed only potential), authority to start a valuation service, and carte blanche to hire people as needed, within reason. The offer sounded great and a 39 percent increase in salary. I didn't ask him about the Mercedes; he didn't seem to have the authority to do much else, particularly a Benz.

Connie and I talked it over one last time, and we agreed that it might be a terrific opportunity. I accepted the offer and started January 2, 1983. And that was the launching of my new career, one that would take me far beyond anything I had ever dreamed of.

I was given a windowed office on the thirty-second floor, a personal secretary, and the personnel of the Closely Held Business Group, a raggedy group of three analysts including Ralph Cox who was on the brink of retirement. There was also a nervous Nelly type who was constantly knocking on my door with one problem after another. She turned out to be a hypochondriac who was out more than she was in. After much planning, we finally terminated her based on her poor performance. I hated to do it, but she was disruptive and unproductive.

One thing about Chase was that it gave me the income to buy a beach house in Southold, Long Island. When I finally closed on the house, I told Dick Vartebedian. He congratulated me and wished me good luck. But what he said next was something I hadn't expected. He said, "Now I have you where I want you." It meant very clearly that now I had additional financial responsibilities so I would be forced to work harder in order to make sure I was able to keep the house. I would have never thought to say something like that to anyone working for me, but that was the reality.

The next six and one half years turned out to be a major challenge for me. It was a lot of hard work, meeting an awful lot of people, giving speeches, and generally getting my face and name known around the country.[109] There was one stretch of a week in Florida in February 1985 or 1986 when I gave three speeches per day for four days straight: breakfast, luncheon, and finally dinner. Believe it or not, I loved it. There is nothing more invigorating than speaking about something you know very well in front of a room full of people whom you know don't know much if anything about the subject matter; I can see how teachers get stimulated by that feeling every day.

I also spent some time in San Francisco when Chase opened an office there. I loved San Francisco—the trolleys, the bay, the Golden Gate Bridge, the mix of people, and the weather even though most people who live there would disagree with me. I've only been there when the weather was beautiful, never when it was cold and foggy. As the comedian W. C. Fields once said, "The coldest winter I ever experienced was a summer in San Francisco."

Since I had in fact put myself into the valuation business, I then felt that I had to show that I had the proper credentials as a business appraiser. I first applied for accreditation with the American Society of Appraisers (ASA) and found out that it would take me a couple of years to accomplish the background work they required. So in place of that I applied to the Institute of Business Appraisers (IBA). They only required a written exam and copies of a few reports. The written exam was mailed to me to complete and send back; how easy is that? I thus became a certified business appraiser by the IBA with the designation of CBA. I followed that up a year later with the designation of accredited senior appraiser (ASA) from the ASA, which was far more difficult. It required that I have five years of full-time business valuation experience (which I had accumulated through the many years at UST) plus a grueling all-day written examination and the submission of two valuation reports for review. As it turned out, I was the first person to hold accreditation from both the IBA and ASA.

---

109. Mostly in New York, Florida, and California.

After I joined the ASA, I was invited to give a talk on basic business valuations at the Annual ASA Conference that was being held in White Plains. It was at the start of that conference that I was scheduled to take the all-day written exam for the ASA designation. The exam was scheduled for Monday morning one day in June 1984. My talk at that conference was scheduled for the next morning. I spent the night before at the conference center hotel, studying for the exam only to find the next morning that the exam had been rescheduled for Sunday, the day before. The problem was that no one advised me of the change. I asked to speak to the organizer of the conference and quietly explained that the rescheduling of the exam was not my fault and that if I couldn't take the exam on Monday (today) then I wouldn't be available to speak on Tuesday. The reaction was immediate. I was led to the president of the ASA's suite at the hotel and at the dining room table was given the all-day exam. Somewhere that morning as I was struggling through the problems, the bedroom door opened and the president's wife staggered out in her bathrobe and slippers and was surprised to see me. The rest of the exam was uneventful, and I passed with flying colors. The Tuesday speech also went well.

The late 1970s and the mid-1980s were actually the beginnings of the growth of the business valuation industry. Shannon Pratt, the so-called Father of Business Valuations published his first book on the subject in the late 1970s, but it wasn't until the mid-1980s that it got anyone's attention. Then memberships in the business valuation associations started to climb as people around the country realized that this was an area in which they could make a living. Little did I know when I first joined Chase that business valuations were actually a growth business that had already been targeted by the "Big-Eight" accounting firms. They each had very advanced business valuation departments offering their services around the country.

Hiring the right people to fill in the workforce was difficult, particularly when I myself was not a really technical business appraiser. But we managed to get a couple of good technicians with Paul Mallarkey, Scott Vandervliet, and Nick Alexiou. They were all prima donna types, but they got the job done and we wound up being quite successful.

In the midst of all this, I paid scant attention to the small administrative aspects of the department, relying instead on my trusted personal secretary to see that all the i's were dotted and all the t's were crossed. My secretary was a hardworking black lady who

I trusted implicitly. Unfortunately, she turned out not to be terribly trustworthy. Over a period of about a year and a half, she had been cooking her overtime records to the tune of about $18,000, which came to light in an examination by some auditors. I had no choice but to summarily fire her on the spot and have her escorted out of the building. I was shocked that this lovely lady would resort to such a tactic. When I confronted her, she merely said that her rent had gone up and she saw no other way out. There was no remorse, no sorrow, not even a concern about another job. She knew the system. She knew that the bank would never tell a soul about what she did. She even used Chase Manhattan as a reference for her next job, which she got the following week. And why? Because we now have to be politically correct, we can't tell the truth about people because they'll sue you for defamation of character. So life goes on and no one knows the real truth about anyone—with one exception, what you read here is the truth.

Chase was a strange place for me. There were so many layers of management that decisions just never got made. No one was willing to put his or her neck out for anything. Everyone was watching out for their own job, their own piece of turf and their own ass. The top guys were those who had been willing to stretch a little and they "made it." But they were few and far between. And it all depended on where you were in the hierarchy or what I would refer to as "the food chain." My bosses were down at a much lower level so while they liked what we were doing initially, as time went by and we weren't actually turning profits, they began to distance themselves, but not too far because we may fool everyone and make it big. So we were caught in the middle. We had to survive on our own; no one was going to back us all the way. But other things happened in the early 1980s.

O. Onward to Alaska

Alaska has been an exciting destination for us for the last twenty-eight-odd years. Mark's decision to go to the University of Alaska at Fairbanks (UAF) certainly changed his life and in the process gave Connie and me a totally new perspective on that state.

Mark started at the UAF in 1980 and was lucky to land a summer job with the Alaska Geological Survey that first summer in the Brooks Range, the job I mentioned earlier. But it wasn't until 1984 that he

could squeeze in a week with his parents at his cabin in college. We used part of our time to first visit Janet in Canada and then jumped aboard the *Sheltered Seas*, a sixty-foot yacht in Ketchikan and cruised up the Inland Passage for four days. We slept each night in different ports: Wrangell the first night, Sitka, the next, Juneau the

third night, and then on to Haynes where we took the *Sheltered Seas* back to Juneau and stayed by ourselves for two days. We then flew to Fairbanks and finally met Mark and were introduced to his new way of life. It was certainly a lot different from what we were used to: a tiny little log cabin, no running water, an outhouse, giant mosquitoes, and almost twenty-four hours of daylight. It was thrilling and invigorating. We were immediately struck by how talented Mark was in building this cabin with a friend and proud of what we saw our son developed into. That first year we also met Sharon for the first time and were delighted that Mark was dating such a beautiful and talented girl. We also met Thule for the first time.

Before Mark graduated, he and Sharon were married in Minnesota on December 27, 1988. Connie, Sophie, Janet, and I spent the weekend in Minnesota meeting Sharon's parents and relatively celebrating the wedding. We enjoyed meeting Margaret and Jake Snyder and Sharon's family. After their honeymoon in Jamaica, they were able to spend a weekend with us in Garden City where we had a family party so that the Lockwoods and Geberts could meet Sharon and see Mark again. It was a wonderful occasion.

Socorro, New Mexico, became the next interim location where Mark and Sharon spent two years getting their graduate degrees. We visited them several times and again saw a different part of the country that had been totally foreign to us: the Bosque del Apache National Wildlife Refuge just south of Socorro, Carlsbad Caverns in southern New Mexico, and the beautiful mountains to the west. Mark and Sharon showed us as much as they possibly could in the time we had available. We enjoyed every moment being with them and their gorgeous dog, Thule.

We also met Mark and Sharon in Mexico one year and Hawaii another. These were years that I will cherish always. We had so much fun with them, exploring various parts of Maui, Hawaii's big island, and Kauai and/or touring the Mayan ruins south of Cancun.

Back in Alaska, Mark and Sharon settled into a small cabin they had built on three acres in the hills around Ester, about eleven miles outside of downtown Fairbanks. Again, a small cabin, no running water, outhouse, etc. My times there were filled with wonderful memories of working side-by-side with Mark in a variety of projects: putting a railing around the deck, closing in the storage shed and the ultimate siding of the cabin with spruce lapboards. I'll never forget going home after those two weeks. My hands were so sore that it took about a week to get the feeling back in my fingers and to be able to hold a pen to write with. It was worth every minute just to be able to help them get their lives in order and their home fixed up. I still don't think Mark cared one way or another if the cabin was sided, but once it was done, it looked great. This was also a monumental time in our lives because it was June 17, 1994, that Robin came into this world and we had our first granddaughter. Oh, what a gal! She was a gorgeous baby. We couldn't take our eyes off her.

The birth of Robin basically forced Mark to think about a bigger and more complete house (one with running water and toilets). The house was completed in 1995 or so and Mark and Sharon's lives settled into a more conventional-style house with two bedrooms, two baths, a very comfortable living room, kitchen, etc. Our trips continued and my work on the house became my goal for being. I wanted to see the house finished. Mark's work and his attention to his daughter took a lot of his time. The siding of the house and  other details were not his priorities; they were mine.

Our trips to Ester, even to this date, include a good deal of work in finishing certain aspects of the house or garage. I actually threatened not to come unless the materials were ready for a specific project for the house or the new garage, which was built a few years after the house was completed.

Then Pearl arrived in 1998. A real "Pearl." Mark and Sharon could not have asked for a better child than Pearl. Together, Robin and Pearl are today the main reason for all of our being. We adore them and can't wait to see them every summer or Thanksgiving in Ester or winters in Hawaii or other places. They've even blessed us with trips to Garden City for Thanksgiving or in summer at the shore. We can't get enough  of them. Ten days with them in Orlando in 2007 was one of the real highlights. Most recently Robin and Pearl spent a week with us during the summer of '08 when they flew to New York by themselves. Robin's interest in tennis got us out on the courts every day with lessons to boot, and they just loved riding in the Audi convertible. Swinging over the top of the car door rather than opening it was one of their enjoyments. The water park, the beach, *Mary Poppins*, and shopping—what fun!!

My fondest memories are my days in Ester with Mark, Sharon, and the girls. One of the most memorable two weeks was in March 2000 when Mark and I entered the ice-carving competition at the World Ice-Carving Contest in Fairbanks. Only days before the start

did we finally decide on the subject of our ice sculpture. Mark had mentioned that B. B. King was performing in Fairbanks on March 19, the day after the finals of the carving competition. "Why not a life-size sculpture of B. B. King?" I asked. You can't imagine how great it was working alongside your son in a project that neither one of us knew much about. The thinking that went into developing the size, the template, the tools needed, the timing. We worked together beautifully. I was so proud of his abilities to figure these things out. Even as the form developed out of the ice, Mark's eye found bad surfaces and disproportionate legs and arms that had to be corrected. We developed a template for Lucille, BB's guitar and figured how best to attach the neck. How do you make an Afro do in ice? We found out from one of Mark's ice-carving buddies. We had B. B. King's records playing on our portable CD in the background. It was wonderful. Mark worked every morning then joined me for lunch and stayed the rest of the day to finish up. We were somewhat taken aback near the end of our work when a black guy approached our site, heard the music, examined the sculpture, and asked, "Who's that?" He was probably more into hip-hop and rap than "good ole blues."

When the winners were announced, I was terribly disappointed; we came in second, but Mark showed a great deal of self-control. I guess I wasn't a good example for the girls but I couldn't help myself. The couple that won first prize did not deserve it. We did. But we had a lot of fun, and it certainly was a new experience for both of us. Would we do it again? I would, but Mark showed no interest when I broached the subject in later years.

A real memorable time was an overnight fishing trip to West Lake due West of Fairbanks and north of Mount McKinley. With us were Terry Gacke, Mark's close friend and the father of another of Mark's friends, Joan Walser, I can't remember his first name. We were flown in by the guide on Saturday morning and fished all afternoon of the first day catching only a few small pikes. The next morning, Joan's father went out before breakfast and came back with a forty-three-inch northern pike. After breakfast we scurried out to get a few hours of fishing in before the guide was to pick us up at around noon. About eleven o'clock, I hooked what felt like a whale on the light tackle we were using, which I was not at all used

to. It was a classic battle of reel in and tug, reel in and tug and keep the head up so you don't lose him. Eventually I landed a very similar-sized pike to that of Joan's father. Since we were running out of time, Mark decided to clean the fish on the boat heading back to shore. I'll never forget Mark cleaning that giant northern pike in the little boat as the guide was landing his floatplane to pick us up. We were frantic to get back to the beach and clean the boat out before the guide saw us. He was a tough taskmaster about everything and warned us not to clean the fish on the cabin side of the lake because it would attract bears to the cabin. Fortunately he didn't notice what we were doing as he landed. I hope no bears showed up at his doorstep.

Another memorable weekend was fishing in Talkeetna with Mark. The fishing wasn't that good, but I was able to spend two full days with him all by myself. To me, that was precious time that one can't replace.

In recent years, we've settled in to visiting Ester for Thanksgiving or Christmas. Ironically, we've been there on two record-breaking days: the coldest Thanksgiving at forty-five degrees below zero and then nine years later when it was forty-five degrees above. They've all been wonderful experiences.

Our early trip to Circle Hot Springs over one Thanksgiving was another experience of swimming in a one-hundred-degree pool with the temperature outside of five below zero. Hair froze immediately into icicles, but the body enjoyed the warmth. We were joined that weekend by Terry Gacke and his wife, Leslie, and her dog team of about eight huskies. We even had a couple of rides ourselves. Connie drove the team as though she had been doing it all her life. When I was running the dogs, they ran over Terry's dog as though she wasn't there. None of the dogs were hurt, but it shook me up seeing this dog being trampled by the team.

We also spent a weekend with the girls in Anchorage and Seward in 2005. Robin was a little homesick and I probably overreacted a little too much because she was so upset. While the rain continued unabated for the whole day on our boat trip, we still got to see some puffins and seals. But I think the sea-life aquarium was the highlight for Connie and me and the girls. Robin clearly has a love of sea life and maybe she'll wind up doing something connected to the sea. Her scuba certification in March 2005 gives her the first tool toward that endeavor if she chooses to go in that direction.

Thule was Mark's first dog. A Chesapeake Bay retriever, Thule was a wonderful companion and fetcher. She was a pest in that she always wanted to fetch something. When I would be working on a ladder I always had to watch out for the sticks that Thule placed strategically on the last two rungs of the ladder to remind me that she was there and was waiting to fetch something. When we used the outhouse, which by  the way had a full-length glass door, Thule would sit outside looking in, waiting for you with a stick in her mouth. If you took too long, she'd push the stick through the air vent near the floor. She went everywhere with Mark and Sharon. Mark even brought her to New York with him. She scared the daylights out of Khan Singh when she arrived. We didn't see the cat for the entire visit.

Thule was put to sleep in December 2003 at a ripe old age when Pearl was five. I'll never forget the telephone call I got from Pearl. She said, "Gramps, Thule died." Knowing how sad she was at losing her friend, I tried to console her with some comforting words about how she will miss her but she'll be in her thoughts, etc. Her response was, "It's okay, Gramps, I can still see her, she's downstairs in the freezer."

Thule's daughter, Ginger, was quite similar to her mother although a bit more rambunctious. She was basically under "house arrest" for a time because of her fighting with neighbors' dogs. But Ginger was also a fetcher and actually had the identical traits to her mother in strategically placing sticks for you to find on the ladder and the outside steps, etc. Ginger, as well as Thule, were not cuddle-up type dogs. They didn't require a lot of hugging and petting, but they liked to be around.

For me it's difficult not having Mark, Sharon, and the girls nearby to do more things together. Gramps and Grammy would love to dote on them, take them places, babysit them when they were young, etc. But Mark has made his life in Alaska with a wonderful wife and two beautiful children and he has always had the support and uncompromising love of his parents. What more can anyone ask for?

P. Southold

After renting in Montauk Point, East Hampton, and East Marian for a couple of years, we decided to look for a place of our own on the North Fork. Having moved to Chase Manhattan Bank in 1983, we were now able to afford something extra. Our first shopping excursion was a Sunday afternoon in March. That Saturday had been an awfully rainy day, but Sunday was clear and chilly. The realtor from First Town took us around to a dozen places in the price range of "up to $150,000" which is what we thought we could easily afford. The places she showed us were, for the most part, junk and, not surprisingly, their basements were filled with water from the giant storm the day before. And everyone had an excuse as to why his or her basement was flooded. Mostly, it was because of the high groundwater levels, etc.

As we were getting close to calling it a day, the realtor said she had one more house to show us. "It was a little out of our price range," she said. It turned out to be the house we fell in love with. It was a brand-new house high on a hill overlooking the Long Island Sound with gorgeous sunsets directly out in front of us. The price was indeed out of our price range, but not by that much. The house was built in the summer of 1983 and went on the market in September 1993 at a price of $240,000. When we saw it in March of the following year, the builder was ready to unload it. He had had to carry it through the winter and was now even having to cut the lawn as spring approached. He wanted to get his money out of the house so he could move on to another project. We got it for $190,000 and moved in, in late July 1984 and enjoyed it for ten years.

Southold was a lifelong dream for me. It was a sense of achievement. I had arrived. I could now afford a summer home. But this wasn't just any summer home. This was a beautifully landscaped modern home with a great big deck and a fantastic view. Connie enjoyed it for its beauty and location and the nearness to the beach. She had gotten to love the water and swam daily in the fresh, clear waters of the LI Sound just a short walk down from the house. In many respects it was lonely, however. There weren't a lot of people around. The beach was deserted most of the time. We used to laugh that on Fourth of July weekend we would often be the only couple on the beach.

We had plans for the house too. The lower level was not landscaped. But we soon figured that we could build a wall at the bottom of our property, fill it with sand and dirt, level it off somewhat for a lawn, and build stairs down to the lawn. The slope above this lawn and below the deck could be planted on both sides of the stairs.

 On one side we made three levels for vegetables and flowers. On the other side, Connie planted an English garden of perennials. After a while, plantings became a problem because of the humidity in the air and the exposure to the sun; everything grew like wildfire. In front of the deck the landscapers had planted Russian olive trees. They grew so fast that we spent an enormous amount of

time cutting them back every month or so. For me that was one of the things I least enjoyed. Because of the slope of the ground, it was difficult to get to the top of the olive trees that needed to be cut. I wound up developing a long pole with a hedge clipper attached to get to those elusive branches. One year, George Perla came up with the idea of pruning away all the branches below the top layer, making them looking like trees with nothing but top growth. Another time we hacked them down almost to the ground. But they grew back before we could say "nice sunset."

We had great vegetables too, tons of tomatoes, squash, some peas, etc.

Southold was a great retreat, a getaway to an island where we could do exactly what we wanted. The water was great (except in

August when the jellyfish were ever present). Our neighbors turned out to be wonderful. Ron and Jeanne Lowell became our closest friends. As years passed however, their friendship became one of the reasons we decided to sell. But in those early days we enjoyed their warm and close friendship. We sat on the beach with them, we raced our Sunfishes, we went fishing, we competed on who was a better windsurfer. Ron became quite proficient on the windsurfer while I struggled mightily. The problem I found was that if there was enough wind to power the windsurfer, there was also a chop on the water. The chop was what I had problems with. I couldn't keep my balance in the rough water and also turn around, etc. What became really challenging was windsurfing when the jellyfish were in season. One had to be very careful not to fall on one of those Portuguese man-of-wars or swim into one trying to get back onto the board.

Ron and I got along so well together like we knew each other our entire lives. Coincidentally, when we were buying the house, I happened to be on the board of directors of the W. A. Baum Company, a firm in Copiague, Long Island, that made mercury blood pressure machines used by doctors and hospitals around the world. Well, when I was telling the Baum people at one of our meetings that I had bought a house on Horton's Point in Southold, they all got interested and asked, "Precisely where is your house?" When I told them, they all laughed because the outside advertising guy that Baum used for its marketing and ads was none other than Ron Lowell. So that was the biggest coincidence.

Ron had a twelve-feet Grumman aluminum rowboat with a little outboard motor. It was too heavy to always be dragging up or down the beach so I wound up buying a battery-powered wench from a marine supply client I had in  Freeport. That worked great for a few years until it was swept away in one of the hurricanes we lived through. Ron then devised some other contraption with a hand wench, which worked perfectly well. We still had to drag it into the water but were saved from having to pull it up the beach.

Jeanne Lowell also insisted on buying a kayak one year, but she didn't use it very much. In fact, no one used it very much. It was a novelty at first, but it was actually quite uncomfortable for me to use so I preferred the Sunfish.

I left my Sunfish on the beach for the entire summer and only brought it up to the house for storage over the winter. What fun we had with that boat. I could sail for hours on that little thing up and down the beach. Ron actually kept a blue fish rig in his Sunfish, and when he went out he'd throw the line over and hope to land a nice blue fish. He wouldn't know until he brought the boat to shore. He was often surprised to find a nice big blue on the hook.

After the gardening chores were completed, our main activity was sitting on the beach or on our deck. It was this sitting around that got me into carving the Christmas gnomes in earnest. I was able to make them connect with friends: a tennis-playing gnome;

a gnome with a calculator; a gnome making a list (I made that one for Patricia because she always seemed to have lists of things that she needed to do, etc.); a whole band of gnomes playing drums, guitar, horn and accordion for Mark. I made several for Ron and Jeanne. One year, Ron broke his Achilles tendon and also had surgery on his knee so I carved him a gnome with crutches and its heel in a cast and his knee all bandaged. Another was a gnome holding three large striped bass. Jeanne loved to play golf so I made her in a golf outfit (a female gnome) that she cherished. (Parenthetically, I was told that that gnome was displayed at her coffin at her wake because she loved it so much.) That was probably my most active carving period for gnomes. There was no question but that I had a lot of time on my hands and nothing else satisfied me as much as carving and creating those little figures.

The one big negative about Southold was that although it had fantastic views of the Sound and wonderful sunsets, there was practically nothing ever of any interest appearing on the water. It was not an active boating area at all. The most we got were a few fishermen floating offshore for fluke. If I had it to do it over, I would opt for a place on Peconic Bay where there was a very active boating community. I would have loved to have had a boat on Peconic Bay as well. In fact, I had suggested it many times, but Connie wouldn't hear of it. She felt we had enough to do on the Sound and having a boat would drive us away from the house (and all the chores we had in the garden). I think now that we have a boat and she sees how much fun it is, I think she would have a different view today. And with a boat, we may have even kept Southold. (How dare you say that; that's a sacrilege.)

The other big negative in owning a summer home is that unless you invite your friends to visit, your social life comes to a grinding halt except for the people in Southold that you know. We often had Tom and Marie Ramos or George and Celia Perla for weekends, and that was fun. We also had Jack and Eileen and Patricia and

Mike a few times each summer, and I really enjoyed that. Once we had Jack and Eileen's kids but that got to be too much for us to handle. We also invited some of our other friends from Garden City to come just for the day. That I did not find too enjoyable. I would have preferred to have them spend the night and make a weekend of it, but Connie felt it was just too much and that it was no trouble for some people to drive out for the day. I continue to think it is too far to go round-trip in one day to visit anyone.

When we had friends or relatives out to Southold, we loved to have lobsters out on the deck. Once, when Jonathan and Betsy Blattmachr visited, we barbequed a weakfish; it was the first time we had ever done that and it was delicious. For whatever reason, we never did it again; however, I think it was because every time we went to the fish store, they didn't have any weakfish in stock. It had become a very sought-after fish on the North Fork.

What we missed a lot in Southold was being able to play tennis. There weren't any good tennis courts to play on. The high school was the only place, and those courts were in terrible shape and you had to wait until someone got off and there weren't any real rules (i.e., you can only play for one hour). We made an effort to play when Tom and Marie and George and Celia came out anyway.

During the ten years in Southold, we experienced two huge hurricanes. Both brought massive destruction to the North Fork and caused power outages, downed trees, damaged beaches, lost boats, and untold property damage. Ron Lowell lost his Sunfish in one of them. We had trees down on our property from the vacant lot next to us. Every time that happened, power was knocked out because the power lines separated our house from the lot and the trees from that lot came down on the power lines. In the first hurricane, a huge locust tree fell over the entire lower part of our property, actually touching the deck. That time the police actually came through before the storm struck and made us go to the high school during the worst of the storm. We watched from the high school gym as massive trees fell over as though they had no roots to hold them in the ground. The winds were tremendous. When we returned to the house, we found several trees down in addition to the big one I just mentioned. At the beach, the surf was ten feet high and the beach itself was devastated and practically washed away.

The LI Sound is actually a very rough body of water. This was so evident in the winter when we would occasionally go out for a

weekend. (We didn't use the house very much in the winter because it was heated by electricity and it was very expensive. So we would shut the entire house down, drain the water, and come back in the spring.) But occasionally we would leave the electricity on or visit the Lowells. During the winter, the beach would be practically washed away, totally leaving large ruts that revealed buried tree trunks, huge boulders, etc. Then summer would come and, lo and behold, the beach would be miraculously restored to its original level simply by the movement of the tides and the waves of the Sound.

In the beginning of summer or in March and April when we would start to go back, I always made it a point to clean up the beach. It would be covered with what's called flotsam and jetsam, the junk that floats up to the beach, some of it is thrown overboard by passing ships while other stuff is just in the water. Every year I would collect at least two large garbage bags of junk that I hauled to the dump for disposal. This was something that Ron Lowell never did, and I never understood why. He loved the beach but he never did anything to clean it up. Evidently that didn't bother him. But when I started doing the cleanup, he would rave about how great the beach looked.

Poison ivy was a lurking enemy in Southold. Poison ivy was on the edge of the beach; it was on the edge of the wild woods in the next lot from ours and it was in the trees in the form of large branches wrapped around the trunks. Every year practically without exception, I would contract a case of poison ivy. Many times it would spread to parts of my body I would never have thought it would go. But I guess scratching my behind or my genitals should not have been eliminated from possibility. Connie got poison ivy too but usually not that bad. Once, she got it so bad on the top of her foot that she had to go to the doctor over in Southampton.

We ate out a lot when we were in Southold. Unfortunately, there were not a lot of good restaurants around. We loved the Hellenic Snack Bar. It was a Greek restaurant that had great souvlaki and spinach pie and their fish—mostly porgies—were outstanding. We also liked a family place (the Silent Man) that had great hamburgers. We used to go there mainly on Friday night when we drove out to Southold. Other than those few, there wasn't much to rave about. I would say that most of the others were mediocre at best, and expensive.

Besides the Lowells, there were several good people in our little community. There were the two gay guys, Dan and Don, who built a house up on the hill above us. The way the property was once owned, they wound up having right away to the beach over our and the Lowells' properties. Dan was a magazine editor and violinist. Don was an architect. One of his firm's specialties was designing prisons. Both Dan and Don loved plants, flowers, and vegetables. Dan swam three or four miles in the Sound every day. Another gay couple lived up on the hills, Irene and Isabelle. They were somewhat ordinary. Irene was a pianist who worked as a nurse. Isabelle was a television editor. One of the first people we met was Bill. He was a retired sales manager from Kraft Cheese. He had a wonderful house on the water way up high on the cliff. I remember him saying that he had so many stairs going down to the beach that when he felt like a swim, he'd think about the stairs and go take a shower. His wife had died several years before we moved to Southold. Not long after we met him, Bill married a wonderful lady (Elizabeth) from the church and they had several wonderful years before he died. She continued to live in the house.

Our next-door neighbor was Bonnie Bauman, a JAP (Jewish American Princess) who had been married to a television news anchorman from channel 7 by the name of Steve Bauman. They had one child, Beau. Bonnie divorced Steve and got the house as part of her matrimonial settlement. Eventually she married a local character,

Paul Stuart. He was a real lady's man and was known for "sleeping around." Bonnie had no money; her mother lived in Florida and came to stay with her in the summer. We're pretty sure that her mother was actually supporting her and Paul. Their house was on a full two-acre lot that went from the road to the water. (Our lot was split between us and the Lowells' property—we had the lot on the road.) Bonnie's mother gave her enough money to put in a heated swimming pool and Jacuzzi because Mom liked to swim when she came up from Florida but hated the jellyfish in August. Bonnie tried to be an artist and painted some very unusual, if not bizarre, paintings that were quite grotesque. I don't believe she actually sold very many of them although she told me that some sold for as much as a few thousand dollars.

We had been told that we could use the pool and Jacuzzi whenever we wished. I can't remember once actually going in when they weren't home. Once, when I thought they were out, I did start over to the pool but oops, to my surprise there were Bonnie and Paul making it in the Jacuzzi. Somehow I lost the desire to jump into that warm swirling water after that.

In 1994, Connie shocked me by announcing that she no longer enjoyed going out to Southold every weekend and wanted instead to stay in Garden City so she could play tennis with her friends on the weekends. Connie had retired from the board of ed a few years before and had gotten back to playing tennis at the Garden City Casino during the week in the spring. Yes, I was shocked. I thought I really loved Southold. But as we talked about it, I realized she was right. Southold had become a weekend chore in more ways than one. The greenery was growing out of control and frankly it was becoming more and more boring just sitting on the beach, particularly since there wasn't anyone else on the beach.

But one of the most overwhelming problems we were having was with the Lowells. Ron and Jeanne were ten years older than us and retired. They had been retired since about 1986 and lived in Southold full-time since then. While they had a strong connection with St. Patrick's RC Church and belonged to the North Shore Country Club, they looked forward every Friday night to our being there. We got to a point when we literally couldn't do anything without having to include them for fear of hurting their feelings. When the weather was bad particularly in the spring and fall, we liked to go to the movies on Saturday night. The Lowells, on the other hand, didn't like going to the movies on the weekends because they would have to pay full price. Senior citizen discounts only applied during the week. Consequently, they were always urging us to go to dinner with them instead of seeing the latest flicks. This was beginning to annoy us more and more as the summer wore on.

When we finally made the decision to sell, the buyers came fast and furious. Eventually, a female gay couple fell in love with the place and we got the price we were looking for ($300,000).

The Lowells were devastated. They at first couldn't believe that we would actually sell the house since we loved it so much. But eventually they came around to the realization that we weren't kidding. The next thing was telling them about the potential buyers coming to look at the house. They, of course, were concerned that it could be some family with a load of kids or a Greek family with a lot of relatives that visited on the weekends. I could actually feel their concern because their and our property was bordered on both sides with tall, thick locust trees that converted our property into an acoustical channel. We could practically hear them whisper and they could hear us. So with a large noisy family sitting on our deck, the noise would be awful.

But fortunately the couple who bought the place wound up being very quiet although somewhat annoying according to Ron because of some of the things she wanted him to do—I don't remember what they were, but he wouldn't do them in any event.

As an epilogue, a few years after we sold, the man who owned the vacant lot just to the north of us sold it to a Greek doctor and her husband who quickly cleared the trees and constructed an ugly house with a wrap-a-round porch. They had three little children who continually ran around the porch with their heavy shoes on; our buyers were furious and wound up putting in a group of trees to block the noise and the view of this ugly new house. The Lowells had their problems with the doctor and her husband during construction because the loss of the trees caused rain runoff which flooded Ron's property. The Lowells eventually also sold their house—also to a gay female couple (for a reported $600,000-plus price).

So that ended a period in our life that we will always cherish. We had great fun with friends, beautiful sunsets, wonderful sailing and swimming, and a thoroughly relaxing time. Do I regret selling the place? Maybe a little, but it was counterbalanced by a return to the Garden City tennis scene which has given both Connie and me a new lease on life: meeting new friends and being able to play a lot of good tennis as our bodies get older with every passing day. If we had continued owning Southold, we would have had more anguish and torment from the new construction to a point that it would have probably driven us out of the place in any event. Could we have rented it? Sure, but we decided we did not want to be landlords and have to worry about the plumbing, heating and appliances, and the landscaping. The house was actually pretty fragile. It was built on a slab with little installation; the fireplace was corroding as we sold the place, and soon after, we learned that the washing machine and dryer had some sort of plumbing problem. So it's over and we moved on.

*   *   *

While I was enjoying Southold, I was also having a load of fun at Chase where the valuation business was growing as I had predicted at 40percent per year and my bosses loved it. The crazy part at Chase was that the marketing people were not concerned with profits; all they wanted to show was "Are you making your sales quotas or not?" That part turned out to be easy. As a result of our steady growth, I was awarded all kinds of bonuses and special incentive items. For example, when Leslie Bains was running the marketing program, she came up with a marketing program she called "Go for the Gold." This was a special event that if you met your goals for the year you would be rewarded with gold coins. I was included in the program even though it was my job to reach my goals. I didn't need to have this special incentives; I was being rewarded with a special bonus unrelated to her "Go for the Gold" program. But I got it anyway. We reached our goals for the year, and I got awarded with seventeen American Eagle gold coins worth at the time about $444 each or a total of $7,500. I actually had to lug them home on the LIRR one night. With gold now at $900 plus, an ounce of those AEs are worth a cool $15,000.

Leslie Bains, it turned out was a number one "bitch." When she eventually got promoted and moved to another department of the bank, she held a special farewell party. It was Christmastime and she chose to read "T'was the Night Before Christmas," but she put her own words to the rhyme and with it pointed out all the negatives that just about everyone in the department had. Her administrative assistant, Karen, who was not going with her to the new assignment, was a short stocky girl with very large breasts. For Karen, Leslie hoped that Santa would bring her weights for her back to offset the weights of her breasts in the front. Karen was standing next to me when Leslie said that and she was physically shaken by it, saying,

"How could she be so mean to me, I've spent three years working side-by-side with her. I thought she was my friend." That was Leslie Bains. Leslie's wish for me was pants with an expandable waistband to accommodate my ever-changing waistline. Hmmm, thanks, Leslie. I needed that. As she moved through Chase and onto Citibank and eventually to HSBC, her style remained the same and she left a path of destruction wherever she went.

As things go with big corporation, and Chase was no exception, Hans Ziegler wasn't around for very long. He had left to take a job in Philadelphia; Dick Vartebedian only looked out for himself and for those who could help his career. So if there was any question on how we were doing, Dick always hedged his bet. He would always stick up for us because we were making our numbers. However, as the "numbers" guys began looking at our size, Dick waffled to please them. The numbers guys were interested in having business entities that had annual revenues of at least $5 million. We didn't reach $1 million until 1988 so we weren't even close to acceptability. And for all intent and purposes, we showed no profit because we were allocated all kinds of expenses from rent based on the number of people we had to divisional and corporate overhead, both based on numbers of people. The results were that we were never profitable and never expected to be profitable because as we grew we needed to add more and more people. Every time we added people our noncontrolled allocated expenses rose disproportionately. It was a losing battle and only a question of time before the ax would fall.

The ax fell in March 1989. Dick Vartebedian basically cut the cord, and the division executive at that time, a woman by the name of Gail Schneider, told us to close up shop. While I didn't realize it then, it was actually one of the best things that could have happened to me.

The History of the Times—1980s and 1990s

The 1980s marked an abrupt shift toward more conservative lifestyles after the momentous cultural revolutions, which took place in the '60s and '70s and the definition of the AIDS virus in 1981. Political events and trends of the 1980s culminated in the toppling of the Soviet Union and European communism in the last months of the decade. The 1980s saw rapid developments in numerous sectors of technology which have defined the modern consumer world, particularly electronics like personal computers and gaming systems.

In electronics we were introduced to the Walkman, VHS videocassette recorders, and compact disc (CD) players. The IBM PC came out in 1981.

In politics, the "Reagan revolution" begins with the election of Ronald Reagan as U.S. president and the introduction of neoconservatism to Washington. He eventually tells Russia's Gorbachev to "tear down that wall," which leads to the reunification of East and West Germany. Francois Mitterand, the most politically successful Socialist in French history becomes France's president. Philippine dictator, Ferdinand Marcos, is toppled. The Soviet Union ends its disastrous military campaign in Afghanistan which eventually led to the rise of the Taliban in that country. We see the noticeable rise of the terror groups of Abu Nidal and the Hezbollah.

In mid-1986, crude oil prices drop to below $10 per barrel.

October 19, 1987, Wall Street experienced Black Monday as the stock market dropped more than five hundred points, the largest one-day drop.

The Rubik's Cube, Cabbage Patch Kids, and the Trivial Pursuit game capture the interest of the American public.

No-fault divorce laws pave the way for increased divorce rates.

In entertainment there were such movies as *Aliens* (1986); *Back to the Future* (1985); *Batman* (1989); *E.T. the Extra-Terrestrial* (1982); *Indiana Jones and the Last Crusade* (1989); *The Empire Strikes Back* (1980); and *Top Gun* (1986).

Television saw the introduction of shows like *Cagney & Lacey, Cheers, The Crosby Show, Hill Street Blues, Late Night with David Letterman, Miami Vice,* and *Saturday Night Live.*

Q. Empire Valuation Consultants Inc.

Gail called me into her office in mid-March 1989 and told me that she was closing the valuation group and asked me to finish as many jobs as we could in one month and suggested that we tell our clients for any other pending work that Chase was getting out of the business and they would have to find another source for getting their businesses valued. The Closely Held Business Group which I also headed would continue to manage the business interests in trust and estate accounts, and Gail made it clear that I was welcome to continue to stay on at Chase to manage that small group of people that would remain. The other guys in my group would be given opportunities to find other jobs within Chase if they wanted them. As the ship was going down, I realized that I could not be happy managing this ragtag group watching over trust and estate assets now that I had seen the other side of the business. I had seen what I could do in attracting people to use me to do business valuations and I didn't want to give that up. So I personally called the clients and told them the news of our closing and told them that I was leaving and would finish the appraisals myself. Not one client turned me down. That amounted to about $250,000 to $300,000 of valuation work. Chase agreed to accept letters from the clients authorizing Chase to hand over the files and the retainer checks to me for all these assignments. I was instantly in my own valuation business. Now what?

The next hurdle was to find people to help me get the jobs done. Paula Heermance and Terry Griswold had been doing valuations in Rochester for Chase Lincoln Bank and Trust Company, a Chase subsidiary, but had left to form Empire Valuation Consultants in June 1988, nine months before this. I had actually put Terry into the valuation business when Chase bought the Lincoln Bank in 1983, and we remained both friends and colleagues during his stay at Chase. I called Terry and Paula with the idea that I could subcontract the work to them. They said that they were willing to do some subcontracting but were more interested in having me join them in expanding their business. I flew to Rochester, and we worked out an arrangement whereby I became a 40-percent shareholder in exchange for the $250,000-$300,000 of business I had in hand and they would each have 30 percent. My remuneration would be 25 percent of the fees I generated. That worked for only one year. As our business grew, we had to hire new people, buy computers, rent space, etc. Eventually, Paula and Terry realized that I wasn't sharing in any of the increased expenses since I was getting my 25 percent right off the top. Since I needed these two people as much as they needed me, I graciously agreed to split the profits with them on the basis of our share ownership. And that's how it all began.

Ninety eighty-nine was a tough year. I started with Empire in April and immediately was thrust into having to host the 1989 ASA Advanced Business Valuation Conference at the Marriott Marquis Hotel in Manhattan, which I had agreed to do when I was at Chase, knowing I would have a staff of people to help me. Without Chase, I had the awesome task of having to arrange for all the speakers, the artwork, the hotel arrangements, the entertainment, and  breakfast and lunch for 350 people for a three-day conference. I think I learned more in those 6 months than at any other period in my life. Not only was I able to pull off the most successful (and most profitable) ASA-ABV conference in the history of the American Society of Appraisers, I was also able to do it while bringing in an ever-increasing book of new business to Empire.

I realized after that conference that I could do anything I set my mind to. I also realized that I had done the only right thing in leaving Chase and going with Paula and Terry who incidentally turned out to be the two smartest people I could have ever found to work with. Not only were they smart, they were also personally great to work with. I'm saying that now even after having experienced heavy-pitched battles with Paula almost on a weekly basis because of her superiority complex pitted against my own. I generally won because of my sheer pigheadedness and the fact that I controlled the company's purse strings. Without the large volume of business I was bringing in,[110] Paula and Terry would have only been a very small two-man shop barely making a living in Rochester, New York. Terry was and is now

---

110. Which was about 95 percent of all our business.

an analytical and valuation genius while Paula was more of a stickler for accuracy and good English, but she was also a good appraiser. The combination was perfect.

My role in building EVC was more of a marketing one although I had a lot to say in the overall running of the company and its operating and valuation policies. While I knew how to do business valuations, I was even more valuable being able to tell people how good we were and

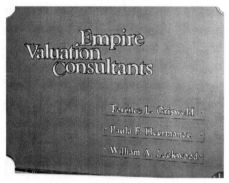

explain valuations in an intelligent but almost superficial way—enough to persuade them that we knew what we were talking about. Terry and Paula, on the other hand, had the technical knowledge to write the reports and do the research; but when it came to explaining the process to clients, they generally went much too deeply into the technical aspects of the assignment and wound up confusing everyone. We made a wonderful team. I also brought to the table management and marketing skills that we continued to expand upon. Terry was not interested in managing people; he wanted only to do valuations. Paula was good at giving orders and bossing people around, but she lacked the sensitivity to deal with people in a positive way.

One thing we needed was a brochure; the one Paula's friend had put together was awful, and I was able to convince them of that quickly. I encouraged the brochure designer to concentrate on our name and come up with a design with our name all over the brochure. She did just that and it developed into an extremely attractive brochure, which we used for many years. I was very proud of that item.

For me, my handicap was in not knowing how to run computers. I literally had to start from the beginning. I knew how to type, which helped, but everything else was Chinese. I wound up finding

a little office in a shared office facility on Sixth Avenue, a block from Penn Station. The room was so small I could not keep both a file cabinet and my desk. I opted for the desk and the computer. Fortunately, the corner office in that complex became available about six months after I moved in and I was able to move there. Rent was only $400 a month and there was a central switchboard that answered my phones and delivered my mail, what could be better than that?

Empire continued to grow in Rochester. We had been continually hiring analysts. Andy Hock and Tom Evans were hired in mid-1989 right after I joined the company. And I think every year thereafter there were one or two people hired. By 1991, we had a staff of three analysts and a receptionist. In the adjoining picture left to right in the front row are Paula, Patty Bruno, and Andrea Hock; behind them are me, Nelson Campbell, Tom Evans, Terry Griswold. The sign behind everyone was carved by me and still hangs in the Rochester office.

One thing that Terry and Paula insisted upon was that we hire smart people. In finance, that means we had to hire MBAs. We've essentially stuck with that policy and it has paid off royally. As of this writing we are able to hire graduates from the William Simon School of Business at the University of Rochester. It is considered one of the top business schools in the country. Rochester is a difficult place because we have to find people who want to live there. Rochester is becoming a depressed area with the decline of companies like Xerox and Kodak. As it has turned out, we have done extremely well because we have a full team of people who indeed want to live and work in Rochester because they were brought up there or because their wife's family is there, etc. What makes it much better is the fact that we have no competition in Rochester, so if anyone wants to leave us but stay in the valuation business, they'd have to leave Rochester or start their own business.

In the early 1990s when things were going well, I started thinking about the continuity of the business and where would we be if something happened to me. I was approaching sixty and looking for retirement at sixty-five. And then in 1992, I met Scott Nammacher at an ASA meeting in Manhattan and liked him immediately. He eventually joined me in New York and became a partner in around 1995. Here too, we have worked together extremely well, never a harsh word. We might not see eye to eye on everything, but we've been able to work things out sensibly. I suspect part of that is the fact that Scott was only a 10-percent partner and he didn't really want to buck heads with the people who could throw him out if they chose to do so. But here again I've been blessed with a fine friend and colleague who also developed into a superior business appraiser and a recognized expert in the field. I don't know what I would have done without him since business valuation has become more and more complex and frankly I have not been able to keep up technically on everything that has developed. Scott is my technician and has covered the truly deep technical assignments we've had. I don't want this to sound like a testimonial, but you can't imagine how delighted I am to be able to have these people around me supporting me every day. How else could I have done it otherwise? On my own, I could only go so far. I needed their help, and thank God I got it when I did.

Married with two children, Scott lives in White Plains. He was raised in Minnesota in a fairly wealthy family. His father owned a string of publishing businesses among other things and he enjoyed a large wooded private campground for hunting and fishing in northern Minnesota as well as the family yacht and summers on the lake. Scott tends to be very technical almost too much so. His reviews of contracts, leases, etc., are generally bogged down with minutia, which turns people off and frankly also pisses off a lot of people. But he makes some good points and generally benefits us.

With Scott aboard, we were squeezed into this corner office on Sixth Avenue and really needed more space. We decided to look around for a small office uptown. Scott commuted from White Plains, which was serviced by Metro-North trains coming into Grand Central Station at Forty-second Street while I came into Penn Station, which is at Thirty-fourth Street. To our surprise, a real estate advisor that we hired came up with the Empire State Building, which is on Thirty-fourth Street and Fifth Avenue. The space on the fifty-seventh floor was adequate for our purposes and allowed for some small expansion. The walk from Grand Central for Scott was acceptable to him. My walk from Penn was two blocks.

 We soon needed to hire more people, and within a short time, we hired Bill Johnston and a secretary and then came Tony Paddock. We wound up breaking through the wall and taking over another small office space next door. Tony is a year younger than me and in 1995 was forced to retire from the accounting firm of KPMG Peat Marwick, one of the "big five" accounting firms in the world. Tony had headed up their New York City valuation group. He too has become a really good friend and advisor. He works on a commission-only basis and was an invaluable addition to the team. His contacts are several prominent law firms which eventually will continue to business with Empire after Tony retires.

Tony also comes from a wealthy background. His father was president of American Standard Company's overseas operations prior to World War II and actually fled Paris as the Germans moved in. Tony and his sister and mother left just before the Germans came and moved to the family's house that they had maintained in Larchmont, New York. Tony went on to Harvard College and Harvard Law School and worked as an attorney before going into investment banking at Chase Manhattan and Merrill Lynch. He wound up at Standard Research Consultants, the most prestigious business valuation firms in the country at the time, which later turned into KPMG Peat Marwick where he spent the rest of his career. Married without children, Tony and Wendy spend most of their free time on their forty-foot sailboat moored at the Larchmont Yacht Club.

Tony is a great example of what you might call the upper crust of society, having attended Harvard and before that some well-known prep school.[111] He has a huge number of friends from around the country. They are a disproportionate number of well-heeled folks from all walks of life. In fact, Wendy's family was also quite well-off, having had a shipping business carrying goods back and forth to the Far East. I once brought back a can of macadamia nuts from Hawaii for everyone in the office, and Tony's comment was "Thanks for the nuts. Wendy will enjoy them. Her family owned the largest macadamia nut plantation in Hawaii for many years."

[111.] I believe it was Exeter.

Tony has been a great asset to Empire. He is an unofficial advisor to the firm and is invited to sit in on our quarterly board of directors' meetings. His insights reflect the broad experience he has had in his forty-plus business career which we highly respect.

As we have grown in Rochester, we have actually had to move three times since starting the business. Originally we had a couple of hundred square feet on Cambridge Street in downtown Rochester. Then Paula's dentist had an opportunity to buy a small office building on Winton Road outside of downtown Rochester and asked us to join her in taking the first floor and she the second. We soon grew out of that space, sold our half to the dentist, and moved to a building on Brighton Henrietta Town Line Road. We eventually took over the entire two floors of that building except for the owner's small office, which he was willing to give up for us if we wanted it, but it was just not going to be enough. In 2004, we leased eleven thousand square feet in a fairly new one-story office complex almost across the street from where we were. Even there we have had to convert our storage space to offices to accommodate the added staff.

In New York City we now have close to 5,200 square feet and have sublet some of it pending our expansion there.

In about 1999, with Scott's help, we embarked on a new marketing strategy by developing a new logo and a fancy new brochure with pictures, which has proved to be the right move. It gave us a new image of professionalism[112] and brought in a different line of clients.

[112.] We were told by some of our clients that the look of our old logo came across as "vampire consultants" because of the way the words were next to each other.

History of the Times—1990s

The 1990s are generally classified as having moved slightly away from the more conservative 1980s but otherwise retaining the same mind-set. The '90s were marked with rapid progression of globalization and global capitalism following the collapse of the Soviet Union and the end of the cold war. While optimism and hopes were high following the collapse of communism, the backlash of the cold war's effect was only beginning, precipitating the continuation of terrorism in third world regions that were once the frontlines for American and Soviet foreign politics, particularly in Asia. In the '90s, many first world economies such as the United States, Canada, Ireland, Australia, and South Korea experienced steady economic growth for nearly the entire decade.

Many countries, institutions, companies, and organizations also viewed the '90s decade as "a prosperous time" meaning that almost all of them rebounded after many years of failure.

In technology, the World Wide Web was born, the Pentium processor was developed by Intel, and Microsoft introduced Windows 95 to the market. Web browsers such as Netscape and Internet Explorer were developed, making surfing the Web easier. Pagers and PDAs became popular communication tools along with e-mail generally. The year 2000 problem (Y2K) emerged.

In science, Dolly the sheep was cloned, DNA identification became more widely used in criminal law, and the Hubble Space Telescope was launched, revolutionizing astronomy.

In politics, the first bombing of the World Trade Center in 1993 raised the awareness of international terrorism as a rising threat; Rwandan genocide killed one million people in 1994; the United Kingdom handed sovereignty of Hong Kong over to the People's Republic of China on July 1, 1997; Bill Clinton's sex scandal with Monica Lewinsky came to light in 1968 along with his impeachment.

In economics, the North American Free Trade Agreement (NAFTA) phasing out trade barriers between the United States, Mexico, and Canada, was signed into law and Alan Greenspan coined the memorable phrase "irrational exuberance."

In culture, rap music gains widespread mainstream acceptance throughout the decade; black becomes the dominant color in fashion; extreme sports reached a new height in popularity; and cartoons aimed at adult audiences became popular such as *Beavis and Butthead, South Park,* and *King of the Hill.*

Movies of the 1990s included *Forrest Gump* (1994), *Goodfellas* (1990), *Jurassic Park* (1993), *Men in Black* (1997), *Pulp Fiction* (1994), *Sleepless in Seattle* (1993), *The Matrix* (1999), and *Unforgiven* (1992).

Other notable events in the '90s were O. J. Simpson's "trial of the century"; the Oklahoma City bombing; the Waco massacre; Princess Diana's death in a car accident; winner of the Nobel Peace Prize Mother Teresa's death at age eighty-seven; Tiger Woods's winning the Masters Tournament by a record of twelve strokes, becoming the youngest and first black person to win the Masters; and finally, John F. Kennedy Jr. and his wife Carolyn's death in a private plane crash off Martha's Vineyard.

In 2002, we brought in Mark Shayne, an accredited business appraiser and CPA who was a partner in an accounting firm a couple of floors above us in the Empire State Building. Scott and I knew Mark from our local ASA chapter meetings.

Scott and Mark have brought a whole new dimension to our business. It was essentially business coming from trust and estate lawyers dealing with estate planning and gifting of assets and estate administration. Scott's and Mark's knowledge of accounting requirements that call for valuation techniques has brought us into that field where we now get business from accounting firms and corporations needing these different kinds of valuations. Fees tend to be much higher, but the time frame for completion of the jobs are shorter.

With the talk of eliminating federal estate taxes in Congress during the Bush administration, there was the thought of less need for estate and gift-type valuations, which were a major part of my portion of Empire's business. We therefore have been expanding beyond the trust and estate area into these new accounting-type valuations. In addition, we are seeking bigger fee jobs in preparing fairness opinions in corporate merger/acquisition deals. Another area we've gotten some good business from are banks looking to value intangible assets for lending purposes. All of these require a more sophisticated approach to valuations which these young MBAs are able to deal with in a much more technical way.

Many more people have come along both in New York and more so in Rochester since then. As of this writing we have a total of seventy-seven people and have opened an office in West Hartford, Connecticut. Our success has truly come from a cooperative effort of everyone working very closely together to produce a fine product at a reasonable fee. This is not a commercial.

Empire is like a large family now. Most of the people, both men  and women, are in their twenties, thirties, and forties, some are married and building families. Our annual Christmas party in Rochester has become an event that everyone looks forward to the entire year. It's a chance to see the kids growing and meeting new family members. We've actually had two young people meet, fall in love, and get married while working together in Rochester (Terri Wagner and Kevin Kane). We attended their wedding in Buffalo in 2002. We also have a wonderful Friday afternoon picnic in August in Rochester every year. In 2004, we reached our current number of shareholders of ten. Above are left to right: me, Joe Eckl, Bill Johnston, Mark Shayne, Chuck Coyne, Andrea Hock, Scott Nammacher, Hugh Lambert, Greg Sullivan, and Terry Griswold. In 2007 we added Keith Smith (not pictured).

At our summer picnic, the annual tennis tournament, which started in 1999, has become a big event. The first year, Scott and I challenged any three people in the Rochester office to a tennis game. The weather was very hot and humid, but we won against two guys who really hadn't played much tennis in their life. As purely a lark, I bought a Rochester City

coffee mug at the airport as we were returning from that picnic and it has developed into a large trophy with the mug sitting on top. It has become a great talking point and item for fun and banter between the two offices.

I actually turned a twelve-inch block of wood into a trophy base, painted it with white enamel with some areas of gold leaf, which matched parts of the porcelain cup, and left flat areas to screw on brass nameplates showing each year's winners and losers. One of the gals in Rochester actually found a three-and-half-foot Grecian column on which the trophy now stands in a prominent alcove in the Rochester office. Surrounding it on the walls are pictures of the annual teams and write-ups of the event. At the 2006 Rochester Cup event,

Jason Ross and I lost to Mike Manjerovic and Scott Cunning in a really close match. One of the running jokes in the company is that the NYC office is "headquarters" and Rochester is just a support office. So to spice up the competition, I bought polo shirts for Jason and me with "NYC" on the chest. There were no "Rochester" shirts on the market in New York City, but I was able to pick up "Rochester" T-shirts at the Rochester Airport for our competitors.

The tennis match, as small as it is, evokes a lot of discussion and goodwill and everyone looks forward to it. We're not large enough to field a softball team or something like that, but as we grow, that might be the next endeavor. Whatever it is, it seems to bring us all closer together as people and develops friendships and a esprit de corps that money can't buy.

That in a nutshell is the story of my business career. It's been a great ride. I have no words to describe what it has meant to me to be able to achieve these things in my life. They weren't planned. I didn't start out saying I'm going to achieve this or that. I had no target, no destination, nor real goals that I set for myself, at least not at this level. If I had, maybe I would have been disappointed in not having reached the highest level of those expectations. Or maybe I'd be driving a beer truck in Ridgewood for the rest of my life. Instead, I guess I just did what looked like the right thing to do and did it. If there are any regrets in looking back one last time at all this, I would have to say it would be that Empire didn't happen earlier. But then, what does that mean? Someone once said, "Timing is everything." Had it happened earlier, would I have been able to join up with Terry and Paula? Would I have met Scott at a time in his career when he was looking for a position in business valuations? Would Chase have been as receptive to starting a valuation service at an earlier date? In fact, I think the timing was just right because it was at a time when business valuations were just beginning to come into their own. Attorneys and accountants were recognizing the need for competent, well-written, and researched valuation reports to satisfy the growing numbers of privately owned business clients emerging in the market. Let's leave it at that. It worked great and I'll be eternally grateful for having had the opportunity to participate in it.

History of the Times—2000s

Thus far, the 2000s has been marked with generally a continuation, if not escalation, of the social problems the world inherited from the 1990s and the post-cold war era which included rise of terrorism, globalization, the rapid expansion of communications and telecommunications with cell phones, international pop culture, and the expansion of Corporate America around the globe.

In technology, there was a huge jump in broadband Internet usage from 6 percent to what's predicted to be 62 percent by 2010; a boom in MP3 music downloading and audio data compression; digital camera revolution; USB flash drives replacing zip disks and 3.5 inch diskettes; liquid crystal displays began to replace cathode ray tubes; DVDs replace VCR technology; LASIK eye surgery becomes popular; GPS becomes a must-have piece of equipment and is showing up not only in automobiles but also in cell phones; DVRs introduced by cable companies; and self-service kiosks become standard for airline check-ins, hotels, and car rentals.

The United States is sent into shock by the attack on the World Trade Center by terrorists on September 11, 2001, killing close to three thousand people; American troops invade both Afghanistan and Iraq in response to 9/11.

In economics, China continues to expand rapidly to become one of the leading economies in the world.

Culturally, newspapers decline as the major distributor of information as digital media takes the lead; reality television becomes a well-established sector of TV programming; and Pope John Paul II dies at age eighty-four on April 2, 2005.

Hurricane Katrina devastated the Gulf Coast of the United States with winds of 175 miles per hour. New Orleans sustained catastrophic damage with 80 percent of the city underwater as the levy system failed.

The 2008 presidential race becomes the most prolonged, expensive, and bitter races in the history of this country, pitting two of the most unqualified candidates against each other.

CHAPTER VI

Odds and Ends

Those are certain things during my life besides what I've already talked about that have also brought me a great deal of pleasure and happiness. I've kept them separate from the rest of my story because they didn't seem to fit in any chronological order. I share them with you here.

A. Wood Carving

For as long as I can remember, whenever I was in a hardware store or craft-type store I would look for wood chisels. It was sort of something in the back of my mind that said "try wood carving," "get chisels." It wasn't something that ate at me or kept me awake at night, but it was obviously something I must have spoken about because one Christmas, in around 1970, Connie presented me with a catalog from a company called Garrett Wade in New York City. It was a magnificent catalog with a full array of wood chisels and other finely crafted but expensive woodworking tools. Her Christmas present to me was "whatever you want from that catalog." I promptly ordered a Henry Taylor starter set that included a dozen varied-sized chisels, a mallet, sharpening stone, and a can of honing oil. That's how it all began. When the chisels arrived, I was thrilled to find that they were razor sharp. A picture of a carving of an owl impressed me and  with a piece of wood from our woodpile, I set out to carve that owl from the picture. Voila! It turned out to be pretty darn good in my opinion. I was pleasantly surprised that this wood carving stuff seemed to come pretty easily to me.

When I look back at my interest in wood carving, I can actually trace it to when I was ten or eleven years old or even younger. One of my pastimes was working at our workbench in the basement, carving faces in sticks of chalk. I expanded that into making the whole cigarette holder, also out of a whole stick of chalk; and with a very thin drill bit, I was able, some of the time, to drill the length of the chalk to make a hole all the way through. I must have had a dozen or more chalk sticks with funny faces on them. Unfortunately, they were very delicate and tended to break easily. Beside the chalk carvings I also had a cheap set of miniature chisels that I used to carve faces and male torsos in a small piece of mahogany scrap wood I found in the basement.

In the late sixties and early seventies, when I went to scout camp with Mark, I used to whittle things in branches and pieces of scrap wood—names, faces, and other things. So I was always using my hands for something although I wasn't always consciously thinking that I like to carve. It sort of came naturally.

It was in the early seventies that we visited the Daleys on the Jersey shore, and over their fireplace was a large carving of a whale that had been carved by Jim's father who was a retired pattern maker for some manufacturer in New Jersey. The whale was flat, but the eye was carved very nicely. Jim gave me a drawing of the whale that his father had worked from and that led me into a whole series of whale carvings with which we eventually decorated the kitchen.[113]

Peter Becket who worked with me at U.S. Trust also liked to carve and we wound up going to the Garrett Wade store in Lower Manhattan to look for more tools. Ironically, Peter recognized the owner as one of his classmates from Columbia. His name was actually *Wade Garrett*, and the business was a venture he started out of business school, which became very successful. Besides buying more tools, Peter and I wound up also taking a carving lesson from a professional carver in Greenwich Village, and after a couple of months the teacher essentially told me that I knew how to carve. I knew how to hold the chisels, how to approach the wood, i.e., with the grain or across it to achieve the best results, etc. From those lessons I gained confidence and sort out ways to expand my knowledge and meet other carvers. Someone mentioned that there was a wood carving store in Huntington which I then visited and met Gerry Holzman

---

[113.] Mark contributed a neat whale in tin from his shop class.

and Jim Beatty and they in turn introduced me to the Long Island Wood-Carvers Association. I joined the group immediately. There were about fifteen to twenty guys who met every month at a high school in Deer Park, Long Island. I was thrilled to meet these fellows, some of whom were excellent carvers. One man carved exquisite miniature birds and was more than willing to show everyone his techniques. Some of the members were not very good carvers but gradually they learned and their pieces developed character and took shape in different ways. I eventually became the president of the group and was able to expand the breadth and interest in wood carving on Long Island. The membership expanded, and at one point we had probably about fifty carvers every month. We encouraged everyone to bring to the meetings the pieces they were working on or finished pieces that they either wanted to have critiqued or just shown off. It was a great way for those guys who were more tentative in their carving to gain confidence that what they were doing was good.

In 1979, with encouragement from the guys in the club, I started carving decorative duck decoys, which had become enormously popular throughout the country. From as far back as the twenties or even earlier, the U.S. National Decoy Show was the largest such event in the country and it was held on Long Island, attracting decoy carvers from afar. At that time the concentration was on "working decoys," i.e., those that hunters put out in the water to attract the ducks into their blinds so they could be shot. This show was the biggest and best in the country. But, as decoy carving increased in popularity it evolved into something much more than just working decoy carving. Artists and just regular wood-carvers like myself started carving decorative decoys; i.e., decoys that were not just a faint silhouette of a duck but rather a life-like replica of each specie with all the accurate feather detail and coloration. This was a phenomena that came, I suspect, in the sixties and just kept growing. At the same time the Long Island show was losing its appeal because hunting on Long Island had dwindled and sponsors were able to develop bigger and better shows in places like Ocean City, Maryland and New Orleans and in the Mid West where duck hunting was regionally much more active.

I love to carve but I don't consider myself especially creative; thus, decoy carving was attractive to me; because it is basically copying from drawings and pictures to create a life-like image of a duck or other bird. My first attempt was a small bufflehead, which turned out to be very amateurish and stiff. I next tried a mallard, which was somewhat better. After seeing the mallard, my friends encouraged me to enter the real competition so I decided to carve a full-sized Canada Goose. It took me about three months of working practically every  night. I even bought a small airbrush setup to try for better coloration. When it was completed, I entered it in the U.S. National Decoy Show in Melville, Long Island, and to my surprise won "best in class" in the goose category and then the "best in show" in the amateur division. I was elated and quite surprised, to say the least. In fact, I was not expecting to win anything and actually went home for lunch before the judging began. As I finished lunch, Joe Durso called me. "Where the hell are you? Get out here you've just won best in class." By the time I got back to Melville, I could not believe that I had also won best in show. It was even more surprising knowing that the feathering on the goose was entirely wrong. I had not bothered to check on how the feathers lay on the back of a goose or for that matter on the back of any bird. I just never thought about it even when I was copying from pictures and plans. I was more concentrating on getting the body, neck, and head in the right shape. And that they were.

I then carved a colorful wood duck for the next year's show, but unfortunately, the seam between the body and the bottom opened up and the decoy sank and was immediately eliminated from the competition.[114] After that I went back to carving another Canada goose. It was the best thing I've ever carved. However, the judges didn't think so. I didn't even get an honorable mention. It was then that I realized what was happening: what had generally been a hobby for most people like me was quickly becoming a full-blown moneymaking industry and the professionals were taking over. The pros were giving lessons and entering their students' birds into the competition and several also acted as the

---

114. The birds are judged floating in a large tank of water so they have to be hollowed out and weighted in order to get the proper balance and floating position. A false bottom is then attached.

judges for these shows. One of the judges for the goose category had several of his own students' birds competing with mine and naturally favoring them over mine (sour grapes on my part, perhaps). The fact of life was that there was no way I could ever compete unless I was willing to devote more time to the hobby. I decided it was time for me to look for other things to carve and forget about competing. I just didn't have to time to go that extra mile. Here's a miniature wood duck I carved for Ducks Unlimited fund-raising event.

By then, wood carving had taken off across the country with books being published almost weekly on "how to" carve this or that, "how to" sharpen chisels, "how to" set up a shop and so on. One how-to book that caught my eye was Tom Wolf's book on funny little Christmas gnomes. It was something that just struck my funny bone. I started copying Wolf's little gnomes and thoroughly enjoyed the results. I then branched out with my own renditions of Christmas gnomes. I did it for relaxation and to entertain my friends. It was a great way to fill up a day at the beach in Southold. I would take a standard gnome and have it in tennis shorts holding a tennis racket or in camouflage carrying a shotgun in one hand and a dead goose in the other. I carved five gnomes playing different musical instruments for Mark; a gnome with a large fluke fish for Hank Schneider. Today, I would guess I've probably carved a couple of hundred of those little guys. The biggest collection is, of course, in Fairbanks. I try to do at least one or more per year, depending on the occasions.

 I also enjoyed special carving projects like the one I did for Al Cacamo's front bumper for his Subaru. That was followed with what I think is a great carving of  the front jacket of the Grateful Dead's *Blues for Allah* album which I did for Billy Porzio's front bumper of his Jeep.

Another type of wood carving which originated in Germany and Switzerland is called chip carving or *Kernschnitzen* which means "engrave carving." Chip carving is a way of decorating wood with small incise designs. A special knife is used, and the results are attractive. I started chip carving also pretty early in my carving career by carving a number of small jewelry boxes and decorative wooden plates. My biggest chip-carving project came in the mideighties when Gerry Holzman approached me with a project. Gerry and Jim Beatty, two fine wood-carvers from Long Island who had introduced me to the LI Wood-Carvers Association, had conceived of a special carousel project, one  that would be special for New York State made with only New York animals and all the appointments would be related to New York State and its history. Inside the carousel there would be scenes of different regions of New York State painted by high school kids from those regions. The frames surrounding their pictures would be carved by carving clubs from around the state and would also depict the specialty of the region. Around the top of the carousel frame would be songbirds of New York, and bas-relief scenes of historic events in New York history would decorate the body of the carousel.

What Gerry had in mind for me was to chip carve one of the three-by-four-feet picture frames that would be used as the frame for the main entrance sign. The frame took me about two years to complete. I copied intricate chip-carving designs around the frame. When it was stained and finished, I must say it was beautiful and Gerry loved it. Gerry also asked me to join the board of directors of the carousel, which I accepted.

After more than twenty years of working on the carousel, the real problem came in trying to find a home for it. The town of East Islip on Long Island had set aside parkland specifically for the project, but when the time came to set aside money for the building to house it, the town reneged. I won't bore you with the details, but eventually it was acquired by the Farmers Museum in Cooperstown, New York, where it proudly displays the magnificent carvings and dozens of wood-carvers from across the state. Gerry, of course, was the biggest contributor, carving more than half the animals himself. This was Gerry's lifelong dream. He quit his high school teaching job to concentrate on the carousel when he was in his midfifties. In addition to designing and carving the pieces, Gerry devoted the rest of his time to raising money and talking to politicians. In the end, neither was altogether successful; the money did not come easily and the politicians were empty suits with empty promises.

Carving has been good for me because I can be a little bit creative with my gnomes and make something that everyone will enjoy for the rest of their lives. When I see friends getting enjoyment out of one of my gnomes, I make sure they get more. What it really is to me is my legacy. My friends will remember me, hopefully for not only my glowing personality and sense of humor but for the joy I brought them through my carvings. They will always have those gnomes to remember me by. I can think of no better token of my love than with one of my gnomes carved especially for that person.

Gerry Holzman wrote a book *Us Carvers* about his relationship with Gino Masero, an Italian master carver with whom he studied wood carving in England every summer for five years. In the book, he said he felt that he was meant to be a wood-carver since his name in German was "woodman." So too I believe that *Lockwood* means locking something in wood. Ancestry.com has the origin of the Lockwood name coming from the old English *loc wudu* or "enclosed wood." Whatever the meaning, I feel I was destined to carve.

Time is the only thing that prevents me from doing more carving. That's not to say that if I had the time I would do more carving because I know I have other interests and other things I want or need to do. But carving has been a wonderful outlet for me, and as long as I'm able to hold a chisel or a whittling knife, I will be working on a new project. Like so many other things in my life, I will never become a master carver but I will do my best.

I should say a few words about my tools. I eventually found other sources for carving tools than Garrett Wade and their Henry Taylor chisels. One of the best sources turned out to be Woodcraft Supply Company from Massachusetts. I found their chisels superior in many ways to Henry Taylor; they fit in my hands more comfortably and they held their edge longer.

My most cherished tools are my whittling knives that were made for me out of old straight razors by my friend and fellow carver, Carl Johnson. Carl was a retired patent maker for Grumman Aviation and was a master at whittling small people with a lot of character or nicely carved animals. He would also make whittling knives for $15 for anyone who had old straight razors.[115] At our LIWCA monthly meetings, we always had a "Dark Horse" raffle of items donated by members. Raffle ticket proceeds were used to pay for coffee and donuts and books for the club's lending library. Carl regularly carved a piece for the Dark Horse, and for some reason, most members didn't catch on that the item in the brown paper bag was his monthly contribution. He never disguised the pieces with different packaging or anything like that. So when I was lucky enough to draw a raffle ticket, the first item I would select was Carl's "brown paper bag" if it hadn't already been taken by someone else in the know. I will forever remember Carl by way of my collection of his Dark Horse contributions and his whittling knives.

I also learned a lot of different kinds of techniques and carving skills from other members of the LIWCA. One guy was Greg Krokta, a young man who didn't know what he wanted to do in life. He took a job working for a sign carver in Northport, and after realizing that he was a better carver than the boss, he quit and started his own sign-carving business. He became a very successful carver, creating signs all over Long Island. He gave the club numerous demonstrations on incise letter carving and gold leafing techniques, which I continue to use. Gerry Holzman and Jim Beatty are all friends from whom I've learned a lot about carving.

The club had demonstrations of carving techniques and lectures of one kind or another practically every month. There were sharpening techniques, marquetry, face carving, hands and fingers, how to carve hair, chip carving. I gave a lecture on ice carving from my experience with B. B. King. The most memorable evening I can remember was a lecture by Armand La Montagne, a master carver from Rhode Island who carved full-sized sports and other notable figures in a most realistic technique. Armand's skill is unbelievable. He not only carves the subjects but also makes all the specialty tools that he needs to achieve a certain effect. If there is anyone I would like to emulate as a carver, it would be Armand La Montagne. Google him sometime.

Connected somewhat with carving is my affinity to working with wood in other ways. I like carpentry although I never took a shop class in high school and was never taught formally how to operate power

---

[115.] I got my straight razors by asking my barber for all of his old rejects.

tools. Growing up, Uncle Will had a ten-inch circular table saw[116] in the basement which I can remember cutting wood on when I was probably ten or eleven and older. My first big project was making that cabinet in our living room in Ridgewood after we were married. Gluing these large pieces of plywood together required some creativity since I didn't have any large pipe clamps. I remember using ropes, straps, and an old carjack up against a wall in the basement and it worked.

The only other big piece of furniture I made was the entertainment unit in our den in Garden City. I actually had to assemble it in the den because it turned out to be bigger than I thought. Today it is still in use although true to my nature I have never finished it with proper draw handles and decorations on the TV section doors. I also never stained the cherry wood because we could never agree on what stain to use.

The rough carpentry work at Mark's was most enjoyable for me. Building the deck and railing, putting doors on the shed, siding the cabin, working on the garage, they were the types of jobs I thoroughly enjoyed doing.

I also get a great deal of satisfaction out of doing projects at the Casino: redoing the front sign, building the table under the awning to which I added my own touch by getting round newel heads and painting them the color of tennis balls—I still get compliments for that nice addition. Last year, I noticed that the Casino's empire chair was in deplorable shape, the wooden steps had rotted out and the chair seat itself could not be sat on for fear of falling through. I wound up making a whole new chair from the seat right down to the steps and the storage area under the seat (the frame is metal). Here too, I added my own touch by making the arms of the chair out of real thick wood which I stained and varnished and also for the right arm I cut it out to match a student's chair that would enable the Empire a larger writing surface. I memorialized it by attaching a plastic-engraved sign on the back that read "Compliments of Bill Lockwood, August 2007." I went further with the chair by buying a tarp to cover it when it's not in use. If they continue to cover it every year when it's not in use, it will last forever. Why don't other people think of these simple things.

[116.] The saw sat on an old Singer sewing machine table, and the motor hung off the back which kept the belt tort.

I pride myself on being able to tackle difficult projects that no one seems to have a solution for or simply don't know how to proceed. I even have guys from the Casino asking me about how to repair broken furniture or how to finish a certain project. If things had been different, i.e., if Empire had not taken off as it had, I could easily become a full-time handyman around Garden City and be fully employed. However, it wouldn't be the same and I probably wouldn't enjoy it. Thank God for Empire!!

B. Tennis

The seventies proved to be a wonderful period for socializing for Connie and me as we exercised our newfound interest in tennis from our summers "at the farm." To hone our untrained skills, we even spent a grueling week at a tennis camp during two separate summers following our two weeks at the farm. When we moved to Garden City we quickly learned about the tennis club in town and joined the **Garden City Casino**. Structured originally for working men of Garden City, weekend mornings are reserved for men playing doubles and then afternoons playing mixed doubles and the occasional tennis parties that ended at someone's house for dinner and drinks. It was so easy to meet a huge number of people with the same interests in tennis, and they have essentially stayed close friends ever since. Tennis has proven to be a great sport for me that I hope to be able to play on into my senior, senior years. Having never been particularly athletic, I find tennis suiting me just fine.

The Perlas, as I mentioned earlier, became very close friends, and we would visit them on Staten Island and play tennis with them at the Richmond County Country Club. There we met many of George and  Celia's friends and actually went on a one-week tennis trip to the Dominican Republic sometime in the midseventies with them and two other couples whose names I can't remember. Celia was a travel agent at the time and was able to get us all a great package deal for a week in the DR in early December, which was considered the off-season. We played tennis every morning for two or three hours, had lunch, and then sat by or in the pool the remainder of the day. We were all very compatible and wound up having a great deal of fun. I remember being so sore from tennis that I had to take hot baths to soothe my legs and back muscles.

Back in Garden City, in the winter I played tennis indoors at Mid Island Tennis on Post Road in Westbury. I played there every Sunday morning from 10:00 a.m. until noon from October through mid-May starting in 1973 up until the mideighties. Some of the players are still around and continue to be good friends, like Cyril Smith and Ken Bolte. Over the years, I also managed to pick up games during the week after work or on Saturdays at indoor courts during the winter.

More recently I continue to play on the weekends both in the summer and most of the winter months. In the late nineties, I got invited to join a group of old Jewish guys in Great Neck, one of whom was a client of mine, Marty Bergstein. While some of these men are very old—like in their eighties—they still play very good tennis. We've become good friends as well and I cherish our relationships. Morrie Yohai is the so-called manager of the group. He is, as of 2008, I believe eighty-six years of age. He's a Sephardic Jew, about five feet two inches tall and wears a ponytail and long beard. He actually was a Marine pilot in the Pacific during World War II, dropping supplies and picking up mail throughout the South Pacific islands, a most unlikely background to look at him. His family started the Old Dutch Melba Toast Company in the Bronx, which was eventually sold to Kraft Foods sometime in the fifties. Morrie stayed with Kraft as a marketing executive and wound up being credited with the creation of the Cheese Doodles snack. Morrie has been taking a poem-writing class every Thursday for as long as I can remember, and from those classes, Morrie writes a new poem which he e-mails to his friends on a weekly basis. His "Life and Memories" stands at the front gate of this book as a tribute to my good friend.

Marty, on the other hand, is an accountant/lawyer who has been very successful. His son Ivan is a doctor performing cancer research. Both of his daughters are also lawyers. Another player is Dave Burghardt, the youngest member of our group. He is a professor of engineering at Hofstra University. The fourth regular member of the group is Herb Behrins, a stockbroker from White Plains. Others have come and gone, but this core group still remains. How long will it last? No one knows. As the new winter season begins, I've heard rumors that everyone is hurting.

The Garden City Casino has been a centerpiece of our social life for at least the last fifteen or so years since we sold Southold. From attending the various dinner dances and parties to the weekly tennis games, we are there most weeks of the spring, summer, and fall. Most of our friends also belong to the Casino. Connie actually became active on the board of governors several years ago and just retired after two years as president. In a quirk that reminded everyone of Bill and Hillary Clinton, I was elected president—or should I say "tsar" which I'm trying to change my title to—for the 2008/2009 fiscal year and have taken on the challenge of restoring the Casino's Sanford White landmark building to its earlier grandeur, a project which Connie initiated. After three months in office, I'm beginning to think it will never happen.

Tennis is still the major activity of the Casino, but there are periodic dances, parties, and other events. In the early part of each summer, I participate in the Long Island Senior Men's Club Tennis League which includes about twelve other tennis clubs located in Nassau County. The Casino actually fields two teams since we have so many guys over sixty (which is the minimum age requirement for this league). Except for one year, 2006, the Casino has won the title, I believe, for the last nine years. I personally have only won a few of my matches in about ten separate contests. But everyone still loves the competition so it's a fun program. Playing a bunch of people you don't normally play against makes tennis even more challenging and interesting.

We also have a friendly relationship with a community in Manhasset called the Stratford-Vanderbilt. The club is housed in an old Whitney family mansion which boasts a pool and about fifteen tennis courts. Twice each summer, we go to their club and play or they come to ours. The games are extremely competitive and invigorating.

The Casino also has internal competition in a series of seeded doubles, mixed doubles, member-guest, and other events. On a more social note, the Casino holds round-robin nights every Friday where twenty or so couples mix up with their spouses and others after which they have dinner under the stars. The club has 200 tennis member families and about 30 house members. Connie and I can truly say that at least two-thirds of those 230 families are our friends.

My involvement with the Casino goes far beyond just being its president or tsar. I have twice restored the three-by-five-inch sign at the corner of the Casino's property. The sign was originally carved probably in the seventies. I first restored it in the nineties by bringing it down to the raw mahogany wood, painting it with good epoxy marine paint and gold leafing the lettering. That lasted until 2008 when I noticed how bad the finish had deteriorated. One of our members, Bob Chlupsa, provided me with exterior sign painter's quality paint from his wife's family's paint business, which Bob claims is supposed to be superior to any other paint products on the market. He also provided gold paint which is supposed to hold as well as gold leaf. Time will tell if his claims are authentic. As of this writing the sign has been reinstalled and the gold paint looks very much like gold leaf. I've also made several other gold leaf signs, repaired chairs, built a sturdy table, built an expanded shed for tennis grooming equipment, installed a bike rack, and a host of other things. Why? Because I take pride in doing things right, and what I've seen at the Casino is a bunch of guys who love to play tennis and as long as the tennis courts are open and playable, that's all they care about. The building could be falling down behind them and they could care less. I'm trying to keep that from happening, trying to get them to take pride in what we have at our disposal and keep it in good repair. My close friend, Joe Geraci, is working with me in this effort and we work well together.

I have also become the unofficial photographer for the Casino, taking pictures at a number of social events and sending them into the local newspaper to publicize what is going on at the Casino. I started in recent years to take action shots of members playing in tournaments. That has been very effective. In 2007, I took over six hundred pictures during "finals weekend" and set them up on site on Snapfish so that everyone could view their pictures and order copies if they so chose. I'm trying to make a difference.

C. Hunting

I was introduced to hunting from carving duck decoys in the mideighties. Bill O'Conor, a lawyer from Garden City with whom

I became friends, was an avid hunter and member of the Ducks Unlimited (DU) Garden City Chapter. After seeing my decoys, he asked if I would donate one of them to a DU fund-raiser where they auction off donated items. I agreed to do a miniature Canada goose, which to my surprise was auctioned off for about $150. The following year I did another one and it went for about $250. The third year I did a beautiful canvasback that went for $500. During the auction that night, a 12-gauge Browning Autofive shotgun came up for bid and Jonathan Blattmachr and Bill O'Conor encouraged me to go for it, promising to take me hunting with them. I bid $350 and got it.

Keeping their promises, Bill and Jonathan invited me skeet shooting in Manorville, Long Island. They were surprised at how good a shot I was, and this led to invitations to shoot pheasants at Spring Farms in Sag Harbor. Since Jonathan is by far my best client, our hunting relationship has shifted to a point where I now take him and his son and other contacts and potential valuation clients hunting at Spring Farms at least four times each year. Scott Nammacher is a regular whenever we go since he was brought up hunting birds at his family's estate in upper Minnesota. On one of our early hunts, I complained (to anyone who would listen) that the Browning 12-gauge shotgun I was using was so heavy that I was thinking of getting a 20 gauge. To my surprise, the following Christmas Eve, after I agreed to forgive a $16,000 note Scott owed Empire for the shares of stock he acquired two years earlier, I received a 20-gauge Beretta over and under Silver Pigeon shotgun in thanks from him. It's now my all-time favorite shotgun.

Spring Farm is a private pheasant-and-duck hunting operation owned and operated by Dave Skellenger. Dave breeds about 175,000 pheasants and ducks each year for use in his own hunts and/or he sells the birds to other hunting clubs around the country. When we go pheasant shooting, I set the date well in advance and call Dave with how many birds we want (cost $35 each). Typically we order 30 birds for a pheasant hunt and usually don't miss too many. Dave and his staff put the pheasants out in the field in the morning before we arrive.

We then go into the field with a guide and his dog(s). The dog(s) are specially trained bird dogs, primarily German shorthairs. When they find a pheasant, they stop dead and point toward the bird. The guide then makes sure the hunters are placed strategically around the area then flushes the bird. If the bird is shot, the dog finds it and brings it back to the guide. Over the years we've been lucky to have Stan and Jimmy and their fine shorthairs as our main guides.

On most pheasant hunts we have to amuse Jonathan Blattmachr with his bow and arrow effort. It's become a fun event. Jonathan  hunts half of the day with his bow and the other half with a shotgun. When he's shooting with his bow we have to be sure to stay clear of the area he will be shooting into. Over the ten years or so that he's been using the bow he has actually hit five pheasants as of this writing. I've witnessed at least three of those and have the pictures to confirm one of them. The only other target Jonathan has downed with a bow and arrow I believe is a caribou in Alaska. He is fun to be with when hunting because he has had so many fascinating tales from his myriad of hunting experiences. Many of his clients take him hunting whenever he visits them so he winds up hunting elk in Montana or wild boar in the Florida Everglades or doves in West Texas.

At Spring Farms we sometimes participate in a "continental shoot." Hunters are placed in a very wide circle in the woods; they actually can see the other hunters from their location. The birds, pheasants and/or ducks, are released from the middle of the circle and they fly in whatever direction they want. Chances are they will fly over or close enough to one of the hunters that they will be a flying target. After about ten birds are released, the hunters move clockwise to the next location (or stand) around the circle. Because of the number of birds that are ultimately released—perhaps several hundred during a three-hour shoot—there is a good deal of shooting for everyone.

In 2006, Jonathan invited Scott and I to join him and his son and other friends on a trip to Delta Wings, a duck-hunting lodge outside of Stuttgart, Arkansas, that is owned by Dick Farmer, a client of Jonathan's who is chairman of the board of Cintas Corporation, a large public company that provides uniforms of all kinds. We have now been invited back three years. The lodge has eight bedrooms, a game room,  living room, and dining room. A staff of people prepare brunch and dinner.

Delta Wings has one thousand acres of flat, partially wooded land, which is flooded during the hunting season. In the summer, the land is drained and planted with rice and corn, which is the feed that attracts the migrating ducks coming down from Canada in December and January as they fly south. Several "blinds" have been built at strategic locations around the property and, depending on the ducks' activities on any given day and the amount of wind and other weather factors, the blinds are selected for us by the Delta Wings director or the head guide for that day.

Different from pheasant shooting, duck hunting is a hide-and-seek type of sport. The hunters are totally camouflaged, including covering their face and hands. The blinds are especially made so that the hunters are out of sight. In front of the blinds are usually placed a number of floating decoys to attract the ducks to the area. At times we actually have to wade into the water and stand at the edge of the tree line if the ducks prefer feeding in a certain area where the blinds are not close enough. Each pair of hunters is accompanied by a guide and his retriever.

Hunting starts at sunup; the hunters are transported to their blinds by boat by their guide at about 6:30 a.m. before the sun rises. Once daylight arrives, we can begin shooting, which is at about 6:50 a.m. or so. There are limits of six ducks per hunter per day. Hunting ends at 10:00 a.m. whether you reach your limit or not and we return to the lodge for brunch. The rest of the day we spend skeet shooting or doing sporting clays or shopping at the local hunting equipment store. Dinner is served at 6:00 p.m. A bar, pool table, and two televisions get the attention of everyone after dinner.

The number of ducks flying over Delta Wings is nothing short of awesome. The sky is actually black with just about every known species of duck that inhabit North America: mallards, green-winged teals, wigeons, wood ducks, pintails, gadwalls, shovelers, canvasbacks, and more.

I particularly enjoy bird-and-duck hunting because of the skill needed in bagging these targets. It's not all that easy because of the speed of the bird, range at which it is flying by, even the type of bird is important since you are only allowed to shoot drakes (males). There is a strict limit on the number of hens (females) that can be taken. So as you are aiming at the birds flying by, all of these things have to be taken into account. The comradery of participating with a bunch of guys is also to me invigorating and special. While I only see several of Jonathan's friends once each year at Delta Wings, we all feel like close friends for those three days.

D. Fishing

From the time I was old enough to hold a rod and reel, I was fishing or catching worms for bait to go fishing, but I never was an avid fisherman nor did I ever consider myself a good fisherman or even a mediocre fisherman. Some guys spend all their leisure time surf casting or fly-fishing or going out into the ocean shark or marlin fishing; my father loved cod fishing and would drive to Montauk Point, sleep in his car until 4:00 a.m., then catch a charter boat that would take him four hours to Cox's Ledge. He would fish for four hours and then spend another four hours getting back to the dock. He did that in the middle of winter. When I returned from the air force, he invited me to join him on one of these trips, but when he described the schedule I graciously declined the offer. That kind of fishing trip was not something that turned me on.

When we had Southold, there were times when the blue fish were "running" or at least swimming right along the beach in front of our house. The beach would be swarming with fishermen all surf casting for blues. In the ten years we owned Southold, I never caught a fish off that beach. The one time I tried, I ran down to the beach with my surf casting rod and reel and began casting. The guys on both sides of me were pulling in huge blues which they threw up onto the beach. I didn't have the right hooks or lures and there was no way I could get them that evening. I was so discouraged I vowed never to try surf casting again.

After we sold Southold, Joan and Charlie Moran regularly invited us out on their twenty-feet runabout. When they decided to give the boat to their son, we found ourselves without a boat to enjoy as we had the Morans'. So we bought a new twenty-feet IO (inboard/outboard engine) Four Winns. That was in about 1999. Talking with Hank Schneider one day about fishing, I invited him to join me as an experiment. That one trip turned into a weekly habit that has lasted until today.

The Four Winns was eventually found to be inadequate for fishing, and I upgraded to a 20-feet Grady White with a 150-horsepower four-stroke Yamaha outboard, a fisherman's fishing boat. Now, if it's Tuesday it's fishing. This starts in late June and continues into early September. Would you call me an avid fisherman? Actually, we're not too avid. Hank and I go out of habit and the fun of being out on the water on most nice summer days to enjoy each other's company, bullshit about the problems in the world, tell jokes, and hopefully catch a couple of flukes. However, in recent years, more and more restrictions are being placed on the size and numbers of fluke sports

fishermen are allowed to take out of New York State waters. For the 2008 season, fishermen may only keep two flukes per day and they can't be smaller than twenty and a half inches in length. An ideal fluke for eating is about fifteen to seventeen inches; the larger ones tend to be too thick and the meat less tasty. So Hank and I spend the day catching "shorts," sea robins, sand sharks, and annoying crabs. Is that fun? We think so. For three to four hours or so, we are out in the open waters in fresh air without a worry to our souls.

Occasionally, I've taken others along: Larry Riccio who spent four years in the navy but still gets seasick. Tom Burke, who has now moved to Connecticut, used to love fishing with us. Unless he is in

Garden City visiting, it's now not convenient for him to join us. I have also taken Ira Fisher, my chiropractor, and his staff and will most likely continue that on an annual basis.

What makes boating attractive aside from the fun of being out on the water is the convenience of owning a boat in what's called "high and dry." The boat is actually kept on a shelf in a building; when I want to use it, I call and they put it in the water with a huge forklift truck. When I return, the boat is lifted out of the water, washed off, and placed back on its shelf until I want it again. There is nothing better than that.

E. Khan Singh

It was 1982 that I got the bright idea of giving Connie a special present for her birthday. Not any present, but a live one—a CAT. She always admired those pretty Siamese cats so why not one of her own. I found a Siamese cat breeder by the name of Judy Singer in Port Washington. The timing was perfect; she was expecting a new litter soon and called me a few weeks later. I went to her house and there were several little beautiful Siamese kittens running around. I selected what I thought  was the most beautiful one and then waited until his mother released him from her care—toilet training, etc. That took about four weeks.

Connie was of course surprised and, to my chagrin, not very pleased to have this new baby to care for. I hadn't realized that she wasn't ready or willing to have something else to take care of since she was busy with her job. The first couple of weeks were stressful as we really didn't know what to do with the animal. We put it in the basement at night, but it cried the entire time. Eventually, we let it roam the house. That in itself was okay, but then we discovered that he was clawing all the furniture and the carpets. The litter box was in the basement and he found that right away without any trouble.

Next we had to name him. Since he was Siamese, I suggested we look for a Siamese name out of one of the *National Geographic* magazines floating around the house. In retrospect we're not sure it was a Siamese name, but we hit on "Khan Singh." Because he was a pedigree cat, Judy needed to get his name for her records. Because she was the breeder, he was officially named "Singer Khan Singh."

It was strange getting used to him around the house, but he really took to Connie and became "her cat." They were almost inseparable. At night he would sleep under the covers next to her or on top of her or between her legs or even on her chest. He eventually took over the house. He went wherever he wanted, and for the longest while he was actually a house cat, never venturing out on his own. Then the first year we were in Southold he happened to slip out when the door was ajar and we were frantic. We combed the beach and walked the road calling for his name. Connie was beside herself. We had come in separate cars that weekend so Connie stayed in Southold and I sent back to Garden City. Sometime in the middle of the night he returned and from that moment on he became an "outside cat." He would go and come as he pleased but always came back. That went for Garden City as well. Occasionally he would come home with a few wounds, but he survived. He would even bring home his prey from time to time, mostly little mice.

We loved Khan Singh. He was beautifully gentle, smooth, and one of the family. He spoke to us and we spoke back as though he could really speak. When we got home at night, he would greet us at the door with a big MEOW.

The funniest thing was when Mark came home to visit with Thule. Khan Singh was actually coming down the stairs to greet the newcomers when Thule came though the front door. Khan Singh took off like a bullet with Thule right behind him through the living room, the den, the kitchen, and then down the basement steps never to reappear while Thule was in the house.

Khan Singh traveled to Southold with us every weekend, usually on Connie's lap and spent his time sunning himself on the deck or on the steps going down to the lower lawn. After many years in Southold he eventually would venture down to the beach when Connie was  there, but he was very skittish doing that; perhaps the beach was too wide open for him.

Khan Singh eventually grew old and sick and we had to have him put to sleep and that in itself was not without an incident. We were going to Hawaii on vacation with Mark, and Connie had made arrangements to bring the cat in to the vet to be put to sleep on the Friday before our flight on Saturday morning. That Friday morning opened with a huge snowstorm, enough so that we couldn't make it to the vet's office. Frantically, we called other vets in the area and found one nearby who agreed to take him. Connie said her farewells with tears flowing down her cheeks and I drove through the snow to the vet's office. When I arrived, he looked Khan Singh over and pronounced the cat in fine shape and would not agree to euthanizing the little fella. So home I went with Khan Singh in tow. We were able to get MaryAnn to take care of him during our trip. It was several months after our return that we finally were able to get back to our original vet to finish the job.

Khan Singh brought us a lot of joy. He was a calming factor at home. He strutted around the house as though it was his. He loved to sit on Connie's lap and hum away, singing his happiness for all to hear. I think he added another dimension to our lives. He was someone we cared about and had to watch over but not enough to have it bother us. He was one of us and we loved him. I would consider him a major part of our life for the fourteen or so years we had him.

F. The Perlas

I was promoted to assistant secretary at U.S. Trust in 1969 and was awarded an automatic five-week vacation, which included a one-week winter vacation which had to be taken before May otherwise it was lost. Since Connie was off for the Easter holidays, each year  we decided to go to the Royal Caribbean Hotel in Montego Bay, Jamaica, that year to celebrate the promotion and naturally use the winter vacation week. There we met George and Celia Perla and wound up becoming fast friends and stayed that way until the present time (at least with George).[117] In the years that

---

[117.] Celia and George were divorced in the late '90s.

followed, we saw a great deal of each other both at their home on Staten Island and in our house in Ozone Park and later in Garden City as well as vacations in Montauk, East Hampton, East Marion, and also in Southold. We even went to Disney World with them over the Thanksgiving weekend in 1973 before much of that amusement park was even finished.

We would meet George and Celia in Brooklyn or Manhattan for dinner practically every couple of weeks or so. George knew an awful lot of people with Italian restaurants and we always had great meals and a lot of fun. George loved to cook and throw parties so we were regulars at their house.

George and Celia were avid tennis players and were pretty closely matched with our level of play. We spent a lot of time with them on Staten Island and played tennis at the Richmond County Country Club, which was almost around the corner from their home on Todt Hill. There we met all of their friends and played a lot of tennis. We were all about the same level. As I mentioned earlier, we even went for a week to a resort in Santa Domingo with the Perlas and their friends.

Several years later, we also spent a weekend in the Bahamas with the Perlas. Unfortunately, Celia was wrapped up in herself and for some reason felt she was better than George who somehow was not good enough for her. They fought all the time and it was always about the fact that he hadn't finished college and was screwed by his father in having to work long hours in the family meat store. The big fight came when George invested in a new venture selling frozen packaged meat in concept-type stores. Prices would be lower, and the meat was prime cuts, which the marketing people had emphasized was what "the market" wanted. Unfortunately, the marketing people located the first two stores in the wrong neighborhoods in the beginning of the summer, prime time for outdoor barbequing. The problem was that the neighborhoods they had selected were both Jewish communities and Jews don't barbeque when the kids are away at summer camp;[118] they eat out. George ended up losing about $500,000. It greatly affected his standard of living because he had to pay it off over the next ten years.

[118.] Which is what all Jewish kids do in the summer.

George was in fact a very bright guy who had "made it" in spite of not having a college education. He was smarter than most college graduates that I know. But Celia put this stigma on him, especially after the new venture failed. Nothing was good enough; she had to have a Jaguar or she had to have a BMW. Meanwhile, George was struggling to pay off the huge debt he just acquired. How and when it happened I don't know, but we saw less and less of them and eventually George announced that they were getting divorced. She was sleeping with an insurance executive from the club. She put the screws to George in the form of a divorce attorney who was out to get everything he owned. George wound up being able to keep a few of his rental properties, but lost his house and just about everything else. It was a sad story; George deserved better.

After his divorce, George and I drifted apart for a couple of years; but recently, through a strange twist of fate or coincidence, we contacted each other again. It happened like this: I thought of George a lot and felt guilty that I had left the relationship cool. In the summer of 2007, I was visiting a client on Fourth Avenue in Brooklyn and recognized that I was only a few blocks from where George had been living. "He had moved," said the doorman but didn't know where. I tried getting his telephone number, but that didn't work and I gave up. Then on a Sunday night in January of 2008, remembering that his son, Jack, had a Web site with an e-mail address, I sent him a note asking him to give me his father's telephone number. The next day when I got to the office, there was a message on my voice mail from George with a telephone number to call. We spoke that morning and made a date for lunch for the following week. As we were parting, I marveled at how quickly he heard from Jack since I had only e-mailed him the night before. "Jack? What about Jack?" he said. "I haven't heard from Jack." I then told him about my e-mail to Jack and we both were amazed at the timing of our calls. I truly consider him one of my best and closest friends and hope we can continue to see more of him in the future.

G. Friends

During the last fifty-odd years, looking back we've had a few good friends with whom to share good times and many laughs. But there haven't been a lot of lasting friendships as some people have in their lives. The Perlas were the exception. Through thick and thin we would see them. A couple of months would not go by without our talking on the phone or driving to Staten Island or Brooklyn for dinner. We enjoyed being with them and they with us. I consider that special.

Other friends have passed through our lives at one time or another. The Howaths, for example, were great friends when we first got married, but they had other interests and as their life progressed there was less reason to get together with them. And before you know it, ten, fifteen and twenty, thirty years have slipped by and we haven't seen them. There's always the annual Christmas and anniversary card with a little note, but we never had the spirit to make an effort to see them personally. It's our fault and theirs.

Tom and Marion Burke came into our lives in the early nineties. They were members of the Casino and played bridge with us. Tom and I saw eye-to-eye in so many things it was frightening. Tom's tennis was better than mine, but we managed to play from time to time. I just enjoyed his company. We played mixed doubles with him and Marion from time to time too. Several times each month we would spend the night with them for dinner and bridge. The Burkes had five daughters: three lived in the Boston area, one in London, and one in California. Marion couldn't stand not being close to at least some of her daughters so they wound up buying a house in Litchfield, Connecticut. We still talk from time to time, but it's tough being two and a half hours away and carrying on a meaningful relationship. We still consider them good friends.

We now have a group of friends from the Casino that we enjoy. Everyone has his or her idiosyncrasies that you either like or dislike or just learn to ignore and put out of your mind. Connie had a great friend with Marie Ramos, a truly close friendship that goes back to the early eighties or even the late seventies. We played tennis together every weekend; in the winter we played platform tennis on Sunday afternoons and then went for hamburgers at Leo's. We went bird watching, and when we had Southold, the Ramos couple were weekend guests on a regular basis. The friendship has cooled over the past couple of years and we're not sure why, but Connie and Marie keep talking about getting close again. I don't know if it will ever happen. For one, Tom has become even more difficult to tolerate as he has grown ever more self-centered and demanding of everyone's attention.

We're blessed with other good friends: Helen and Hank Schneider, RoseAnn and John Palmer, Marge and Les Schnell, Jonathan and

Betsy Blattmachr, Joan and Charlie Moran, Grace and Larry Riccio, Roberta and Joe Geraci, Carlos and Maria Arevelo, Helene and Ken Bolte, Carrie and Bob Flapan, Sue and Tony Giangrasso, Judy and Ray Feeney, Mary and Al Cosenza, Pat and Jim King, Betty and Bill Lake, Phoebe and Bob McMillan, and Eileen and Cyril Smith. Art Boddicker lost his wife, Mary, a few years ago and we miss her. Phil Franzese lost his wife Annette whom we also loved. Connie is also close to Sandy Sununu and others with whom she plays tennis. Tom and Bambi Doran have been loyal friends from the seventies when I worked together with Tom at U.S. Trust.

We still keep in touch with Jack Lynch from the air force and John Perri, Joe Brocco, and Dick Roethel from high school days. I had dinner with John Perri last year in Atlanta, but he had to decline in 2008.

I consider some of my closest friends the people I work with on a daily basis: Scott Nammacher, for example, is someone with whom I have shared ideas and business decisions, family stresses and joys, and the day-to-day problems of running a successful and growing business. My other colleagues in New York City, Bill Johnston, Tony Paddock, and Mark Shayne are also among my closest friends as are Terry Griswold, Hugh Lambert, Andy Hock, Kevin Kane, Chuck Coyne and Greg Sullivan, Keith Smith, and the many dozens of folks in both the New York City and Rochester offices. My life would be far less complete without having had these folks by my side in helping to steer Empire to where it is today.

Not surprising, our circle of friends has come from our membership in the Casino and the others I play tennis with—particularly in Great Neck. We have not made an effort to meet other people in other areas. If we have met nice people, we have not followed up to keep the relationship alive. I am convinced that friendships have to be nurtured like houseplants. You have to continually fertilize and water them to keep them strong and viable. We have done a lousy job of that over the last fifty years.

H. Where Were You When—?

On the seventh anniversary of 9/11, I noticed that that was a question that people ask each other and this memoir would not be complete if I left out the answer. Tuesday, September 11, 2001, was a beautifully clear day in New York. If it was Tuesday, it was fishing day. Hank Schneider met me on the dock at Grover's for our weekly morning of fishing. Grover's opened at 8:00 a.m. and we timed it so that I'd pick up our lunch at the local deli, call Grover's to put the boat in the water just at 8:00 a.m. as I waited for the sandwiches to be made and get to the dock about 8:15 a.m. When I arrived at the dock, the boat was just being lowered into the water by the giant forklift. Jose, the boat guy, eased the boat into the slip as if he was performing a delicate brain operation. The boat hardly touched the wooden dock on both sides.

With little preparation other than putting away the gear and stowing the sandwiches and cooler below decks, we were off to Scotty's, the bait store located in Reynold's Channel on the north side of Point Lookout. As we motored up to the dock at Scotty's, the boat handler pointed west, down Reynold's Channel. "Look," he said, "there's been an accident at the World Trade Center!" We looked and saw the North Tower billowing black smoke. Just then Scotty came down the gangplank and beckoned us up to the bait house where he had a television. As we watched, the second tower was hit and we stood in shock trying to figure out what the hell had happened.

We got back in the boat and started down the channel to our fishing spot for that day but kept the radio on to find out more. As the news expanded, we learned of the massive tragedy and the catastrophic event that was unfolding as we listened to eyewitnesses on the radio. It was then that Hank became very concerned because his daughter, Diane, had mentioned to him the night before that she was meeting someone at the WTC in the morning. He frantically tried to reach her on her cell but there was no signal. We then decided to go back home to try to learn more. Later that day or the next morning Hank learned that Diane had arrived at the WTC moments after the first crash and ran away because of the debris and excitement in the street.

I can still see those two towers billowing black smoke and then only large clouds of smoke and ash as the towers disappeared.

The stories of what happened over the next several days after the disaster are well documented. Airports were shut, subways were down, communications were disrupted, and people were suspicious of every Arab male in the city and around the world. It has changed our lives beyond what we ever thought.

Another fateful day that I can remember as though it was yesterday was the landing of our troops on D-day, June 6, 1944; I was ten years old. I came home from school to find my mother ironing in the dining room with the radio blaring a strange sound that I had not heard before. Normally it would have been soft-spoken actors talking of love and desire on the afternoon soaps that my mother loved to listen to. But this noise was of deep voices with a great deal of crackle as Edward R. Morrow told of the landing on Normandy that morning. We were glued to the radio for the rest of the day and days later as one report after another told of what they saw from the ships delivering the troops.

Another significant event I can remember was when the lights went out in New York City. I don't remember the exact date, but it was in the early sixties. I was working at U.S. Trust on Wall Street. Suddenly, all the lights went out, the elevators didn't work, and the subways stopped. UST had its own emergency lighting system which at least lit the hallways and the dining area. In fact, the kitchen which usually provided all employees with hot lunches each day stayed open and provided all the stranded employees with sandwiches and soup. The blackout lasted all night and people tried to sleep just about anywhere they could find a comfortable corner. Days' later, stories emerged of how people left their offices and walked home to Long Island or New Jersey across the George Washington Bridge, etc. There was also some looting of stores, and traffic was in chaotic conditions with no traffic lights and people desperately trying to get home.

I. Religion

While Mom was a devout Catholic and we were all brought up Catholic and attended at least grammar school with the Sisters of Mercy nuns, I can say pretty unequivocally that religion was never one of my strong points. When we were kids, it was required of us to go to Mass, go to communion, go to confession, etc. It was probably in the air force that I first started to realize that I really didn't believe a lot of the hocus-pocus stuff the priests and nuns had been feeding us: not eating meat on Friday, having to attend Mass every Sunday, going to confession, etc. I didn't believe that stuff anymore. I didn't believe that all of those things were totally necessary for a person to go to heaven. In fact, people who where not Catholic would not get into heaven. How could that be? The letters I was getting from Patricia in the convent contained nothing but spiritual gibberish that frankly I didn't even understand. Nor did I feel guilty about not believing what she was writing to me about.

In the early sixties when the ecumenical movement gained attention, I saw that there were others who questioned the authority of the church and I realized that organized religion was not something I needed in my life in order to "survive" or to give me the leg up I supposedly needed to get me into heaven. I saw so many people going to church and being so overtly "religious" then going out and getting laid every night, cursing and swearing, cheating at cards, telling bold-faced lies and a bunch of other stuff, and concluding that I did none of these things and felt I could be a good person by myself. I didn't need a priest or a nun to tell me what was right and what was wrong. I had learned that early on from my mother (and probably from the nuns in grammar school). But now that I was out on my own, I felt I knew the rules and regulations for leading a good life and being a good person. I didn't need to have lectures every week to reinforce those codes of ethics.

And when I got married, it wasn't long before Connie seemed to take the same position although I think she was more bound to tradition of Sunday church, etc., but eventually came around on her own. We didn't push religion on Mark. He was in a parochial school, but I didn't sense that religion was pushed on the kids as much then as it was when I was in school. I'm not sure where Mark is on religion today and frankly it's his life and he needs to do it his way. Sharon, I sense, is much more religious, much more of a believer, and that's okay too.

So where am I today? I profess to be a Catholic if someone asked for my religious affiliation, but I do not attend any services other than weddings, christenings, and funerals. I believe there is a god but I'm not sure what that means or how it relates to me. I try to be honest, righteous; I try to treat people with respect; I try to support charitable causes where I think support is needed; I try not to lie or cheat others; I don't steal from anyone; I generally follow the Ten Commandments; and I do unto others as I would want them to do unto me, my one strong humanitarian belief being that abortion is wrong. The act of abortion is the killing of a human soul and should be stopped except in unusual circumstances.

J. Regrets

Everyone looking back at his or her life must think about what could have been, what was done poorly, what was missed; the old "coulda, woulda, shoulda" stuff. And I'm no different although I must say my regrets are few and basically insignificant in the grand scheme of things. Oh sure, I should have bought real estate back in the sixties and seventies; I never should have bought the IBM stock for Mark when he was born (and then hold it as long as I did thinking it would recover); I should have kissed that girl I went out with in Shinnecock when I was thirteen (but I was too scared). But I don't sit around moaning about those things. For other things I do however.

The worst faux pas by far that I ever made was throwing out my mother's stash of my letters from four years in the military. Those four years were meticulously described on a week-by-week basis for the entire four years. The letters were filled with names of all my friends, places we visited, things we did on our days off, pictures of people, places, and things. It would have made a book all by itself. Anyway, it's gone and I will truly regret that mistake for the rest of my life.

I almost hate to admit it, but on a lighter note, one big thing I regret is never learning how to two-finger whistle; you know, that loud whistle that guys do at ball games, etc. It makes me feel inadequate not being able to do it. I remember trying to learn it, but I guess I never spent enough time at it.

Knowing what I know now, I'm also sorry I wasn't a better athlete when I was young. I was talking with someone recently who went away to camp for two months every summer. He learned to love playing basketball, baseball, soccer, etc. Patricia and I went away to Bayville and we didn't have that structured playtime or the number of kids around with whom to play. All we did was swim and fish, etc.

By the same token, I never learned how to jump rope and I'm frustrated by that too. I'm having difficulty coordinating my arms with my jumping. It's the same with juggling. I guess I just have to practice more.

Had I only known that all my old toys, games, and Captain Midnight rings and Dick Tracy wristwatches would now be worth about the same amount of money as my house, I would have carried them into the twenty-first century somehow or other. I can't boast that I would have had a large collection of baseball cards because I can't remember ever having any when I was a kid. I did have Wings cards that were contained in the packages of Wings Cigarettes and a couple of other kind of cards and they too are probably now worth a small fortune. I also had a fair number of comic books from the late thirties and forties. Those, I'm sure, would fetch a good price.

I also have to admit that I have screwed up an awful lot of woodworking projects with my bad measurements. The old saying "Measure twice, cut once" surely applies to me. I can't remember the number of times I cut pieces of wood or even other things too short. Now you know.

While I'm mentioning wood, what a sorry-ass father I was when Mark was four or five; I fashioned a horse out of an old sawhorse for him to ride. Instead of putting some creative juices to work, I wound up making the most unattractive piece of crap for a horse's head that you could ever imagine. I look back on that and say, "How did I ever do something so awful?" I never spoke to Mark about it when he grew up, but when he was four or five, he played with it in the backyard and evidently liked it. But to me it was so unimaginative as to be ugly. I could have made him great toys during those early years if only I had dredged up some of the carving talent I found six and seven years later.

As I mentioned about friends, I would have liked to have had more and closer friends during my lifetime.

I also regret not learning a real musical instrument, one that I could play tunes on and entertain people with, like the xylophone (although I would have had trouble taking it around to parties at friends' houses) or the piano. I'm thrilled and delighted that Mark is playing the guitar and Robin and Pearl are playing the harp. I hope they stick with their music because they will get much more enjoyment from playing when they get older.

In retrospect too, learning another language would have been a challenging thing to undertake. The fact that I failed Spanish two times in high school tells a lot about my language skills but nevertheless would have been nice but probably totally impossible given what I had to work with.

While outwardly I don't regret it, inwardly I really do regret selling Southold. That was such a great location, one that can never be duplicated, and while the house and its surroundings had problems, they were not insurmountable. It would have been problematic, but renting was an alternative that we may have been able to live with. But here again, I don't spend time moaning about it. It's done and over.

Healthwise, there were all those years that I smoked with a passion and addiction that could have had and may still have lasting impact on Connie and Mark and a lot of other people I came in contact with on a regular basis including myself. I certainly hope I stopped short of imparting any lasting damage to anyone. That, by far, was the stupidest habit I ever had. Biting my nails is the next stupidest, and I still do that, but it doesn't harm anyone else; at least I don't think so.

Oh yeah, there are probably a half dozen or so other things I could dredge up that if I had them to do over I maybe would have liked to have done them differently, but they are so insignificant that mentioning them would be a total waste of time.

Life has been too good to me! My regrets are minimal. My rewards have been overwhelming. Let's leave it at that.

Some autobiographies end with the age-old question: "What would you like your headstone to say?" The answer is this: "There won't be a headstone." I insist on being cremated and my ashes used to fertilize the flowers. If that won't work, then bury them next to Thule and Ginger so I'm close to my two good friends and near to Mark, Sharon, Robin, and Pearl.

K. Final Comments

I want to conclude with some final words:

From 1957 to today, I can honestly say that I could not have done what I've reported in these pages without Connie's love and support. She has been an inspiration for me to continue in any and all things. She accepted my idiosyncrasies—and I understand they are numerous—she put up with my many years of smoking, she hung in there when I was depressed, pulling me back to reality, she supported me on a daily basis in those early years of Empire when it was still in its infancy. She was the saver in our early years when we had nothing but our dreams to keep us going. She was the best and most devoted mother Mark could ever have. And in the last fourteen-plus years she has also become a most loving grammie to Robin and Pearl and mother-in-law to Sharon. We have all learned to count on Connie whenever it's necessary.

Connie and I have been married now for close to fifty years. We've known each other for over sixty years; and while we've had, like most married couples, our ups and downs, I have truly cherished each and every one of those years with her. I could not have asked for a better life, more loving wife, or a more wonderful family. I have truly been blessed beyond my wildest imagination. This autobiography is a tribute to Connie and the family she raised. Connie, I've never stopped loving you.

ADDENDUM A

(cover letter)

PATRICIA LOCKWOOD DAVIS

September 23, 2003

Dear Bill,

Here are my notes on your Memoirs. Please don't gasp when you see how many pages there are. I was surprised by all the memories your writing evoked. I had a great time writing what I did and I appreciate all that you wrote. You did a great job, which makes one more item to add to the list of why I'm so proud of you. Thank you for asking for my comments. Your memoirs are delightful. I smiled often while reading them. They made it possible for me to relive numerous great times and a few painfully sad ones.

The problem is that memories are funny, in the sense of "strange." Memory and imagination play tricks on us. We remember selectively with our senses, with our emotions. Or we repeat stories the way they've been told to us, or we take stories we've told once and whether they are true or not we just keep repeating them as if that's exactly what happened. Sometimes our stories are a lot more interesting than what actually took place.

For myself, I'm somewhat suspicious of my own recollections. I found myself sometimes writing as if what I was writing and recalling was absolute truth. That's why I'm suspicious and skeptical. So if anything I wrote sounds too good to be true, or completely contrary to your recollections, you know my imagination got the better of me, even though what I wrote is how I remember it.

After completing my "comments," I found that I was sad. Sad because of all I could not remember, all that I'll never recall—all the blank spots. As in works of art, there are "negative spaces" which enhance and enrich the whole picture and the details take on more importance. No amount of memories can replace the actual living that one does which is experienced in countless rich experience—both mundane and sublime. Thank you Bill for the pleasure of commenting on your (our) memories.

Lots of Love,
Patricia

Dad's Family

I remember reading Sunday "funnies" on the living room floor of Richmond Hill house maybe we were 4 or 5 years old. Once you find out when our Grandparents died it will be easier to know how old we were. The house had a strange cooking smell, not when the meal was being cooked but when you walked into the house, maybe it was cabbage or pork. I remember being nauseated by the odor. I don't remember having any kind of affection for our Lockwood  Grandparents nor do I remember looking forward to seeing and being with them. Grandma Lockwood's death was the first time I remember someone in the family dying. We had to be quiet and not bother Dad because his Mom had died. I thought Grandma Lockwood's ancestry was Scottish and Grandpa Lockwood's English.

I hated Uncle Joe. He'd be sitting in his living room, and say something like, "Come on over here, Pat." (a command, an order, almost like an "or else . . .") I reluctantly and shyly approached. I was only about as tall as he was when he was seated. He'd put his arm around me and then pinch me so hard on the outside of my right thigh, the one furthest away from him. I can almost feel it still. That was no ordinary pinch! When I went to bed at night, my thigh was still sore. To me he was sneaky and mean. There was a lot of yelling and shouting in Uncle Joe's house. Everyone used what we called curse words which we never would dream of using. Mom would not let us. We were quickly corrected if we did. The cousins all seemed to be smart alecks, rough and ready, not like anyone I would want to be friends with. I didn't like them at all. Robert was called Sonny and Sally was called Sissy or Sister. I thought they didn't like us because Mom was Catholic. I don't remember Uncle Joe's wife at all.

Uncle Ted was quieter. He had what I think was a burn scar on the right side of his face. Margie Lockwood married Paul Lemieux, who died September 2001. They have a daughter Patricia and a son Theodore. I think Aunt Gertrude was British. When we visited them once when we were young, Margie was jumping all over the place. Margie & Paul visited me when I was at Our Lady of Wisdom Academy in Ozone Park. We continue to send each other Christmas cards.

Mom's Family

I remember Mom telling me that Grandma Stumpf had lost her first 3 sons, either in childbirth or when they were very young making Mama the youngest of seven children and the only girl. I've seen a picture of Grandma and Grandpa Stumpf, both with very round bellies. The story I've heard was of the one-legged mother with 13 children whose eldest son inherited the farm when the father died (a Bavarian custom). The eldest son threw her and his siblings out and so they came to the USA. This was the Kress side and Grandma was one of the 12 kids. I think the Stumpfs had been here in the States longer.

Uncle Gus

What I remember about Uncle Gus was how big he was and how he would let a cigarette dangle from his lip as he spoke. Everyone in the family smoked. He seemed to be gentle, smart and hard working. Everyone thought very highly of him. Toys from Uncle Gus' store: dolls with porcelain heads. I had numerous Shirley Temple dolls of all sizes. There were many sets of men and women dolls, maybe about 5" or 6" tall. Each set was dressed in the particular costume of the country they represented: Greek, German, French, Chinese, Turkish, and Japanese. The costumes were very ornate and detailed. Each couple had its own little box and I had to be sure and put them back into their boxes. We wanted them to last a long time. I have a vague memory of little carved scenes of interior of houses, with great detail in both carving and painting. It was something you could hang on a wall.

Bea and Tom

Growing up Bea was my ideal. In my eyes she could do no wrong. I knew she and Mom were very close. Around Christmas time she'd come over to Linden Street after work to wrap presents. One year she wrapped everything in white tissue paper and I helped her paste colorful "5&10 Cent Store" stars all over the tissue paper. These gifts were probably for the Whites. She and Tommy were great dancers. She sang beautifully. Tommy made me several gifts while he was in the Service: a pinkish Plexiglas cross is one I remember well because I remember the panic I experienced when I thought I had lost it in my bedroom. Mom and I searched the floor inch by inch until we found it. Tommy wrote me long hand-written letters while he was in the Army Air Force and I wrote to him. I felt so special having a "service man" writing to me and he was so handsome. I thought they were the greatest couple I knew. Didn't Bea work at various veterans hospitals or was it just one hospital? She always had stories of wounded men and where they had been. She traveled a lot with her girl friends, driving to different places all over the USA. She loved to see and visit all kinds of places (as she and Tommy have done for years). She has an extremely ready laugh and has a way of being interested in many varied and diverse things and people. She's a very good listener. She has a way of being in the kitchen and cooking that's like an artist working on a masterpiece, concentrating on every detail and humming along. During the months before she got married she spent many evenings in our living room, biting her nails, crying and talking to Mom. She often came to visit me in Litchfield. During the summer after I left the convent she invited me to stay with her in Southold. We also shopped together. She's great to be around. She and I visited each other by bus when I lived in Brookline. And when I first started to go to "The Conversation toward Autonomy" Seminars in NY City I stayed with her (Mike & I both stayed with her for several years while attending those weekends). No matter how much we insisted that she not cook for us and let us take them out to dinner, she always refused. Of course, she's a magnificent cook—a real artist.

When I came out of the convent (and was staying with Bill and Connie in Ozone Park), Bea took me shopping and we had such a great time together. I stayed with her and Tom at their place in Southold for a either a weekend or a week before I moved up to Boston in the summer of '68.

There was a time after I bought the condo in Brookline that she came up to Newton by bus and we walked all over Brookline together, never running out of topics to talk about.

Uncle Will and Virginia

Uncle Will was a constant presence in our house. He was kind, good humored and generous. I don't remember him ever raising his voice. It was he who got me to taste baby clams on the half shell. We were sitting out on the small back porch in Bayville, I have no idea how old I was, probably between six & eight. Anyway, he got the clam all ready with lemon juice and sauce and told me how to swallow it whole. That was my very first baby clam on the half shell. After that I ate them just like everyone else did.

Uncle Will used to pick us up and throw us up to the ceiling and catch us, with every one screaming and laughing around us. Probably Mom was saying something like. "Now, Will, be careful." He was careful and he was strong. Uncle Will was all heart. He was gentleness and kindness personified. I actually think it is because of him that we were able to have a much different idea of an adult male in the family (as compared to Dad). Uncle Will spoke quietly and rarely lost his temper. In fact, I don't remember ever seeing him angry except that one time when he hit George who must have been in 7th or 8th grade in St. Bridget's and had not walked us home from school one day. I can't imagine that George got hit for only having done it once. I don't remember anything except seeing Uncle Will raise his arm and George falling against the radiator in the dining room.

In fact we could probably say that about our three Stumpf Uncles. They had really great dispositions; at least that's how I remember them. They were readily there for Momma.

Virginia was 10 years older than we were. There was a time when she and I shared the front room on the second floor as a bedroom. We had twin beds. She had one of those kidney shaped dressing tables with a mirror top and with a flouncie type skirt all around it and a triple folding mirror that stood on the dressing table. It had to be while I was in sixth or seventh grade. Because I think she got married when we were in the 6th, 7th or 8th grade. A woman across the street made a dress for me for the wedding. It was a pale turquoise woolen material. I think she made a dress for Mom, too. Once she married, Virginia & Joe lived upstairs on the second floor. I remember rushing home from school & going up to play with Virginia's daughter, Barbara. I know the second baby was a boy named after her husband, Joe, but they did not live upstairs then. Virginia died when she was about 31 years old. She was in a Catholic place up state New York for incurable cancer, I don't remember its name. I think she had cancer of the bone, which was extremely painful. Little Joe was only about a year or so old. I did not have the same emotional attachment to her as I do for Bea. Virginia was quiet. There was something about her not getting along with Dad, or not feeling part of the family.

Uncle Harry

The story I like best about Harry was that he and Margaret "ran away" together after one of the movies he was showing. Margaret's husband was the organist in the movie theatre where Harry operated the camera. Margaret didn't get custody of her son, (I thought his name was George not Henry) because she left him in one of the seats in the movie theatre waiting for his Dad to finish playing the organ while she and Harry went off together.

Uncle Harry, after his beard-stubble-rubbing kisses always gave us a quarter or two. Both he and Uncle Will were generous and my memory of them was fun-loving. They were the "good guys" in comparison to Dad and his brothers. I loved them my Stumpf Uncles, was not afraid of them and looked forward to seeing them.

You know that Uncle Harry had typhoid fever when it ravaged NYC or maybe it was when he was in the service, and he lost all his hair. It grew back absolutely white and curly. I think he was in his 20's.

Margaret was somewhat of a "seer." She was interested in horoscopes and astrology. She could tell people's birthdays when she first met them. I remember going to their house with Dorothy Jacklovich (spelling?) after school one day and Margaret told her what month she was born in.

Early Childhood

Mom didn't know she was having twins until she was coming out of the anesthesia and heard someone say, "Wait a minute, there's another baby here." How's that for a surprise! She said she wanted a girl and Dad wanted another boy, so they were both happy with the two of us. I imagine some of the difficulties Mom and Dad had between them had to do with her and her brothers owning the house, her Catholicism and the problem of birth control as well as finances. I guess we were poor, only I never realized it. In our neighborhood everyone seemed to be about on the same economic level. Only when we visited the other Lockwoods or Aunt Peg did I realize that other people were better off than we were or that other people made more money than Dad did and had "professions." The families of my girl friends from St. Brigid all seemed to be about on our economic level.

Linden Street

What I remember about the Linden Street house was that the outside doors had many panes of glass and they were painted to resemble wood grain—today it would be like the faux finishes that Jennifer and Juliet make. The vestibule was also done that way. Mom scrubbed the stone front steps every week, usually Fridays and when I got old enough and to earn an allowance, I cleaned to stairs and front hall and vestibule. I think there was a rubber mat in the vestibule. The halls had some sort of printed fiber rugs that shed. The floor of the vestibule was small white, maybe black & white tiles like in the bathroom, or were they octagonal shaped?

I really liked the awnings that got put up in the summer time—making the house cooler. I think Uncle Will used to put them up & take them down as the seasons changed.

Mom did spring-cleaning rigorously & religiously: washing everything—all the windows, the curtains, the walls, woodwork and floors—everything got moved around and shook out and brushed and scrubbed. A big part of this cleaning ritual was washing, starching and then drying the sheer or lace-like curtains on wooden stretches that could be adjusted to the size of the curtain. These stretches had a row of tiny nails all around the edges. They were usually set up in the back yard, in the sun to help bleach the curtains. The house smelled deliciously fresh and clean, and looked so new—she had slip-covers for the living room furniture and lighter weight drapes.

For a time there were bunk beds in the Hall Bedroom because I used to help make it up. I think you and George slept there and Jack had the large room being the eldest. I remember that "the boys" (maybe Jack & George, or George alone, or you and George) mixed all the different remnants of paint that were in the basement and painted that large front room on the second floor—it was a dark greenish-bluish grayish color. That was around the time George had a large drafting table by the window in the front corner.

The black wrought iron gate in the front of the house had these enormous decorative spikes which someone was always getting caught on, or dug into by if they slipped while climbing or playing around on them. I don't think we were the only ones with that type of gating.

I remember the ritual of Saturday night baths but I don't remember ever taking a shower in Linden Street. As I got older, I used to wash my hair in the kitchen sink in between baths. I also washed Mom's hair in the kitchen sink and put those "blue" rinses in it. Depending on the timing or the mix her hair sometimes was too blue, or too purple!!!! I loved to set her hair and comb it out. We gave each other home permanents. I was in 7th and 8th grades and through HS years when we did it. She was so patient and trusted my doing what ever I pleased. But when she worked on my hair I was like one of the wicked step-sisters in Cinderella. I'd comment the whole time—a little tighter, a little looser, don't do this, do that, etc., etc., etc.

Uncle Will's apartment on the second floor, I think still had the dumbwaiter in it when we were growing up. I don't remember his kitchen or bathroom being renovated, but it might have been done for Virginia or for you and Connie.

In one of the writing classes I took, I wrote about being afraid of the Linden Street house basement and how I thought of it each time I went down the basement steps of our Mendum Street house.

When Mom and Dad got married and moved into Linden Street I know Grandma did all the cooking and never taught Elsie anything so that she had to learn on her own after Grandma died. Having not been taught by her mother she probably didn't feel comfortable teaching me. At least, that's what I say about having neither an inclination nor desire to cook. Bill, Jack & George all seem to know how to cook and like to do it, Jack especially. Also, I remember being shooed out of the kitchen while any of "the boys" were allowed to stay.

Since Uncle Will lived on the second floor we seemed to be able to freely go up there. Our bedrooms were in many different places. We slept on the pull out sofa when we were little, then on bunk beds in the small room off of the living room. Before Virginia got married I slept on the second floor front room in twin beds with Virginia. That was before we had bunk beds on the first floor. Jack & George must have always slept on the second floor. Somebody slept in the room off the bedroom I shared with Virginia and also in the small room off of the second floor hallway. Then for a while Jack & George or maybe you and George slept in the second floor front room. I know the bunk beds ended up in the hall bedroom when I was finally got the small room on the first floor.

I both hated and loved the back porch. I liked sitting out there or hearing others out there but I hated its stark ugliness and the hardness of the cement.

I think Dad & Uncle Will did all kinds of wallpapering and painting. I was very young at one time and made a mess with the wallpaper paste. Mom must have gotten me out of their way fast.

The Immediate Family

Mom's death: I never thought she was dying. It seemed so unreal to me that she in the hospital. They gave her Vitamin K to dilute the blood and break up the clot that was lodged in her heart—that's all they had to do in those days. I remember the night nurse saying that all they could do now was wait and see what happens. I must have stayed at the convent in Ozone Park.

To me, Mom, was somewhat melancholy, though she laughed easily. She had an even temperament, much like her brothers, but was a worrier—always worried about something or other. I never got that she worried about me, though. She trusted us implicitly. I don't remember ever having been given a curfew. To me, she was unhappy and there wasn't anything to be done about it. She "offered it up" and expected an eternal reward. She seemed to me to be somewhat naive. It seemed that she never stood up for herself when Dad would criticize or argue with her. There was always something she hadn't done well enough to suit him, she made a mistake or forgot to do something.

I never liked the way he talked to her. There was always something going on about money. He was just too gruff for me. I loved him, but I didn't like him. I never wanted my friends to meet him. I was ashamed of the way he always spoke so loud or asked questions or made him self the topic of conversation. And of course, I compared him to Uncle Will who had such an easy way of speaking.

Mom

I don't remember her being a disciplinarian at all. She was a push-over. I don't remember ever being punished for anything, or yelled at. She must have had a good sense of humor because she really enjoyed her children and her family. She always laughed at the funny stories you would tell. Lots of people loved her and respected her & came to talk to her about their troubles. Maybe Mom could be thought of as unassuming, modest. She was not pretentious. She was not loud nor boisterous.

The house was always less tense while Dad was away. I loved it. As soon as he came home, the bickering began, he'd raise his voice. Dinner times were the worst. No matter what anyone said he'd start an argument or would make a remark that would be a put-down. The last place I wanted to be was at dinner when he was home. We never had any fun when Dad was around. I think he needed so much attention himself it was hard for him to give it to others.

I have my own theory about our parents' relationship: First of all, Mom had more education than Dad. Secondly, they lived in a house that she & her brothers owned. And her brothers were always helping her out and were more "professionally" successful than Dad. Thirdly, they had three really great, smart, good-natured boys and a little girl to boot. Mom was wholly enamored of her children. She was a great Mom, the best. Fourthly, he was not Catholic and Catholics had this notion that no one else would get to heaven and the wife had to do her best to convert her husband if he wasn't Catholic. I think it must have been very difficult for Dad to feel that he fit in or could even compete adequately or hold his own with the good-natured, smart, successful Stumpfs. I think Dad was very unhappy—he boasted so, was loud, had to be the center of attention. I never felt nor thought that he did not love me or us. I felt very much loved by both Mom and Dad. They definitely communicated that they wanted the very best for us.

I remember Pat Plouffe telling me that Mom told Pat's mother that if you can bring up three boys there's no one can hold a candle to you. She knew she'd done a great job of being a Mom to us, especially her boys. (She told me that I was harder to bring up than the three boys combined). I don't remember being that much of a problem, but I've heard others say that girls are harder to bring up than boys. Of course, she was very worried about George—not going to Church, etc., etc., etc.

Growing up, I don't remember ever lacking anything—except for an undertone of "not being able to afford" something.

When I was in 7th Grade, Singer Sewing Machine Company (had a store on Myrtle Avenue) offered to give the 8th grade girls sewing lessons—10 lessons for $10. The 7th grade girls after much begging also got included though they could not compete to get a final prize. I really wanted those lessons. Mom was hesitant and showed so much concern that George got a family meeting together to talk about it in the dining room. I don't remember who paid for the lessons but I got to participate in the classes and learned to cut out dress patterns & use the sewing machine. We had a "fashion show" after the ten weeks. It was said that my dress was by far the most complicated and well done in all its details but I was not allowed to get the prize because I was only in 7th grade. I wonder what the prize was. For sure, I knew I'd done very well and I was happy with what I learned. Those lessens began my long love affair with sewing & sewing machines.

Mom and Aunt Peg, her cousin, where both musicians, as you know. I have a vague memory of a story about Mom and Aunt Peg doing lots of public piano recitals when they were growing up. In Southampton it was a joyous night when they played together and we listened or danced around the living room.

This is how I remember the "no anesthesia" story: she saw St. Theresa's (The Little Flower) face in the light above the operating table. Thus Mom had a special devotion to her and I took her as my confirmation patron.

I never for once thought I was the biggest thing in Mom's life. For sure, she loved her boys—that I knew. And, I knew she loved me very much as I loved her. She was a dear-heart, a gem of a mother. I never wanted or wished she had been any different. I deeply regret never having known her better or longer or as an adult. There's no way any of us can change the past. We each do what we do when we do it for whatever reasons move us at the time. I remember when George died, I could not stop crying. I knew then that I was mourning not only for him but for my lost relationship with Mom which I had not sufficiently realized at her death so engrossed was I in being a good nun, putting God before everything, submitting to His will above all else. I understand how you could have thought I was aloof with a holier-than-thou attitude. I deeply regret that Mom only knew me as I was when she died. And I know the loss it is not to have known her longer and more intimately—all the unanswered questions.

I'm almost certain it was a hysterectomy that Mom had in her 40's and because of all she had to do at home—wash, cook, clean for Dad, Uncle, Will, Virginia, and four kids—the doctors recommended she stay in a recuperating home so that when she did return home she would be well healed and rested. I remember Dad driving us to the place and standing on the road waving to her when she crossed the lawn for meals. When she did return home she was the thinnest I ever remember seeing her before or after. There was a short, fat, robust woman who stayed with us. She cooked, cleaned, did the laundry. She had a wonderful laugh & loved to tease the boys.

I applaud Mom's influence on my ethics, morality, and conscience. It was remarkable, extraordinary, unexplainable. When Esther Hogan and her husband Cliff Laube, years later, were discussing how to educate their children without bringing them up Catholic, I recalled and remembered that the greatest influence for good in my life was not the Church but Mom.

Speaking of Esther reminds me of all my friends who got to know Mom so well while I was in the convent. Even in these later years when we talk about "old times" they say how much they loved Mom. A lot of people loved and admired her and she was so unassuming, so sincere, so good. She was a very good and gracious and generous woman. That's how I remember her.

She was so proud of her children it is not hard to imagine how doubly proud she would have been of her grandchildren and how she would have been triply overjoyed by her great-grandchildren.

Dad

There was a time when I was very young when the best thing in the world was being able to climb up on his lap and cuddle with him in the big chair in the dining room. On the other hand, I also remember Dad taking us shopping to Macy's for a gift for ourselves. We could pick out whatever we wanted for $1.00. The game or toy I chose cost another one or two cents and Dad said I couldn't have it. He wanted to teach us something but all I learned was how rigid, stingy, picky and miserly he was. I learned never to go shopping with him again. Of course, Mom was just the opposite.

Years later when I was in HS, Dad used to give me what seemed like a lot of money (I have no idea how much that was) to get clothes—it might have been a gift certificate at a particular store. I remember getting myself several outfits, especially during my last year in HS. I also stamped cards and envelopes that he used for something while working on his trips for Pullman. Then he paid me $5 for each time I did it, which was almost every week. It was terribly boring work, but I think he was just looking for an excuse to give me something.

No matter where he went with Pullman he always sent me a postcard (the kind that had the name of the city on it with pictures of places of interest in each of the letters). He also brought me a souvenir from all those different cities—a pin or necklace or bracelet—some kind of a memento. I also wonder whatever happened to that shoebox.

Dad must have been a very angry man, unable to express his frustrations. My understanding about the time he punched Mom around in the living room was about his flirting with another woman in the corner bar and Mom saying she wanted to go home. I really never understood it all. Often after their arguments and misunderstandings they would not speak to each other and it wound up that we then didn't speak to him or we would have to relay messages from one to the other. This was very bizarre behavior for any of us. It was the only way they knew how to deal with these disagreements. It was always Mom who patched it up and she'd tell us they were talking again. That beating took place when we were either in the 7th or 8th grade. It wasn't until I was in the Postulate in Litchfield that he moved out which was in he fall of 1952. So those 4 or 5 years were the most unpleasant ones I can remember. I must have always been afraid something like that would happen again. Then I was sleeping downstairs in one of the "pineapple" twin beds in the small room off of the living room. There were several incidents during those years when Mom & Dad returned from an evening out when I heard them arguing & him shouting at Mom. I was frightened that something terrible would happen again and I was alone.

I know Bill wrote to Dad while he was in the service. He told me how much he loved Bill's letters and how well he wrote, what a good writer Bill was. I thought the same thing.

The fight that Jack had with Dad was during the evening of Christmas 1951. It was my last Christmas before going to Litchfield. Dad was traveling and was not there for Christmas dinner, at which I had gotten very drunk, very quickly. I remember drinking lots of white wine but I don't remember eating anything. When Dad did get home I was just getting conscious and was lying across their double bed and had already vomited at least once. I have no memory of anything that happened that whole day except throwing up and being very sick. Dad was furious and then the details get fuzzy. Jack came home and he and Dad started yelling at each other. Dad must have blamed Jack for my drinking. I somehow got in on the argument and fists began swinging. I remember hitting Dad on the side of the head trying to keep him away from Jack. The police came to the house but I don't remember the details. Uncle Will might even have been there by then. Dad must have hit Jack because Jack was the one with the bloody lip.

I remember Dad throwing George out of the house—I don't know for what—They argued and yelled and Dad said something like "Get out and don't ever come back." George was furiously collecting some of his things from around the house. Of course, Mom was frantic.

When Dad visited me in Litchfield many years later he said, with tears in his eyes, how badly he felt about me having entered the convent and hoped it wasn't because of the kind of man he was and what he'd done.

He was very generous with the nuns and brought lots of fish from his latest fishing trip and other things that I don't remember. He was probably a big softy at heart but never knew how to express it. He grew up at a time when the man was supposed to be the head of the household and here he had kids who didn't think too much of him and loved their mother very much and were willing to do anything for her. He was somewhat of an outsider in the family, not being Catholic, being away a lot and not being as approachable as Gus, Will and Harry. I have a lot of sympathy for Dad and given the conditions & circumstances of our lives and that time in history—I don't see how it could have been any different than it was.

One of the trailer parks he lived in was close to the Daughter's of Wisdom hospital—"Good Samaritan" in Islip, NY. Because of his heart condition he went there for treatment & care. He met a lot of nuns there and was a "star" because he always gave brought them something, and because of me they took extra special care of him. The nutritionist was a nun who had been at Litchfield while I was there (I can see her face but don't remember her name). She helped Dad make his decision to become a Catholic and get Baptized. For him it was something he could not have done while Mom was alive. I was always glad he did it because it gave him peace of mind and reconciliation—it might have also allowed him to die more peacefully—we'll never know.

Jack

Jack was always thought of as a "good boy"—he did what he was told—he always seemed to please Mom. Yet, in my memory, he never pleased Dad. For whatever reason some things were never done well enough for Dad.

I guess I wrote to Jack, too, while he was in the Navy but my memory is foggy about it. There's a photo somewhere of Jack's homecoming, you have on his sailor hat & I have on a grass skirt—we were still in grade school, maybe sixth or seventh grade.

On one of Jack's leaves he took me to Myrtle Avenue to an ice cream parlor and treated me to whatever I wanted. I was so proud walking all those blocks with my oldest brother in his Navy uniform.

Once we'd gotten the turntable, Jack would often put on a record and we'd practice some new dance step he wanted to learn, like the Rumba, the Samba, the Polka. Well, one Saturday or Sunday evening at a St. Brigid's dance where I was, Jack came in with a few of his friends (who were a much older crowd and would not usually have been at this dance). He came to dance with me, to put our practicing to the test. The one I remember most clearly was hopping and spinning around the auditorium doing the Polka. We were great and everyone clapped. Jack and I knew we'd done well. I was thrilled having just danced so well with my big brother, Jack.

Mom always waited up for Jack and George when they were out on dates or when George was coming to stay over or coming from night school, and for you when you played with your band. I slept on the first floor and would hear her talking with them/you for what seemed a long time. That must have been on the nights when Dad was out of town.

Jack had a lot of girl friends and there was always someone being talked about as a possible marriage partner. I remember Mom's concern and all her considerations about their religion, their nationality, etc., etc. I don't know what the criteria or the standards were but they were there and they were Mom's.

Whenever I saw him come in after a date (a rare occasion, I was never up that late) he had lipstick all over his collar and his eyes were often bloodshot. It was common knowledge that what the guys did in those days was drink, go out on the town, even if just down the block and have a few beers. Drinking was a form a socializing: relationships got cemented, buddies got created. It was something you could do with a date.

Jack was a very sweet guy. After the first shock of my having left the convent, while I was visiting him in Vernon, he took me into his & Eileen's bedroom and gave me Mom's pinkie ring and my Bishop's School ring, which he'd kept all those years. Family was very important to him.

When Bob Chipman and I broke up, Jack wanted me to come out to Vernon every weekend.

He was steadfast. He finished what he started. He loved to work around his house as we all seem to. Though Bill, Jack & George each spent so much time refurbishing, renovating, maintaining. You were all very responsible.

He was a strong character who tenaciously fought with the cancer that killed him. Even during our last visit together he would not talk about himself even though it was very apparent that he was getting weaker & weaker, thinner & thinner. He kept up the image of the stronger older brother with me. I don't know how he was with you because you two had gotten so close during those last decades.

George

George was very sensitive, philosophical, and extremely creative.

It seemed to me that he'd get an idea and then would set about making it, which reminds me of the way he went about tearing down the barn in Pembroke and building the new two-story studio. One day he said to Jimmy, I'm going to build a larger studio here after

I tear down this old barn. And that was that. Then and there they started to pull down some of the sides of the barn.

This is my memory of what he designed for the living room and dining room while we were in HS. The living room: dark brown wallpapered walls, pale yellow ceiling and drop ceiling, rug ???, turquoise couch (day bed), one chair grey and the other gold, some accents and trim where red-orange. Two of Van Gogh's prints were framed on the walls: sunflowers and I think the one of his bedroom—both of these had the colors he chose for the furniture covers. I remember them clearly because they were the first slipcovers I ever made. And I loved the rope-web-like chair that I used to sit in to watch TV. My room: pale pink walls, navy blue ceiling and drop ceiling, dark blue rug (some old rug cut to fit), white painted furniture, blue plaid & solid white window curtains. The things we remember!!!

He did the dining room, front door & kitchen after I went to Litchfield because Mom sent samples to me in Litchfield.

When George moved to the Greenwich Village I remember how Bill and I guess Jack, too, talked about the loft and the bathroom that had painted eyes that stared at you when you sat on the toilet.

His loft was used as a backdrop for one whole edition of Vogue Magazine. He knew and dated fashion models. I don't remember the name of the fellow who shared the loft with him. Anyway, it was whispered in the family that George was dating a model that he wanted to marry to change her sexual orientation. Those were not the words used but the gossip was that she preferred women to men and George thought he could "help" her change.

Speaking about dating: In HS, George and his friend, Oogie (Gene or Eugene somebody), used to only date red headed girls—Mom was worried as usual about these girls getting to close to one of her sons. George always seemed to be "in love" with somebody.

George got us to think outside the box of the conventional way in which we had been inculcated. It was exciting knowing there was someone in our family who seemed to have so much freedom to do as he pleased. None of this really meant anything to me until I was considering leaving the convent. Then I realized what living could be about and I knew I'd gotten some of that from George. But I want to say it wasn't only from George, even though I knew he was innovative and original and experimental and I loved and admired him for it.

From my perspective my whole family was somewhat different from the families of the other nuns I lived with. Mom, in her early fifties had asked Dad to leave the house and was willing to go it alone rather than be bothered with him any longer. Will, Gus and Harry had all done something uniquely their own. Someone was always asking us kids to try new foods—goat milk, yogurt—are two I remember. Even Dad making that cement deck out back and the weird awnings that had to be looped onto the frame every summer—there were no previous "patterns" for those ideas, no neighbors had done anything like that as far as I can remember. Once Jack and George worked and/or lived in NYC then we heard about a lot of other things and people and foods. Suddenly it became very important to rub the wooden salad bowl with garlic cloves before putting in the salad fixings. Doing, making things was very important in our family. We were all taught to crochet and knit. I was taught to embroider. Mom could tat using a very swift complicated fingering to make a kind of lace, which I was never able to learn. Hand made things were important and greatly valued as were well made, long lasting items. We were rewarded with praise and love and admiration for anything we made ourselves.

George did not want me to enter the convent—no one did. Yet, he took me to NYC for a kind of farewell day. It was a Sunday and the city was pretty empty; we went to see the film "The Red Shoes" and we had a very different and delicious meal in a Bulgarian Restaurant, which we had to go down several steps from street level. He ordered & I tasted whatever was served even the thick black coffee, which came in tiny cups. I was so thrilled to be in NYC with my older brother. We even met someone he knew while we were window-shopping on 5th Avenue.

George almost got dishonorably discharge for not going to his reserve weekends and offering to go to Korea to get it straightened out. There he designed propaganda literature, which was dropped out of planes. There he also frightened Mom by writing about marrying a Korean girl and bringing her home to the USA. I think there were several different girls at different times, always giving Mom something to pray for or against. He always sent us photos of them in their native costumes. He came home just in time to take me to my senior prom. We passed him off as a cousin, because he didn't want me to have to own up to having my brother as a date. After being discharged he went to Yale on the GI Bill where he got his MFA.

He studied with a variety of famous artists. Josef Alpers was one of them. He was one of the original Bauhaus (Germany) founders who taught an innovative course on color and how colors next to each other effect our perception of color. It had to do with the mixing of color wave lengths and how the eye perceives them as the wave lengths make their way to our color receptors. You might remember some of George's painting that are repetitious slanted paint strokes next to each other all across the canvas which were probably done as experiments initiated by Alpers.

Also at Yale, George met a woman who he brought to visit me in Litchfield. I have one of her books in Chapel Hill and I don't remember her name—Sheila ??? She was and probably still is an innovative, creative, famous weaver. She has done some enormous freestanding weavings, some filling whole walls.

While I was at Our Lady of Wisdom Academy, during the year before I left the convent, George would call me up to be sure I was OK, that the nuns were not making my life miserable and he'd offer to send me the plane fare to Boston. I guess he had some notion of the cruel tactics prevalent in medieval monasteries.

The summer before I left (1967), I was allowed to visit George & Margo in Pembroke for a long weekend. I don't remember how this came about but it might have been because some of the regulations had changed and we were allowed to have vacations. Almost immediately, Margo styled my hair and found something "secular" for me to wear. We went out to eat at the Old Oyster House in Boston. It was a wonderful world to my then curious and appreciating eyes.

Once, George came home very intense and concerned that I learn to listen to and be exposed to Billie Holiday singing one of her soulful songs. At that time I thought I'd never forget it, but here I am and cannot recall it—but I do remember being there, in our living room listening to a female jazz vocalist with my brother George, who was interested enough in me that he wanted us to do this together.

I applied to the master degree programs at Boston University School of Fine Arts & the Boston Museum of Art School once I'd planned to leave the convent. When I was accepted at both schools it was George who helped me decide to go to BU because he knew some of the teachers at both schools and thought BU would give me a more solid drawing & traditional base.

I had been in Boston a little over a year, in my third (part-time semester) when I got the call that George had died. Those were very hard times for me. I could not mourn him enough. He, too, had a kind of tenacity. He had the spirit of an artist—art was his whole life.

Patricia's Three Brothers

I thought and still think the world of my brothers. I don't think I'll ever be able to say enough about my three brothers. I've always been very proud to be their sister. They were inventive, artistic, creative, hard working, intelligent, each had/has a good sense of humor. They never got in any serious trouble and would do anything to please Mom. They often tried to wiggle their way out of doing chores or errands but in the end they always did them, or part of them. They are all very curious. Anything that happened in the street, they had to go out and see what was going on. They all loved to fix things up and all took pride in their homes and what they and their wives had done to fix them up. They took pride, too in their work, what they did for a living, in their wives, and in their children. They took pride, too and satisfaction in their "hobbies." They were fascinated by how things worked and how to make things, how to do things. All three of them have always been very generous toward me—

Patricia

Remember the large sleep sofa we slept in together until I don't know when? It was that same sofa that was the background for our "twin" photos. We used to crawl into the space in the back while it was open and play "make-believe" games. We were probably hiding from the bad guys. One game I remember we played what seemed like very often to me was "Cow Boys & Indians." There were always good guys and bad guys. You, of course, were always the good guy, I was the damsel in distress and you always arrived just on time to save me from a deadly end. We used the overstuffed arms of the sofa and the chairs as horses, kicking the sides so often and repeatedly that the upholstery was torn at the bottom.

Bill as my French artist uncle at that dress up party was a blast! We had so much fun, and in my memory of it they believed him.

In 1981 I began asking people to call me "Patricia" rather than just "Pat". I'd always loved the name Patricia and began to introduce myself as Patricia but family and old friends still call me Pat which is OK by me.

The sewing I did was on was Mom's Singer Sewing Machine which she bought in 1934. I'm not sure of who had it when, but I know soon after I left the convent either you, Jack or George gave me that sewing machine. In the eighties, Bob Chipman's mother gave me her old sewing machine when she bought a new one—I still have that one which sews very well and is a giant upgrade from the Singer. I had the Singer repaired when I first got it in Brookline and the fellow who did it said it would never wear out because those machines were made to last. Margo's girls all learned how to sew on Mom's machine when I lived on Davis Avenue in Brookline. I gave it to Jennifer about three years ago when we were cleaning out our attic while preparing to move to Chapel Hill.

Bill

He was an excellent brother. He had amazing good humor, and an even temperament. He was very sociable and loved to entertain and tell stories. People loved him. Of course, I was shy and could only wish I was as carefree as he was. Nothing seemed to bother him. He was fun-loving and knew how to have a good time which I think is very much a Stumpf trait. He was a great playmate. I could always count on him to take care of me and he never let me down. What about the "poison ivy" incident you might ask—that was just fooling around—we did a lot of that. While giving permanents or setting Mom's hair I often tried to put a curler into his hair, NEVER. Bill was a very good boy and a very good brother. As much as we fooled around and wanted each other to stop pestering, or leave us alone, we counted on each other. Except for the time when out of shear meanness and probably jealousy, too, I told Mom that Bill had started to smoke cigarettes. That was me being just plain nasty—maybe I thought "At last, I've caught Bill doing something wrong."

I never realized until later in life how great it was having a twin to play with when we were growing up. None of our friends had a built-in playmate/companion. It was so much a part of who we were I never thought of it as different from others. All my life, from the time I was born, through childhood and schooling, Bill was there. When I went into the convent, I had another group of people who cared and were concerned about me. When I left the convent and stayed with Bill and Connie and then moved to Boston and had a series of roommates—I still had not yet lived alone. Around 1971, I was teaching Art at a Junior HS in Reading MA and moved for the very first time into an apartment (Medford MA) by myself. I was 37 or 38 years old. All those years I had never know what it was not to live alone. Perhaps this is not so uncommon but to me it was a giant step.

I remember how proud I was of you playing in a band. I loved making all those matching skinny inch-wide like bow-ties for all the guys. Also I remember the challenge of sewing denim covers for your drum set—the fabric was so thick I kept breaking needles.

Family Life

At Thanksgiving and maybe Christmas we had martinis and anchovies on Ritz crackers. This was a big treat. We also had very, very, very thinly sliced cucumber in a sour cream sauce. Mom's gravy was the best. As you've written already she was an amazingly good cook.

Dad and/or Uncle Will used to slurp their coffee. They'd pour it in the saucer to cool off and then slurp it from the saucer.

One of my favorite dishes was egg omelet with melted Velveeta cheese folded into it. Mom never burned it, it always turned out "perfect."

Do you remember me not liking vegetables and Dad mixing cauliflower into my mashed potatoes one Sunday?

"Anything for Thanksgiving?" When we were little and had to go around together, I would dress up as a boy beggar and Bill would dress up as Aunt Jemima—blackening our faces. I read about this tradition once and it showed up only in the "neighborhoods" of Brooklyn.

As we got older we took turns washing & drying the dishes. We each had a week for each chore. With the wet towels from drying the dishes there were often the-snapping-towels-to-the-legs "fights."

We ate at 6 o'clock. As I said somewhere else dinners were unpleasant times for me.

We each had our specific seats at the dinner table. Bill & I were against the wall, Bill on Dad's right hand side. Mom was on Dad's left opposite Bill. I don't know how we all fit at the table on the nights that Uncle Will and Virginia were there.

Just a note about the margarine that we got during the war that you used to mix with coloring to make it yellow like butter—in Canada the margarine, no matter what brand, is almost white. It always reminds me of oleo-margarine.

Play

I remember some of the games we played outside in the evenings but during the afternoons the girls jumped rope or roller-skated, but I don't remember anything else that just the girls played, except "pretend school" when we were very young and someone was the teacher and the others where the students.

Do you remember making tin solders in molds? It was quite a process and I used to love watching you melt the metal (I think it was tin) in a ladle from which you'd pour the hot liquid into the molds at the side or at the top.

Radio Shows

I remember the radio shows that you mention as well as: *The Thin Man, George Burns & Gracie Allen, Truth or Consequences*. There were several drama whose names I don't remember accurately like the *Orson Wells Mystery or Theatre*. One of the soaps I remember always started with and "so & so from the Red River Valley." We were not allowed to listen until we had finished our homework. It was during those times that I'd knit, crochet or do embroidery. Each night of the week had its particular show or shows that we'd listen to regularly.

St. Brigid's

I never liked being in school. I felt very inadequate except in Art and math. I know Mom read to us when we were little, especially if we were sick, but I have no recollection of learning to read. I hated to be called on. School made me very nervous and anxious. But I did like my friends and the social lives we had because of school. Do you remember the women teachers who were like Mutt & Jeff? One was very tall and the other short. They dressed meticulously with **everything** matching. I don't think they wore the same color on the same day but no matter what they wore the dress, hat, shoes, stockings, beads, earrings, rings—all matched—all blue, all green, all red, all navy—it was hysterical!

Bayville

It was Uncle Will, I think who would rent the houses we stayed in. Then he eventually bought the yellow house on 5th Street.

I learned to do lots of things in Bayville: lots of embroidery, crochet and knitting. Mom taught me all the different kinds of stitches during those summer days. I learned how to ride a two-wheel bike: up and down 5th Street I'd go, falling off repeatedly until I mastered it. The streets were all dirt with ruts, which were created by car tires.

I learned to swim in Bayville. Remember the balsa wood pieces that were threaded onto a canvas belt; as we progressed in our swimming skills, the balsa wood bocks got removed until we were able to swim on our own.

I was fascinated by the rake used for clamming and the movement needed to turn it over and shake it just the right way. The rake was shaped like a cup.

There were so many things I learned not to be afraid of—except of course spiders.

And I learned to love clams, crabs, eels, fish—I can still imagine the delicious taste of fresh flounder. I learned to eat one side of it, avoid the bones and then turn it over and eat the other side, leaving the spine and bones. It doesn't get any better.

Some of the people who visited us in Bayville were neighbors whose names I don't remember. But I do remember all the cooking, all the meals, all the pots and pans and dishes and I do remember not liking some of the kids who came out with their parents, they weren't good sports and they did not know how to play well.

On rainy days we played board games & cards. The main game we played was *Monopoly* and one game could sometimes last several days. Richie Schwarz was often our buddy in playing these games.

High School

What was it about HS that stood out for me? Well, Bill was in another school, the first time we'd "been separated" everyone said. While the boys in the family were always being talked with about what they were going to do after HS, if anyone ever spoke to me about it, seriously, I don't remember. I talked to my girl friends about it, but we were young, idealistic and didn't know anything. Anne Kelly knew she'd have to work to help support her family and that's why she took the commercial courses when we got to Bishops. I don't remember about Mary Ann but I think she needed to help out at home, too. Joan knew she wanted to teach and definitely would go to college. In a vague way, I thought maybe I'd be a teacher. It was either that or get married & have children. Well, though I had lots of girl friends and a several close friends (Anne Kelly, Mary Ann Toth, Joan Destefanos) and we had a great crowd to hang around with, we mainly were concerned with doing home work, passing exams, going to church dances, having crushes and meeting boys. We were close to the nuns who taught us, not like friends but we knew they were interested in us getting ahead and making something of ourselves. As far as I was concerned it didn't look like I could go very far, nor could I envision a future for myself. I knew I did not want the kind of life Mom had (cooking, laundry, cleaning, shopping, always worried about money). Neither Virginia's nor Bea's marriage inspired me. I didn't want to get married though that's what I was supposed to want. As graduation from HS approached, I had no idea what I could do to earn money. I wasn't ready. I remember there were many conversations with Jack & George and you about what you'd do after HS. I don't remember anyone having those conversations with me except in a very worried tone as if I was supposed to know what to do, and I didn't. Much later I realized how frightened I was of the "the world". Also, I was idealistic, a romantic. I could see myself as a nun: all that quiet time to my self. As a nun I could see myself teaching the way I saw the nuns teaching all during my school years. Even in grammar school I remember becoming a member of some kind of a society where we met after school, prayed and went to Mass everyday.

I wish I could explain my having gone to the convent, having left the family I loved and who I knew loved me and of all things having chosen such a strict order. I was seventeen, immature, frightened, insecure, confused, selfish, thoroughly convinced I had a vocation (a very strong powerful pull in those days), if God was calling what else could I do. Afraid of not "doing God's will", afraid of the business world, of making a living, of marriage, of failing in higher education.

I felt a very strong urge to do some good in the world. I wanted to have a boy friend and eventually get married but my religious feelings were extremely strong and I sincerely thought I had a vocation given what I was given to understand what it was.

It took going to college as a nun to open the world to me in all its glory—of intelligence, art, friendliness, diversity, beauty, creativity, invention, humanitarianism, science, literature, theatre, curiosity. The diversity alone was very attractive. I learned that I could question, doubt, and be responsible for myself, stand on my own two feet as an individual with or without the Church or a God to tell me at every turn what I should or should not do, what was right & wrong, what was a sin or not. I realized how much I loved Anthropology, Ancient History, Art History, Philosophy, the History of Religions, of Catholicism, of the Bible. These were the makers of my secular mind and it was amazingly freeing and exhilarating.

Convent life suited me well for 16 years—until I'd done the maturing I needed to do, gained the confidence and courage I needed. The fears I had as a teenager were no longer there, and I was no longer a Catholic. I do not regret any of the time I spent in the convent and recall it with delight and warmth.

What do I recall about Bill in HS? You were having a great time, had so many friends, played in the orchestra and in the dance band, there seemed to be no end to his friendliness and friends. In today's jargon I would have called Bill "cool." I think we used to have New Year's Eve Parties at one of our friends' houses with people we knew. I think I went to parties at which Bill's band was playing, just to get me to meet some new people.

Southampton

We began to go to Aunt Peg's place in Southampton when Virginia & Joe moved into the Bayville house. We might have been there two to four weeks at a time. Mom was with us for some of the time and other times we were alone with Aunt Peg (after Peggy began to go to College and was taking summer courses). I felt shy and inept in Southampton. Everyone was so sure of them selves, they knew so much and didn't mind telling everyone. Though, we had a great time so often—yet we had household chores and grocery shopping and errands and gardening and all kinds of projects. From what I've heard, Bill, Jack & George all worked very hard with Uncle Ted—and I'm very vague about the years we went & how many. Cousin Peggy (four years older than we were) was a regular "tom-boy" in that she could do almost anything the boys could do especially around boating and fishing and clamming and eeling.

Patricia Lockwood Davis

June 2003

Exhibit I.   The Lockwood/Jenkins Tree

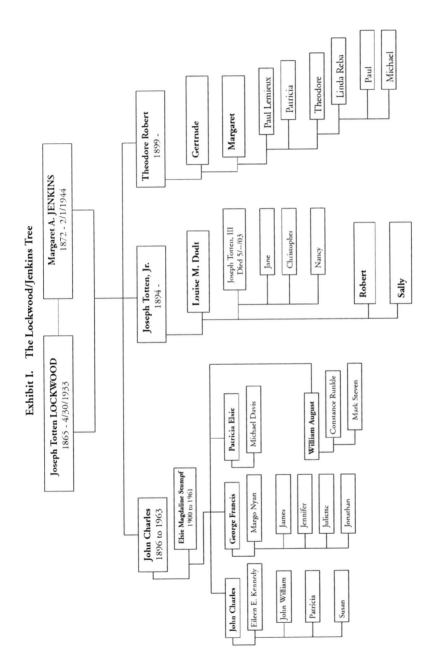

08/29/08

329

Exhibit II.   The Lockwood/Stumpf Tree

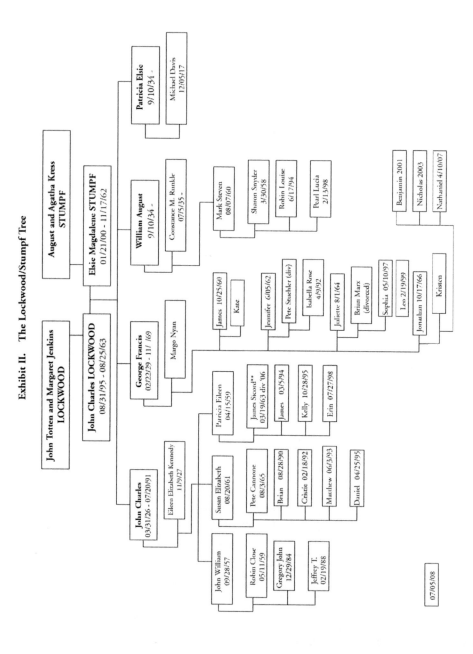

330

Exhibit III.   The Lockwood/Wilson Tree

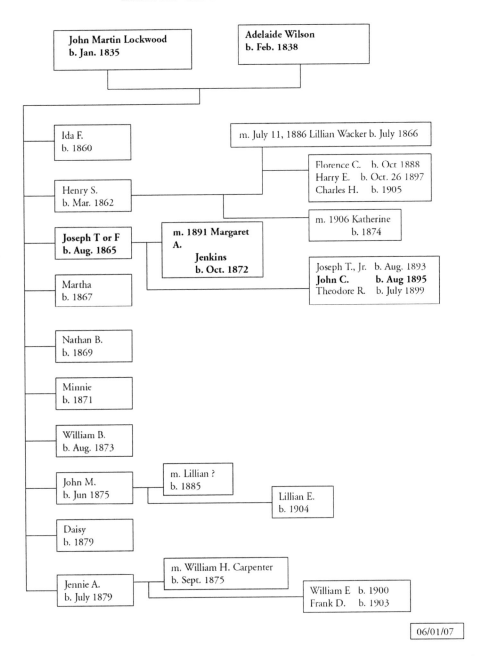

John Martin Lockwood
b. Jan. 1835

Adelaide Wilson
b. Feb. 1838

Ida F.
b. 1860

m. July 11, 1886 Lillian Wacker b. July 1866

Florence C.   b. Oct 1888
Harry E.   b. Oct. 26 1897
Charles H.   b. 1905

Henry S.
b. Mar. 1862

m. 1906 Katherine
b. 1874

Joseph T or F
b. Aug. 1865

m. 1891 Margaret A.
Jenkins
b. Oct. 1872

Joseph T., Jr.   b. Aug. 1893
John C.   b. Aug 1895
Theodore R.   b. July 1899

Martha
b. 1867

Nathan B.
b. 1869

Minnie
b. 1871

William B.
b. Aug. 1873

John M.
b. Jun 1875

m. Lillian ?
b. 1885

Lillian E.
b. 1904

Daisy
b. 1879

Jennie A.
b. July 1879

m. William H. Carpenter
b. Sept. 1875

William E   b. 1900
Frank D.   b. 1903

06/01/07

Exhibit IV. The Runkle/Sullivan Tree

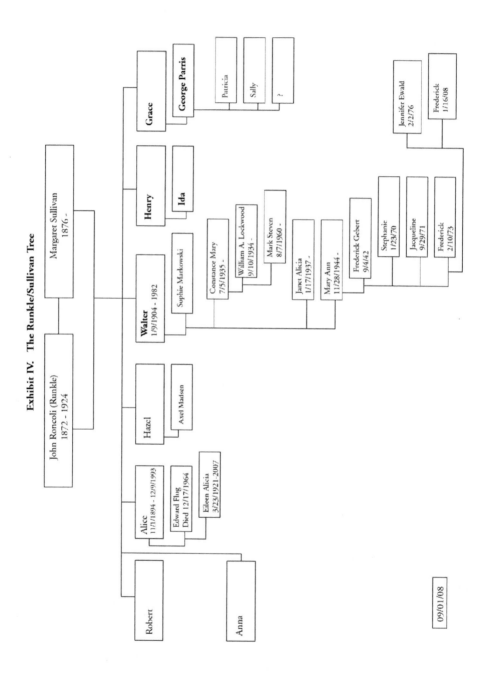

Printed in the United States
151867LV00002B/2/P